THE HUMAN NATURE INDUSTRY

Ward Cannel has been a world-wide roving newspaper correspondent, earning an Overseas Press Club award for his coverage of sub-Sahara Africa. His syndicated column appeared throughout the United States from the New York *World-Telegram and Sun* to the Hawaii *Tribune Herald*. He is the recipient of two grants from the Rockefeller Foundation for this research and report on the human nature industry.

June Macklin is Professor of Anthropology at Connecticut College in New London. She has been chairman of the Ad Hoc Committee on Latin-American Studies of the American Anthropological Association, and has published several papers on Mexican and Mexican-American folk medicine. She took her M.A. at the University of Chicago and her Ph.D. at the University of Pennsylvania.

The Human Nature INDUSTRY

How human nature is manufactured,
distributed, advertised and consumed
in the United States and parts of Canada

WARD CANNEL
and
JUNE MACKLIN

Anchor Press
Doubleday & Company, Inc.
Garden City, New York
1973

150.207
C 164h

First Edition
ISBN: 0-385-07981-8
Library of Congress Catalog Card Number 72–84897
Copyright © 1973 by Edward Cannel
Photograph Copyright © 1970 by Richard Steinberg
All Rights Reserved
Printed in the United States of America

Acknowledgments

The being of this book is attributable in large part to the Rockefeller Foundation which supported much of the research; and to A. I. Hallowell, John R. Everett, Edward Cranz, René Dubos, Anthony F. C. Wallace and many others who took time to share their thinking about this inquiry into the human nature industry.

Among those others are: Richard T. Baker, Peter Berger, William Bradley, J. Bronowski, John Burnham, Victor Butterfield, Harry Demopoulos, Sidney Diamond, Abraham Edel, Loren Eiseley, James Faichney, David Fenton, Arthur Ferrari, Leon Festinger, Martin Freedman, Michael Gazzaniga, Joseph Greenbaum, Eliot Gross, Robert Hutchins, Donald Jason, Julius Korein, Mark Kac, Eric Kandel, Barnaby Keeney, Ruby Jo Reeves Kennedy, Sara Kiesler, David Klein, Norman Lloyd, Borden Mace, Maureen Mahon, Frederick Marx, Edgar Mayhew, Margaret Mead, Helen Mulvey, Gardner Murphy, Ernest Nagel, Eveline Omwake, Roelof Oostingh, Robert Pollack, Joseph Porter, Charles Price, I. I. Rabi, Meyer Schapiro, Carl Schorske, Charles Shain, Roger Sperry, Chandler Stetson, Ivan Strenski, Eugene TeHennepe, Kenneth Thompson, Margaret Thompson, Betty Thomson, Jane Torrey, Gregory Vlastos, F. Champion Ward and Campbell Wyly—and Richard Steinberg, who took the photograph which appears in this book.

Preface

There are only two or three things which still remain unmentionable in polite society. And one of those items is human nature.

As a result, nice people who wish to speak about the subject must resort to euphemisms. Instead of saying human nature outright, they have to use such terms as chimpanzee nature, white mouse nature, computer nature, Norway rat nature and so on. More emancipated people come somewhat closer to a breach of etiquette and talk about the nature of neurosis, the nature of the classroom, the nature of brain waves, the nature of the games people play, the nature of cities, the nature of minority groups, the nature of the unconscious, the nature of children, the nature of parents, the nature of rehabilitation, the nature of women, the nature of the military establishment, the nature of science and, of course, the nature of sexual intercourse.

But when it comes to the other thing, that is simply too disreputable for words. And the reason for that condition is quite easy to see. The general theory seems to be that nobody knows what human nature is.

Well, that is plain nonsense. Everybody knows what human nature is.

But whether people know that they know what it is—that is another matter. That is the subject of this book. And its chief purpose is to open the taboo topic of human nature for public inspection and consideration.

Naturally it may not succeed completely. Human nature is not for everybody.

Chapter One

As everybody knows, for a word to qualify as the Word-of-the-Year, it must fulfill four basic requirements.

The first is that you can find it in the dictionary. And that requirement having been satisfied, the second is that you still do not know what the Word means exactly. True enough, some Words-of-the-Year such as impinge (1949) and serendipity (1956) can be found only in the more expensive dictionaries. But even with cheaper Words like dialogue (1966) and in (1965), the meaning is not much advanced by the definition.

The third requirement for a Word-of-the-Year is that it be used by the people who tell it like it is.

The Word-for-1968, for example, was relevant. During the week of September 30 of that year, to cite a small sample, an eminence in public broadcasting called for more news coverage of relevant issues, a leader of a student activist group demanded that colleges teach more relevant courses, a well-known historian urged the United States to develop a relevant policy toward Asia; and the director of a major art museum said that many of his colleagues across the country had failed to provide relevant exhibitions.

All in all, the Word was so popular that it was held over for another big year. During the week of October 6, 1969, to cite another small sample, one of the best-known anthropologists in the nation predicted that the computer would soon be the means of gaining really relevant sociological data, a leading member of the White House staff said that public demonstrations were not relevant to the making of U.S. foreign policy, and an art critic for a big New York newspaper said that while the new exhibition at a local museum was relevant, many of the works displayed in it were not relevant enough.

The fourth and final requirement for a Word-of-the-Year is that it make some order out of the disarray and disrepair in the human condition, or at least indicate what should be fixed first. But, for some reason, it never seems to do so for more than its twelve-month term. One Year's Word is inevitably replaced by Another that is more profound (1928) or more provocative (1929) with different priorities (1971) of action.

Just how a Word gets started on the route to having a Year of its own is impossible to say. But all at once it is everywhere, and everything is suddenly ethnic (1963) or subliminal (1957) or alienated (1959). The only visible part of the Year's journey is the exit. You can always tell that a Word's career is over when it falls into the hands of management (1938) and is either merchandised or measured.

Take the Word-for-1958. That was the Year of relate, when people suddenly realized that men were actually relating to women and women were relating to children and children were relating to creative playthings, and so on—seemingly forever. But twelve months later, that Word was no longer viable (1964). At lunch on January 2, 1959, a merchandising executive, explaining why he had divorced his wife, said: "She just didn't relate well motherwise."

Or take the Word-for-1967—charisma. That one went out by way of the laboratory a year later. According to a Gallup Poll in 1968, Richard Nixon had 13 per cent more charisma than Hubert Humphrey, who in turn had 4 per cent more charisma than George Wallace. Those figures, the poll reported, showed a 3 per cent gain in charisma for Nixon and a 2 per cent drop in charisma for Humphrey over the preceding measurement made four months earlier. During that period, however, the

10

testing revealed that Wallace's percentage of charisma remained constant.

But as to which of those men *was* relevant—well, it may take decades to find that out. And by then it won't matter because by then relevance will have long since been replaced by a priority more viable or visceral (1970).

That is the whole trouble with telling it like it is. By the time a Word gets in, it is already on the way out. In order to find out whether you are alienated, you have to stop relating. Just as you get a dialogue going, it is time to pull out and develop charisma. So you can see how this thing (1965) not only gives rise to terrible insecurity (1936), but also makes it awfully hard to cope (1951). Here we are, having come through two hard years of relevant, and nothing has been resolved (1776) at all. Have college courses become more relevant? Is television programming more relevant? Is foreign policy, or data, or art or news?

The answer could be yes. On the other hand, it could be no. The trouble is that nobody knows because nobody has ever explained what these things are supposed to be relevant to. All you can find out about them is that they must be relevant to people needs. But just what those needs are, nobody bothers to say. And as for the meaning of that other word—people—it is always left unspecified, too, on the theory that everybody knows what people are. In actual practice, however, it does not seem to work out that way. And consequently, as the old ivory traders used to say, one man's relevant frequently turns out to be another man's umbrella stand.

For a little while it appeared that the situation would clear up once relevant had gone and priorities had arrived. But that one ran into difficulties almost immediately. At the outset everybody agreed that the first thing to do was to establish a list of priorities. The trouble began over what to do second and third, namely, which priority to put at the top of the list and which to

11

put at the bottom. In theory that should have been quite easy to do because the list was supposed to be based on human values. But in actual practice, it soon appeared, nobody had a workable definition of that word human.

"We're not going to bother to define it," said an editor at a major educational materials publishing house preparing a course in human values for sales and distribution to public school systems. "You don't need a definition of human in order to study human values. Just look around you. You'll see that all of us are agreed on certain values."

What values did he mean?

"To take just one," he said, "we're all agreed that 'Thou shalt not steal.'"

If he meant that he and his editorial subordinates in the office did not steal from each other, that may be so. If he meant that he and his wife and her mother did not steal from each other, that may also be so. But as you can see from the crime news in any paper, there are some humans who are not agreed on that particular human value.

That is not to say such an agreement would be impossible to reach. But it would require first an agreed-to definition of stealing among humans. Car theft might qualify. And so might breaking and entering. But what about the other items? What about income tax evasion? What about embezzlement? What about overcharging, cheating on the expense account, pilfering paper clips? Are those acts of stealing according to human values? Or is it human nature to take paper clips, and a violation of human nature to take a portable TV set?

Suffice it to say that a list of priorities is difficult to build on human values without a definition of human. And that would require an enormous scientific undertaking.

It could certainly be done—observing people under this set of controlled conditions and that; keeping minute-by-minute tabs on the nation's behavior, aspirations, fears, guilts, anxieties and other values. What with recent advances in electronic memory banks, sensing apparatus and monitoring devices, the job could be set up as a sort of expanded Dow-Jones daily average of human values.

There are, however, two drawbacks to the scheme. The first is that it doesn't come out with a definition of human. And the second is that the consequences of such a plan are vastly complicated. The legislature would have to be in session at all hours, rewriting yesterday's laws to conform to today's human values report. Even if the average were reviewed only once a month, or once every twelve, human nature would still be defined by fluctuations in the people market. And last year's values would be just that—a closing price. The goods and bads of the year before, the firsts and lasts of the year before that, the oughts and shoulds of three years ago would be statistics only. And in the end history would be looked on as little more than a long series of hang-ups (1972).

And so, like most other Words, priorities had its Year and then went.

Only very rarely does a Word-of-the-Year take root and flower perennially. In fact, there has been just one to do so within the past generation. That one, of course, is communication (1951) which has not only persisted but has also become an organic part of the national perceptual apparatus. Today, few Americans can remember back to the time when communication was not a way of life. But not so long ago it was merely a term reserved for Western Union, Press Wireless, and schoolbook sections about DeForest, Bell and Marconi. A communications breakdown—if the phrase were used at all in those days—would probably have meant that the typewriter repairman's car had a flat tire.

That has all changed now, of course.

13

It is generally understood today, for example, that the UN's business is to keep the lines of communication open among nations, although the organization was not perceived that way when it was founded. It is also common knowledge that New York City is the communications center of the country, a change from its traditional designation as the commercial capital of the United States. There is also widespread agreement today that sex is a means of communication. Dress is another. And so are vandalism, brutality and art, no matter how meaningless they appear to the unready eye at first look, or even at second. As for the widespread use of heroin, LSD, hashish and so on, that depends on whether you listen to the worried Establishment or its critics. Drug use can be classified either as a form of communication or as a means of transportation. But as everybody knows, every little movement has a meaning all its own, which makes transportation a form of communication, too. So it all comes down to the same thing, namely a meaningful dialogue for those who are prepared to hear it. On the other hand, divorce, children, murder and other interpersonal problems can clearly be traced to a failure to communicate somewhere along the line—in the genes, in the nursery or, the popular source as of this writing, in the schools. And in that regard, teachers who used to be called educators now call themselves communicators. And their students go on to take advanced degrees in communications where they learn about the whole subject—neurons, decibels, journalism, public relations, chromosomes, linguistics and advertising.

All in all, the theory seems to be that the human condition is a function of the message unit. And if the bit of information can only be made small enough, transmitted accurately and received clearly, then understanding, cooperation and harmony will surely result, and people will be free to be more human.

But for some reason it hasn't been working out that way, despite great strides in miniaturization, transmission and reception. And a big part of the trouble, as usual, is that neither party on the line has bothered to specify the meaning of people or of human. But without that definition to begin with, it becomes awfully hard to nail down the meanings of the other message units.

So, here we are after more than two decades of communication, and nobody can say one way or the other whether the human condition has been improved. And that is because there is no definition for the word human, and so none for the word improve. Once upon a time improve meant "to grow better." But that was in the bygone day when you were allowed to talk about human nature and whether it was improving or not. In the intervening years, the one term has become disreputable and so the other has lost its meaning. Today, you can open your newspaper to the weather report and find out that the atmosphere is expected to improve from unhealthy to unacceptable.

That's not the only message unit with a leaky definition. Not by a long shot. Most of the human nature dictionary is in pretty bad disrepair, as the following examples of common usage and meaning illustrate:

Antique: (1) Anything over one hundred years old. (2) Anything over fifty years old. (3) Anything over fifteen years old. (4) Anything.

Average Family: The basic unit of society, composed of an average 3.6 persons. They are: 1 schoolteacher, 1 insurance agent, 1 probation officer and 0.6 psychiatrist.

Average Year: That twelve-month period in which a business firm has scored its greatest profit or growth.

Childhood: The period in a human life span covering the first twenty-nine years.

City Planner: (1) A college graduate who has not yet

15

chosen a career. (2) An expert who solves the problem of over-crowding by keeping one-third of the population in transit at all times.

Creative: The innate ability of all humans to follow the directions for living set down by *McCall's* magazine, *Playboy* and *Cosmopolitan.*

Crime Rate: A rising figure, calculated by police to be $25 for sergeants, $50 for lieutenants and $100 for captains.

Decoration Day: An annual holiday celebrated on May 30 when stores put up their Christmas decorations.

Disarmament: (See *Dismemberment.*)

Dismemberment: (See *Retired General.*)

Ethics: An unwritten law forbidding congressmen from stealing money from each other's homes.

Family Doctor: A graduate of a medical school who has a wife and children among other things. (See *Country Club.*)

Five Room Apartment: A dwelling place consisting of a kitchen, a living room, two closets and a built-in chest of drawers.

Future: The present time with its astounding technological and social advances that don't work very well, and the thrilling promise of many more of the same to come.

Generation: (1) A period of time in the human life span covering about twenty-five years. (2) A period in the human life span covering about ten years. (3) The same but covering about four years. (4) Or eighteen months.

Genuine: Sincere. Real. (See *Genuine Silver Plate.* See *Genuine Zircon.* See *Genuine Plastic.*)

Imitation: Real. Sincere. (See *Genuine Imitation.*)

Improved: A product in a redesigned bottle, can, box or other container.

Middle Age: A period of time in the human life span covering the years thirty to thirty-four.

Moral Breakdown: An unwashed girl and an unshorn boy who can't stand each other and are keeping everybody else in the motel awake all afternoon.

New Improved: A newly redesigned bottle, can, box, etc., that looks exactly like the old one but actually contains two ounces less.

Our Thing: An American idiom denoting individuality, creativity and freedom of expression. (See *Cosa Nostra.*)

Prime of Life: The most satisfactory period in the human life span, usually designated posthumously.

Priorities: The twelve things that must be done, listed in order of decreasing importance. They are enumerated as follows— 1, 2, 3, 4, 5, 6, 7, 8, 9, 10, 11 & 12.

Public Opinion: An imaginary ailment, generally characterized by a morbid fear of wax build-up on floor and scalp.

Public Servant: An independent small businessman with a guaranteed annual income and a retirement pension.

Redemption: Deliverance from bondage upon receipt of at least eight filled books of trading stamps. (See *Salvation.*)

Retired General: A former military man who has beat his sword into industrial shares.

Riot: A means of exchange of goods and services. (See *Money.* See *Barter.* See *Mugging.* See *Burglary.*)

Sex: (1) A point-of-sale mechanism. (2) An impulse item.

Sex Symbol: Anything.

Teen-ager: A means of distribution in the clothing, cosmetics and entertainment industries; a TV and radio merchandising aid.

Test Tube Baby: A labor-saving device.

Underdeveloped Nation: A country where it is not safe to drink the water or eat the food. (See *Developed Nation.*)

Victory: (1) A win. (2) A tie. (3) A loss.

17

Those definitions may have changed again since this writing. But if so, that will only further spell out the difficulty in making communication a more human way of life. No matter how small the message unit nor how clear and fast the transmission and reception, there is no sure way to keep the contents from deteriorating en route.

Even if the meanings are hermetically sealed and scientifically preserved it is almost impossible to predict the human value of the data received from people or sent to them. To cite one real-life instance of this problem, set out below is a newspaper dispatch that passes every test for clarity and accuracy. It is not pawky like a dictionary of vulpine usage. On the contrary, every word has an earnest, unequivocal definition. Each fact has been verified. Each sentence can be parsed. The only uncertainty in this report is the human information it communicates:

> CAMBRIDGE, MASS. — Three laboratory-trained pigeons, just back from an experimental tour of duty in the quality control department of a large pharmaceutical plant, have demonstrated that they are 22 per cent more efficient than the three women who usually do that job.
>
> The pigeons, trained by a method known as "stimulus-response," were assigned to watch the capsules traveling down a conveyor belt to be bottled. The pigeons' job was to spot faulty or imperfectly constructed capsules and dispose of them with a flick of the bill. Each time a pigeon successfully identified a faulty capsule and got it off the belt, the bird was rewarded with a grain of feed.
>
> "They performed predictably. And if it weren't for union regulations, they'd still be working," said the man who trained the pigeons. He is Dr.

Now, that is certainly a clear communication assembled in handy, bite-sized facts and transmitted at ninety words per minute. But the information it imparts is another question. Is it a message about three pigeons only? Or is it also a dispatch about the three women who usually perform that task? Or is it really an authoritative report about most people who perform most tasks?—a communiqué regarding human nature that says, "Fred, it says here that you've got a bird brain, and this is how it works . . ."

2

It is unlikely that everything would clear up if the Word-of-the-Year were somehow replaced by human nature. Some things would probably get better, of course. For example, it might turn out that adolescence (1930) does not have to be such a hardship after all. But, on the other hand, some things might get worse. There is no way of telling what kind of epidemic could spring up if a cure were found for society (1893) and civilization (1749). And anyway, it is impractical to get rid of the Word-of-the-Year as it not only provides full employment in art, science, medicine, business and government, but it also gives many other people something to think about while they talk. On balance, it appears to be much better doctrine (1823) to leave the Words alone to come and go annually.

A safer plan is to install human nature in the list for a Year. It certainly can't drive the situation into worse disarray, and it might straighten out a number of persistent difficulties.

For one thing, making human nature a Word-of-the-Year could help to reduce the pressing problem of identification regarding how to tell the difference between a person and a pigeon—or, for that matter, the difference between a person and an ape, a rat, a molecule, a computer, a civilization, a society or a group.

For another thing, there are practical benefits to be gained from even one Year's application of human nature. To mention a few:

It would be very helpful to know whether to hire more psychologists or more neurologists, or to fire both and hire more gunsmiths and locksmiths. It would certainly be very useful to know whether it is more human and natural to be single, or more human and natural to be married, and if so, whether to swap your mate—and if so, on what basis: rental, long lease or full-term depreciation. It would also be good to know if it is human nature to support the general welfare or to cultivate only your own garden (and if so, whether to plant poppies and marijuana as well as corn, tomatoes and juniper). Then, too, there is the ticklish business of who is alive and who is not. It would be a great convenience to know whether a spoonful of scrapings from the uterus is human and should be named complete with a middle initial for the medical abortion records. It would also be a great saving to know when a patient is not human any more and not likely to be so again. You could then turn off the electrical respirator, freeze the body for revival and remedy at a later date when the curing art improves, or remove the beating heart for transplant into a more human system.

This catalogue of advantages could go on at considerable length. But there is nothing to be gained by multiplying the obvious. The plain fact is that a Year of human nature—perhaps Two, if it really catches on—could do wonders for everybody's nerves. Most especially for those who despair at current trends toward depersonalization and dehumanization, it would be a comfort to know once and for all what a person is and what human means. It would settle the dispute over what a human person should know, who should teach it, and how it should be taught. Clearly a definition of human nature would calm angry feelings about human rights, thus resolving the deadlock over women's rights, men's rights, prisoners' rights and the human use of human beings.

And for everybody else in this time of disarray and disrepair when it is such a fearful adventure just to cross the street or even to breathe the air, it would be gratifying to know one way or the other whether to have faith in human nature because it has an automatic drive toward survival—or to give up worrying about the whole matter because human nature has an automatic drive toward extinction.

3

In other words:

Nobody seems to be mentioning human nature anymore, at least not under that name. But somebody ought to. Otherwise the average consumer cannot tell whether the human nature industry is still turning out a product—and if so, whether it is in as bad disrepair and disarray as it appears to be.

As anthropologist Anthony F. C. Wallace puts it: "Hazardous as this exercise may be, it is important from time to time to ask the most general question 'What kind of people are people?' rather than the more specific, 'What kind of people are the Iroquois?'"

Actually, those specific exercises are pretty hazardous, too. You cannot jog two blocks without tripping over still another authoritative discovery regarding pre-Columbian nature, chimpanzee nature, chromosome nature, computer nature, brain neocortex nature, white mouse nature and so on and on. But what about the nature of human nature? What about that neglected and disreputable binding which keeps the rest of the encyclopedia intact?

Antique: Many people certainly feel the anguish expressed by biologist René Dubos "at seeing so many human and natural values being destroyed . . ." But what are they?

Discussing the "human problems of being natural," biologist Marston Bates points out that natural behavior is what is "usual to, or conforming with, human nature—but for that one needs a fairly definite concept of human nature." The difficulty, according to Bates, is that "The human animal is there somewhere, but so deeply encrusted with tradition, with ideas, with learned behavior, that he is hard to find."

Average Family: Oh, he's not all that hard to find. President Nixon's Commission on Population Growth and the American Future has found that the United States should gradually stop multiplying and achieve a zero population growth because "no substantial benefits would result from continued" increased number of humans. In Britain, thirty-three eminent scientists report that unless that country's population is reduced by half, "the breakdown of society and the irreversible disruption of the life-support systems on this planet—possibly by the end of the century, certainly within the lifetimes of our children—are inevitable."

Average Year: On the other hand, if it's inevitable human nature to die of overpopulation or to kill itself off by other means, then there's no point to further inquiry. Human nature and human values left to their own devices bespeak a lethal gene. As Roger Sperry, professor of psychobiology at California Institute of Technology, indicated, there's no need to define the meaning of human in order to set up a system of human values. You merely establish the list of values the way science does, by checking back with nature from time to time.

But what nature do you check back with to establish human values? Take crime. Is it human and natural? Or is it human and lethal? And if so, how much? According to sociologist and student of criminology Arthur Ferrari, it's hard to check back on the nature of criminals. "Only a very small percentage, maybe about 10 per cent, of the nation's burglars and other felons are caught and imprisoned," Dr. Ferrari says, "and most of them are caught and imprisoned over and over again. The successful criminals are seldom caught. We know very little about them, their attitudes and their feelings. Most of what we know about the mind of the criminal is based on our study of the losers, not the winners."

Childhood: And even if you ask people what they think and how they feel, does that tell you anything about the nature of human nature? Feelings of being masculine or feminine may be largely the results of teaching, according to a panel of experts on gender identity assembled by the Association for the Advancement of Psychoanalysis. "Core gender identity is crystallized in children by the age of three," said Dr. Harry Gershman, dean of the American Institute for Psychoanalysis, who has been working on this research for fifteen years. He argued that the important influences on the infant's gender identity were psychological and cultural, not biological. The other panelists agreed. The moderator, Dr. Arnaldo Apolito, struck the keynote of the matter by opening with:

"Good evening, ladies and gentlemen—or, in the spirit of the evening, maybe I should say, Good evening, human beings."

City Planner: But how did he know they were human beings? On what evidence? Because they looked like human beings? Because they behaved like human beings? Or because he had been taught that they were human beings? You can get into a lot of trouble by making pronouncements like that, calling people human beings when you don't know what human means. And vice versa:

Tried for the wholesale killing of unarmed civilians, including old men and infants, in My Lai, Vietnam, Lieutenant William

23

Calley defended his actions in part by maintaining that his victims "were not human" but rather were "an enemy with whom one could not speak or reason." Calley was convicted but not executed. As the Geneva Convention terms make clear, persons suspected of violating the laws of war must be "treated with humanity."

Creative: But how can you invoke humanity or reprimand inhumane behavior if you don't have a definition of human or a notion of the nature of its nature.

A number of branches of the American Society for the Prevention of Cruelty to Animals are under attack because some employees are suspected of inhumane acts such as hosing the foundling animals with scalding hot water or sending them to cremation ovens before their owners can inquire about them. And when the Department of the Interior recently developed a quick method to eliminate some of the nine million or more blackbirds and starlings roosting near Milan, Tennessee, and befouling the hog and dairy farms in Gibson County, a wave of public protest went up to protect the birds from inhumane extermination.

Decoration Day: In many primitive societies, the soul is imagined to leave the body at death or just prior to it. That notion is tied to primitive beliefs concerning the items that constitute human nature. In this part of the world, according to anthropologist Jules Henry, "millions of once-useful but now obsolete human beings are detached from their selves long before they are lowered into the grave."

Dismemberment: A seventy-one-year-old New York psychiatrist who has advocated and practiced sex relations with certain female patients as a means of curing their ailments has been expelled from membership in the American Psychiatric Association. The APA cannot condone such treatment. Said the chairman of the Ethics Committee: "Men of good conscience inherently know what is right and wrong, and what is to be done or avoided."

Ethics: But do they? In a recent, highly-charged study of illness in contemporary society, a psychiatrist and sociologist investigated diagnosis and treatment in a respected medical school. "Should society be content with a score for accuracy in diagnosis of 46 per cent on the medical service and 75 per cent on the surgical service?" ask Raymond S. Duff and August B. Hollingshead.

Genuine: On the other hand, that opens up the question of whether good health care is a human right. And if it is, then why is the median income of medical doctors better than $40,-000 per year? And why is the health care in at least one hospital, according to the director, "geared not so much to the patient's condition as to the patient's insurance coverage."

Imitation: That, in turn, opens up the question of whether good health is a natural right. As Washburn and DeVore put it in their "Social Behavior of Baboons and Early Man"—"We have seen sick and wounded animals making great efforts to keep up with the troop and finally falling behind." The only protection for a baboon is to stay with the troop, no matter how injured or sick he may be. "The whole evolutionary impact of disease and accident on the human species was changed when it became possible for an individual to stay in one place and not have to take part in the daily round of the troop. . . . It is the home base that changes sprained ankles and fevers from fatal diseases to minor ailments."

Improved: "When I was 17, 18, 19, 20, I was interested in sex," says Billy Graham, "and if I had had all of this thrown at me at that time, I don't know whether I could have withstood it. I think about my own sons and my own daughters, and I'm sure that many parents are concerned about what their children are

25

exposed to. Human nature is so built that it cannot resist these temptations when they are thrown from every angle."

New Improved: But, on the other hand, there's some evidence that human nature isn't so natural. Despite all this sexual freedom to discuss and experiment, sex researchers William Masters and Virginia Johnson say that "the younger generation is having the same sexual problems." As Mrs. Johnson puts it, "We are still a society that lives by illusions." Adds Dr. Masters: "The greatest cause of sexual problems is misinformation, misconception and taboo."

Prime of Life: And as for the humanness of crime, "There is no society that is not confronted with the problem of criminality," says Emile Durkheim, an early sociologist. "What is normal, simply, is the existence of criminality, provided that it attains and does not exceed for each social type a certain level . . ."

But what is a normal level of crime? According to the U.S. Census figures, between 1960 and 1966 the crime rate increased by 49 per cent. That is just about the same increase in the population percentage of young, adult males—the most felony-prone category in any population. So, normal being a matter of statistics, you would have to say that the soaring crime rate is just human nature.

Priorities: But that is hardly a workable definition of human. The way people behave isn't the only indication of what they are. At least anthropologists Lionel Tiger and Robin Fox charge that the behavioral sciences have "an incomplete concept of what governs and constrains human action. They fail to take seriously enough the possibility that there is an authentic 'human nature'. . . ."

And it would be a great convenience to know what it is—if only to know whether things were getting better or worse:

Redemption: A London doctor says that prostitutes forced out of business by the inroads of the "permissive society" may

26

one day have to consider the possibility of working for the National Health Service. Dr. Myles Lask predicts in the medical newspaper *Pulse* that prostitutes might be used in the future as a "relevant" part of a medical team to help selected categories of patients who might benefit for physical, psychological or psychosexual reasons.

Relevant: "As President, an individual is expected to maintain a quality of dignity," says President Nixon. "A quality of aloofness. Yes, of course, to be friendly too, but people don't want the President of the United States to be a little sloppy or lewd or vulgar. They want to think he is one of them but not too much so. If they see the President kicking up his heels, eating too much or drinking too much, the confidence factor is weakened. People want to think that if there is a crisis, he will be cool and sober. They also want to think that he's a human guy who likes his wife and kids and a good time . . ."

Riot: A woman who saw a photo of President Nixon and his daughter Tricia at a baseball game wrote to the magazine to say: "How typically American. She, like any other average kid, seemed to be yelling at the umpire, 'Throw the bum out!' That one picture has made me change my way of thinking. It made me realize that the Nixons are really no different from the rest of us."

Sex Symbol: Naturally they're not. But what are the rest of us like? As Noam Chomsky puts it: "A central problem of interpreting the world is determining how, in fact, human beings proceed to do so."

Test Tube Baby: According to a 1971 federal research study, it costs the typical American family between $80,000 and $150,-000 to raise two children and put them through college. According to a husband-and-wife team of anthropological researchers who spent three years in field study among "organized swingers," many of them are people who believe that "it is more

27

fun for people to have sex together than to play bridge and golf together." (Or, for that matter, to go to baseball games together.) Families are shattering at the rate of eighty each hour. A quarter of all people now married have been married at least once before. It's not exactly polygamy, but it certainly appears to be what sociologist Ruby Jo Reeves Kennedy called "serial monogamy."

Underdeveloped Nation: On the other hand, state supreme courts are being asked more and more often to rule on cases of people who have changed their sex and now want to marry a member of the presently opposite but formerly same sex. Single unmarried people are becoming the legal parents of babies because—you know, it's not necessarily human nature to be married, but it is to want children. But if that's so, what about the 35 per cent of the babies born in the United States annually who are unwanted? Meanwhile, unmarried couples with children explain that the marriage certificate has nothing to do with human nature. "Adam and Eve didn't need to go through a ceremony," they tell you, and "It doesn't guarantee a permanent relationship and it doesn't have anything to do with love."

Victory: With the human nature lexicon in such disarray and disrepair, it is not surprising that the General Secretary of the World Council of Churches has recently called for greater cooperation between scientists and non-scientists "in the battle for a more human future for all mankind." What he meant by human, however, he did not say.

But at least the word is starting to get around. And from there it is only one small step to getting human nature into currency, and an even smaller step to having it installed officially as a Word-of-the-Year.

That said, it remains only to arrange the details by trotting around to a few key sectors of the human nature industry—particularly the knowledge foundry where human data are processed into authoritative information. It remains only, then, to pick up the definition of human nature, the expert findings on what it really is, and some illustrative examples of it in operation which have been turned up by the booming information explosion.

Chapter Two

As everybody knows, the earth is tilted on its axis with regard to the sun. And as that angle of declination has a predictable effect on the 43rd parallel, spring came to New England once again as is its nature.

An uninstructed bee collected pollen from the azaleas. A small dog of untraceable ancestry sniffed at another of similar breeding the way dogs naturally do. A cardinal whistled a perfect rendition of an ancient tune from somewhere in the tall, old maple trees that lined Elm Street.

"Let me understand this," the vice-president of Cotton Mather College said, looking out of his window at spring and the new Humanities Laboratory, which had been dedicated the year before with great hope and publicity. "You're proposing an inquiry in human nature?"

That being the essence of the idea, no further explanation seemed to be needed.

"It's an awfully big project, isn't it?" he asked. "Quite overwhelming, in fact."

Why did he think the topic of human nature so large? It was certainly a lot smaller than the nature of the earth on its axis which is 24,902.44 miles in circumference at the equator and weighs 6 sextillion 588 quintillion short tons. Moreover, the nature of human nature is considerably closer at hand than the sun's nature which is 93.9 million miles away. Granted, the nature of human nature is quite a bit larger than the nature of dog nature or bee nature. But that did not necessarily make it an overwhelming project. On the contrary, it had great ad-

31

vantages over an inquiry conducted in whimpers, howls or a six-legged dance. For one, with research into the nature of human nature rather than dog or bee nature, the project would not be distracted by every passing flower or anus, or delayed on account of honey, fleas or bite. And for another thing, a great amount of work on the human nature project had already been compiled in the course of the past several thousand years as a look at the current Mather College catalogue revealed.

But as it turned out, it was not the size of the project that worried the vice-president. It was the size of the school.

"Mather College is very small," he pointed out. "We really don't have the resources for the kind of project you propose."

What about the renowned Humanities Laboratory?

"The purpose of that center is under review by the faculty," he explained. "It may become part of the science complex, or else a residence for graduate students."

But, in any case, that was not the kind of resources he had meant. What the college lacked for such a project, he finally explained, was money.

That, however, was no obstacle. The inquiry had already been financed by a foundation. It required only a university to administer the grant of money and to keep a supervising eye on the work in progress.

"Oh," he said, "it's a grant. I didn't understand that. Send me a letter outlining the project as we discussed it today, and I'll get back to you in a week or so."

Actually it took two weeks and two days for the response—a telephone call. "We've had several meetings on this," he said. "And we can see great merit in an inquiry into human nature. But before we make a decision about taking on this project, we'd like another letter explaining how such an inquiry relates to Black Studies."

* *

Late spring had come to Jay Gould University. There were no trees or grass or ivy to bespeak the season to the city. But a fresh coat of paint on the window trim and doors of the Graduate School of Communication gave a decided green cast to the haze.

"All right, you're proposing an inquiry into human nature," the dean of the communications schools said. "But why come to us with it?"

That was fairly easy to explain, what with the disarray among the Words-of-the-Year, the disrepair in the human nature dictionary, and the uncertain consequences of improved transmission, reception and the other tools of communication among people these days.

"That's a philosophical problem," he said. "This school is concerned with practical matters. We train professional communicators to go out and get answers, and get them accurately."

Looked at that way, then, an inquiry into the nature of human nature was certainly practical. A communicator dealing professionally with the answers was ill-equipped if he did not know what the questions were.

"Well," the dean said, "the proposal is in the wrong place anyway. We don't have the resources to handle this kind of project."

But no resources were needed. The research was funded and lacked only an educational institution to sponsor the work and administer the grant.

He thought about that for a while and then said, "All right. Give me a memo on the project and I'll take it up with the faculty. You'll have a reply within a week."

He beat the deadline by a day. "We've decided not to take this project on," he said on the telephone. "It's too risky. We don't know what this sort of inquiry would turn up, and we

33

don't want to take on any projects where we can't see the end product."

What was the point of starting an inquiry if you knew the end product at the outset? That seemed to deny the faith of scrupulous communication and fearless research in which no stone was to be left unturned in the pursuit of facts, and perhaps of truth as well.

"That's a philosophical matter," he said. "This is a professional graduate school."

*   *

The Institute for Experimental Education looked like what it used to be: an office building in an industrial zone. The lobby was crowded with people registering for the summer courses scheduled to start on the following Monday—the History of Utopias, Writing and Selling Fiction, Remedial Guitar and so on.

"A grant to investigate human nature? I'm amazed," the chancellor said. "Does one wear a toga to conduct this inquiry?"

But in the end he decided not to take on the project.

"If it were administered by Experimental," he said, "it would have to be placed in one department or another. The problem is where to place it. Philosophy? Biology? Chemistry? Religion? It really doesn't belong in any of those. It would have to go to sociology. And if I put it there, the department chairman would take it over and direct the research and the results. There's simply no stopping this fellow . . ."

*   *

By midsummer, Lucy Stone College was empty and silent. The students, having seen life during the academic year, had gone home either to write about it or to breed horses. Most of the faculty members, having seen life too, had gone from the campus. Only a few members of the administration remained

34

to worry about the budget, the freshmen and the antagonisms of the forthcoming fall semester.

"I'm not sure I understand the purpose of the project," the president of the college said. "Or, if I understand it, I'm not sure I agree with it. And that's reason enough to sponsor it and find out what it turns up."

The one remaining obstacle was naming the species of research so as to place it in the academic genus. After some discussion of methods and careers, he came at last to a suitable classification.

"Suppose we call it the higher journalism," the president said, shaking hands to seal the agreement. And with that, the project began its inquiry into human nature.

It is impossible to describe the higher journalism to anybody who has never had a case of it. In many ways it is like the lower anthropology because you are working with natives and taboos and so on. But in many other ways it is like falling into a meat grinder.

Consequently, the real names of the colleges and universities cited in this chapter so far have not been used. In the remainder of the chapter, no names will be used at all. That is not only the privilege of the higher journalism and the lower anthropology, but it is also a necessity if you want to keep enough of your remaining flesh intact in order to go back some day to doing the lower journalism and the higher anthropology.

2

"Human nature?" The elderly man repeated the question. He spoke in a tone so thoughtful that it barely carried across his office. "Why do you bring this question to me?"

Where better to bring the question than to an eminent professor of philosophy who also held a graduate degree in religion? Weren't these the pursuits where the inquiry was stated first in recorded history?

"That may be," he said. "But this question hasn't been the concern of philosophy for many years."

Then what are philosophers concerned with now?

"Philosophy," he said. "If you want to know about human nature you'd do a lot better to talk with a physiologist."

What would a physiologist have to say about it?

"I don't know," he said. "I never talk to those people."

*   *

"Human nature?" the thin man in the white smock asked. "How did you get my name?"

He had been referred by the dean of the medical school as being the best physiologist on the staff, or in the state for that matter.

"Do you know the dean personally?"

It would have been an outright lie to say yes. But the question seemed to demand more than the truth if the topic of human nature were to be opened.

"Where did you train?"

Inasmuch as there are laws against impersonating a doctor of medicine, the safest course was to state the fact.

"I see," he said rather sternly. "Then your Ph.D.—where did you take your degree?"

The penalties are much smaller for impersonating a doctor of philosophy. But what that degree had to do with an interview on the subject of human nature was hard to figure out.

"I see," he said again. "Then your Master's degree? What is your field?"

It was obviously futile to persist. But he did so anyway.

"Your B.A.?" he asked. "Surely you went to . . ."

36

It would have been an outright lie to say no. But by now the questions seemed to demand less than the truth. It was a gamble, of course, as to whether he would explain human nature to somebody whose only credential in the matter was a birth certificate. And in the end it failed.

"I'm getting bad vibrations about this interview," he said. "If you want to talk about human nature, go and interview people of the stature of a Dubos, a Wald, a Dobzhansky, a Margaret Mead."

Did people like that know more about it?

"It doesn't matter," he said. "But they're willing to be visible and make public pronouncements about everything."

*   *

"Human nature?" the biologist said. "That is a very good question."

That was very reassuring to hear, coming as it did from a scientist with a world-wide reputation.

"And I should have something to tell you about it. After all, biology is the study of living things. But I don't see many living things anymore. I spend most of my time at the electron microscope looking at non-living things."

*   *

"Human nature," said the world-renowned geneticist, "is a meaningless question. The term cannot be used."

But he had used it eleven times in a recent book.

"That is just a figure of speech," he said. "There are as many human natures as there are humans. Each human has a different history—personal, environmental, genetic."

*   *

"The question of human nature can't be asked," said the widely-published professor of psychology.

"But aren't you asking it all the time," said the professor of religion. "Aren't you asking it with each experiment you perform on the ways in which humans perceive the world?"

"Well," the psychologist paused. "I suppose that is the question we ask."

"What he means," said the dean of graduate studies, "is that the question can't be answered."

"But don't we answer it every day," said a professor of philosophy. "At least to some extent. Otherwise we couldn't teach our courses in anthropology, economics, sociology, psychology . . ."

"Yes, it appears that we do answer it," the dean said.

All right, then, if the question is asked and answered, what is human nature?

"See for yourself," said the provost of the university, pushing a catalogue of the school's courses across the table. "Human nature is a bundle of electronic circuits with a credit card."

And on that note of jollity and good fellowship, the conference came to an end.

*　　*

"The question is all wrong," said a man whose career in physiology and psychology has spanned five decades, and whose works have been standard textbooks.

"It's too fuzzy. It's too general. It's too personal. You can't ask what human nature is. You have to break the question down into smaller particulars. And even then, the results won't be meaningful. You'll be filtering the answers through your own biases. You'll see everything in terms of your own culture."

*　　*

"You're asking a very interesting question, and potentially a very fruitful one," said the anthropologist who was without any question an eminent figure in the field. "But you're not asking

38

it the right way—going around like this with a pad and a pencil. In the end, you won't have any data to analyze.

"Now, if I were trying to find out what human nature is, I'd do it this way. First, I'd send out questionnaires to 75,000 school children and ask them to write an essay on what human nature is. And then I'd feed all those essays into a computer . . ."

*   *

"It won't work," said a professor of neurophysiology who was now doing his research with the aid of computers. "Asking a computer to tell you what people think—or if they think—is like asking people whether computers think and what they think about. If you ask a computer to read essays, you have to tell it what to look for first. That doesn't make for an impartial reading."

Then how could he get an impartial reading on the human brain and nerves from a computer?

"Because," he explained, "you're not studying thought or will or honor or grace. You're studying a system—the nervous system. The computer helps you to analyze the system."

Was it possible to analyze the system known as human nature?

"Yes, if it's a system. If it is, then you feed the system into the computer and analyze it."

That seemed reasonable. The only problem was how to build a human that could be fed into a computer.

"That's not so difficult," he said. "With a couple of good programmers, you could probably feed Hamlet into the computer in a couple of months."

And what would an analysis of the system reveal?

"I don't know," he said. "But my guess is that Hamlet's trouble was too much negative feedback."

*   *

"Human nature?" The professor repeated the question. His specialty was the philosophy of law. "I don't think that question is allowable. At least not in that form. What do you mean by human nature? That's not a scientific term."

What did he mean by scientific?

"That's your worry, not mine," he said. "I'm not looking for the answer. You are. But you can't ask the question that way."

3

Actually, the question can be put in a number of other ways that will yield much more gratifying results.

For instance, you can inquire into the nature of the bee or the nature of the dog or of the azalea, and experts will stop whatever they are doing to discuss the matter at length, and afterward send you their reprints and references by first-class mail. But while these pleasant exchanges are instructive about nature, they do not seem to advance an understanding of human.

Another way to go about the inquiry is ask such questions as: Are your parents hateful? or Why are you still unmarried? or Do you go to a psychiatrist? This method of research does not require interviews with experts, and moreover can be conducted in buses, on elevators or at cocktail parties. Many people will interrupt whatever they are thinking or saying to answer these questions as truthfully as they can, and never once challenge your credentials. But while information of this sort may be human, it does not really clear up the matter of nature.

In any case, you cannot ask directly, "What is human nature?" The question is simply too intimate. It must be phrased in more tentative terms and asked from a greater distance. One way to do so is by backing up and inquiring:

"Is there such a thing as human nature?"

* *

"I'm not going to answer that," said a well-known cultural anthropologist.

Why not?

"Because your next question will be 'What is it?' And I'm not going to get into that."

* *

"I don't know whether there's such a thing as human nature," said one of the most widely-quoted sociologists in the United States today. "The social sciences haven't done much work on that question."

Why not?

"Because there hasn't been any research grant money for asking it."

* *

"Of course there's such a thing as human nature," said a celebrated anthropologist. "It is the characteristics that are specific to the species known as *Homo sapiens.*"

Those characteristics, the anthropologist said, included such items as the human skeleton, the human heart, the human liver and lights—all those specifics that made people people rather than chickens, say, or chimpanzees or automobiles.

Was that what people meant when they worried about human rights and crimes against humanity and human values and all the other concerns regarding human nature?

"That's not human nature," the anthropologist said. "That's just a catch-phrase—a way to avoid having to think. People are basically very lazy."

Then laziness was a species specific characteristic.

"No," the anthropologist said. "Where did you get that idea?"

* *

"Of course there's such a thing as human nature. But this isn't it," the pathologist said, waving his arm at the activity in the room. It was a very long room, tiled in white. On a dozen tables made of stainless steel corpses of humans were in various stages of autopsy. It was quite difficult to hear the pathologist because of a persistent buzz saw used to remove the tops of the skulls so as to make removal of the brains easier.

"These are bones and skin and organs that once contained humans. Some of these husks may be the results of human nature," he explained, "especially those who died by murder or suicide or misdiagnosed illness, or those who worried themselves to death. But whatever was human about them went when they died."

Then if they weren't human corpses, what were they?

"Medical-legal problems," he said.

* *

"I don't know whether there is such a thing as human nature," said an expert who has applied the tools of psychoanalysis in the study of different cultures. "But there seem to be five or six universals that cross cultural lines."

These apparent universals, he said, included such items as the use of language, a notion of supernatural beings, a taboo against incest, a family group of some sort to rear offspring. But such a list, even if complete and verified everywhere, did not add up to human nature.

"It's not a list that can be added," he said. "It's more like a series of little boxes, each with a label like God Myth, Family, Hero Myth. I haven't looked into it, but it may well turn out that one of those little boxes can be labeled Human Nature Myth."

Was it really possible that human nature might be only a myth?

"If myth is a discouraging word," he said, "then call it Beliefs About Human Nature. But it's still worthwhile to investigate. It's not only interesting, but also some of the beliefs may actually be true."

* *

"Is there such a thing as human nature?" The man repeating the question was an eminent physicist with a long list of prizes and publications to his name. "That's a damn-fool question. I can't imagine anybody's asking it."

* *

"I don't think you can ask a historian that question," said a widely respected historian. "Human nature implies constants and regularities. History studies the unusual and irregular. As the Spanish philosopher Ortega y Gasset says, man has no nature; all he has is a history."

Then how is it possible to recognize the irregular and the unusual without some idea of the regular and the usual?

"Well," he said after a thoughtful pause, "that nature which I just said does not exist seems to have changed quite a bit over the years."

* *

"I don't know if there's a human nature," the psychologist said. "But in our culture some behavior tends to be more predictable than others. For example, we seem to prefer to be consistent rather than inconsistent."

The psychologist cited several laboratory experiments in that regard and then referred to manufacturers who mail free samples of a new product to consumers before introducing it in stores.

"That's not to give potential customers a chance to test the product," the psychologist said. "The free sample gets people to use the product. That makes them users when they go into the store. And rather than be inconsistent, they buy the product they've been using instead of another brand."

*   *

"But did she say why people change brands after years of using the same one?" a neurophysiologist inquired sharply. "Did she explain why many manufacturers don't give out free samples? Did you ask why they change advertising agencies, and why those agencies change campaign tactics? Did you ask if it's possible to predict whether a man will eat prunes for breakfast tomorrow even if he's had a dish of prunes at every breakfast for two years?

"You can't ask these behaviorists if there's such a thing as human nature. They do all of their predicting after the fact."

*   *

"Don't ask me if there's such a thing as human nature," said a professor of economics. "I lie awake at night asking myself that question."

*   *

"That question is all right to ask when you're twenty-one years old," said a professor of neurosurgery. "But I don't have time for it now. I've got other things to worry about. I've got a son who doesn't know what he wants to do with his life. I've got an eighty-year-old patient with inoperable cancer who ought to be allowed to die in peace. But his family is after me day and night to keep him alive at all costs . . ."

*   *

"When is your book due at the publisher's?" The voice on the telephone was very familiar, belonging to a professor of anthropology who appears frequently in public broadcast appearances. No book was planned, however.

"Then what is the purpose of asking if there's such a thing as human nature?" the voice inquired.

The purpose was to open the way to the next question, namely, what human nature is.

"But how will the information be used?" the voice asked.

Inasmuch as the conversation could not go forward until a practical use had been assigned to the project, it seemed harmless and vague enough to say that it was for a movie.

"Well," he said, "in that case I'm afraid I'll have to turn down this request for an interview."

As it turned out, he had recently signed a contract with several businessmen in his city to produce motion pictures on anthropological subjects. And under the terms of that contract, he feared it would be a violation to answer the question.

*   *

"I think there's such a thing as human nature," said an expert in the field of child development. "But I'm really not the one to ask because I don't think that human nature can be measured or predicted."

But what about the way babies learn language? Doesn't it follow certain general paths regardless of what language the baby is born to?

"There may be some evidence of that sort," the child development expert said. "But what does that tell you about human nature? One child will grow up to use the language for dispatching trains, and another will grow up and write books and plays and poetry and change the way humans see the world."

*   *

"I'm surprised you ask me this question," said an expert in linguistics. "If I were inquiring into human nature, I'd be out interviewing bartenders and cab drivers and prostitutes. They see a lot more of human nature than I do."

4

In other words:

If you take a tour of the knowledge foundry where the facts of human nature are processed into information, you would have to come back agreeing with anthropologist A. I. Hallowell who used to tell his students that it's a lot easier to say what human nature is not.

And the same is the case at the other end of the assembly line where the human nature data are manufactured. You cannot get cab drivers, prostitutes, bartenders or their customers to say what human nature is. They will concede that it is there, that they see it every day, that you will be able to spot it if you hang around with them for an hour or two. But as for what the product looks like exactly, the most they can tell you is, "It's awfully big. You'll have to ask the experts to describe it. I'm only a housewife."

Just about the only place in the human nature industry where you can get an answer to the inquiry is in the advertising department—among the doctors, lawyers, journalists, psychiatrists, politicians, merchandisers, book reviewers, TV programmers, judges, educators, publishers and others who have to describe the product publicly and point out how it works in order to do their jobs and get through the day, the week and the year. But it is not so easy to go there and ask your question. Once you have been to the knowledge foundry and can say what human nature is not, you become quite skeptical, if not outright argumentative, regarding the answers you get:

"One thing I would say is, people are basically lazy." Or, as Voltaire put it, "Pleasure is the object, the duty and the goal of all rational creatures."

But a recent study shows that top business executives put in a minimum of sixty working hours per week and frequently seventy-five or eighty, which includes at least one night at the office, two working at home and one spent in business-related entertaining. Did they think they were working too hard? About 90 per cent replied, "Absolutely not," "Of course not" and "It's ridiculous to think I overwork." Their wives, doctors and friends might think so, but that was because other people "just didn't understand." One company president defined overwork as "simply work that you don't like."

"Exactly. Look at the money they get. People are basically greedy. Machiavelli hit it right when he described 'man's envious nature.'"

But the Arapesh of New Guinea, says Dorothy Lee, create a wide gap between ownership and possession which they then bridge with a multitude of human relations. "They plant their trees in someone else's hamlet, they rear pigs owned by someone else, they eat yams planted by someone else." Among the Yanomamö Indians, according to Napoleon Chagnon, a very important value is sharing. A hunter is supposed to give away most of the game he kills. At the evening meal, he may refuse to take even one portion, preferring to go hungry rather than risk the accusation of poor marksmanship or stinginess. About the Kwakiutl tribe, Ruth Benedict reports: "The object of all Kwakiutl enterprise was to show oneself superior to one's rival." That victory could be achieved by two means. One was by shaming a rival "by presenting him with more property than he could return with interest . . . A man who had given away a copper (valued at 10,000 blankets) had overcome his rival as much as if he had overcome him in battle array." The other way to victory over a rival was by destroying your own property. "The highest glory of life was the act of complete destruction . . ."

"Of course. Rivalry and destruction. Human nature is aggression. Hobbes said it: Man's life is 'nasty, brutish and short.'"

But in many primitive tribes, as E. Adamson Hoebel points out, a single murder is usually a private wrong redressed by the kinsmen of the victim, whereas repeated murder becomes a public crime punishable by death at the hands of an agent of the community. Explorer Knud Rasmussen and anthropologist Franz Boas report on primitive tribes in which a unanimous consent of all members was required before an habitual murderer could be executed. And, as Karl von Clausewitz is noted for explaining, says Ralph L. Holloway, Jr., "War is, after all . . . simply an organized extension of politics carried to a different level. It is an organized activity directed by rational decisions by political bodies whose membership is infinitesimal compared to the aggregates involved in actual combat." So, even if the human were innately aggressive, Holloway concludes, the "rational decisions to make war go well in advance of the emotional exacerbations usually thought of as the direct cause of war."

The stimuli that can make a man act aggressively today may not do so tomorrow. Too, the manifestations of aggression can change from day to day. There is very little constant about it. As Holloway says, "The sordid history of man attests well to the fantastic plurality of stimuli that can be cooked up to elicit aggression. How natural are they?"

"But it's basic to fight to defend your territory. Remember what John Locke said about 'life, liberty and property.'"

The indications are that it's not basic to us at all. Human notions of range and territory may well have occurred when people stopped being vegetable gatherers primarily and became hunters of large game, according to findings by Sherwood Washburn and Irven DeVore. "If strangers hunt game, or even disturb

48

it, scaring it from its normal routes, the plans of the local hunters are ruined," they explain. "Hunting man requires a large area free from the interference of other hunters." When man became a big game hunter, two major consequences followed. First, his relation to the land changed; a small range was no longer adequate. And second, his hunting made his children and females economically much more dependent than they had been when everybody lived primarily by gathering food. "A young baboon," report Washburn and DeVore, "receives no food from other members of the troop, and, once it is weaned, it is economically independent. But in a band of hunters, children are dependent on adults for a substantial portion of their food . . ."

"Look. Let's start over from the beginning."

All right.

"Man is basically an animal, right?"

Right. And so is a dog, a white mouse, a zebra, a pig, an amoeba.

"Not so fast. Man is a two-legged animal."

So is a pigeon, a chicken, a turkey.

"Man is a two-legged animal without feathers, as Plato said."

As Diogenes graphically demonstrated in the market place at Athens, you can pluck a chicken but that doesn't make a man.

"Well, man is the only animal who can talk."

Mynah birds and parrots can say words. True, they may be merely, uh, parroting without understanding. But psychologists R. Allen Gardner and Beatrice T. Gardner have taught a chimpanzee enough American Sign Language—the gestural system of communication used by the deaf—to enable it to communicate in symbols. This chimp, named Washoe, can make demands, answer questions and put together gestures in combinations that resemble short sentences with meaning. Other chimpanzees, most recently one named Sara at Harvard, have been taught symbolic language. And John Lilly, after years of underwater research, has surfaced and claimed that dolphins, too, have an audible symbolic language.

"But man is the only animal who can make tools."

Jane van Lawick-Goodall has observed that chimpanzees not only use tools but make them. On several occasions, she records, "they picked small leafy twigs and prepared them for use by stripping off the leaves" to make a termite fishing pole. The stripped twig was inserted into the termite mound and then removed with a good mouthful of termites clinging to the wood. "This was the first recorded example," she writes with italicized emphasis, "of a wild animal not merely using an object as a tool, but actually modifying an object and thus showing the crude beginnings of tool*making*."

"Okay, then. Have it your own way. Man is a chimpanzee."

Either that, or it is necessary to redefine man in a more complex manner than we've been using. Otherwise, as Louis Leakey put it, "we should by definition have to accept the chimpanzee as Man." Philosopher and Rabbi Martin Freedman cautions that it's important to avoid the genetic fallacy of confusing rudiments with developments. A chicken may start out as an egg. But the two are not the same. You have to look at the chicken as well as at the egg if you want to understand the chicken.

"All right. Look at man. 'Born free,' as Rousseau said, 'but everywhere in chains.' Underneath it all, we're really a striving bundle of instincts."

But when you take that so-called bundle apart and list each instinct or human need, you have to keep adding to the tally and correcting for this finding or that. Says Dorothy Lee: "We have now such needs as that for novelty, for escape from reality, for security, for emotional response. We have primary needs, or drives, and secondary needs, and we have secondary needs playing the role of primary needs. . . . Where so much elaboration and revision is necessary, I suspect that the original unit itself must be at fault; we must have a radical change." If it's a list of basic instincts or needs, she asks, how can people abandon them as first causes so often?

Instincts drive a bird to build the same nest over and over. But, says Dr. Harry Demopoulous, Assistant Medical Examiner in New York, "People alter their life styles all the time. Besides, no animal gets a heart attack from non-stop thinking about a problem." Governed by instincts, animals can't put themselves through agonies by the thoughts they think or produce as wide a range as from a Hitler to an Einstein. But man, not driven irrevocably by instincts, "is capable of demonstrating an indomitable spirit in spite of all sorts of setbacks."

"But what about man's basic acquisitiveness?"

Say anthropologists Sherwood Washburn and C. S. Lancaster: "The whole human pattern of gathering and hunting to share—indeed, the whole complex of economic reciprocity that dominates so much of human life—is unique to man. In its small range, a monkey gathers only what it itself needs to eat at that moment." Among the Eskimos, reports E. Adamson Hoebel, "It is the giving away of food and goods, not the possession of them, that wins honor and leadership." It is the entrepreneur accumulating too much property and keeping it for himself, says E. W. Nelson, "who was looked upon as not working for the common end, so that he became hated and envied among the people." He either had to give all his goods away to the community or be lynched.

"Either way, he was looking out for Number One. Self-preservation is the first law of human nature. It's all simply a case of 'Life, Liberty and the Pursuit of Happiness,' as Jefferson said."

Then how can human infants be reared and protected for the years it takes until they are able to take care of themselves? "Altruism, prime requisite for social advance," says Carl O.

51

Sauer, "begins with the mother in the care and affection for her own, extends to the kindred, and becomes interfamilial aid." In the words of Washburn and DeVore, "In the evolution of society, the most important rules are those that guarantee economic survival to the dependent young. Human females and their young are efficient gatherers, so the crucial customs are those that guarantee the services of a hunter to a woman and her children. . . ."

"Right. Human nature is basically jealousy in men and mother-love in women. You know what Freud said about the good old sex drive."

One mate-swapping couple among many reported by Charles and Rebecca Palson answer typically about the practice, but never mention jealousy—basic or otherwise. Says the husband, Glen: "In swinging, you can see people for who they really are—as individuals, without the masks they have to wear most of the time. In a way, I guess I never knew people before, and I'm amazed at the variety. Maybe that's why swinging holds my interest—everybody is different, a challenge to get to know." Says his wife, Andrea: "Swinging has managed to hold our attention for a long time. If you give me a choice between going to South America, night clubbing or swinging, I think swinging is the most satisfying and interesting."

And as for the basic human nature of mother-love, the number of children under five years of age killed by abusive parents is higher than the number of those who die from disease, according to Dr. Ray E. Helfer and Dr. C. Henry Kempe of the University of Colorado School of Medicine. The nationwide toll of child abuse totals two to three thousand children injured each month and one or two killed each day. Child abuse includes burning infants' flesh with cigarettes, immersing a baby in a sink of scalding water, breaking its bones. In the New York City morgue, one pathologist said: "We get plenty of dead infants here—some obviously abused, but many dead of suffocation. It's hard to prove murder in those cases, so the insurance companies have to pay off." And, just for the record, in at least one old version it was the mother—not the stepmother—of Hansel and Gretel who insisted that the children be abandoned to the predators of the wood.

"But they survived. That's what human nature is. As Darwin said, it's the survival of the fittest."

Darwin didn't originate that. He borrowed the phrase from Spencer. And, anyway, when you look at who survives you are not necessarily looking at the fittest. A study of the German soldier by Shils and Janowitz reveals that he was likely to go on fighting "as long as the group had leadership with which he could identify himself, and as long as he gave affection to and received affection from the other members of his squad and platoon. In other words, as long as he felt himself to be a member of his primary group and therefore bound by the expectations and demands of its other members, his soldierly achievement was likely to be good." You can't really say that an individual will do anything he has to in order to survive.

"Not the survival of the individual. Human nature is a drive toward survival of the group."

Then how, asks Dorothy Lee, "could we explain the behavior of certain small nations who chose freely to lose necessary food, shelter, security, etc., rather than join the Axis? Why did whole nations court physical annihilation rather than subscribe to Axis doctrines? Why did fathers and husbands and daughters expose their beloved families to danger of torture or death by joining the underground? In this country, why did millions of people who had adequate food and shelter and 'security' choose to jeopardize their lives? We could say, of course, that they were satisfying their need for emotional response, in this case the approval of others." But in that case, "how could these needs have been the cause of behavior whose goal was neither individual nor group survival?"

"Not the survival of the family, the platoon or the nation. Human nature is aimed at the survival of the whole species."

A major study of world trends has concluded that mankind probably faces an "uncontrollable and disastrous collapse of its society within 100 years unless it moves speedily to establish 'global equilibrium' in which growth of population and industrial output are halted." This study comes from the Massachusetts Institute of Technology where a computer fed with a mathematical approximation of the world system was asked to forecast consequences. Working without a computer, some ecologists are not so gloomy and give people another six generations, or about 150 years, at current rates of progress. Other scientists are not so optimistic and say that unless we change our ways, human nature will be facing extinction within one generation.

And so on and on, from one advertisement of human nature to another.

Only man can remember the past and anticipate the future. But then, what about the computer which does the same sort of work?

It's human nature to want to be clean. But it depends on when you look, and where. An English monk of the fourteenth century took more baths and smelled sweeter than a gentleman of Elizabethan times. A middle-class family in the time of George I bathed far more often than that gentleman—and more often than a middle-class family of the mid-Victorian era. And a study of the United States bathroom in the 1960s points out that bathing habits are not the only indication of cleanliness, as anybody who does the family's underwear laundry knows.

Fundamentally, people are a clutch of fears, anxieties and repressions. But in that case, human nature is a pathological condition, a chronic ailment that needs constant treatment until it is finally cured by death. . . .

After a tour of the human nature industry, it's a lot easier to say what human nature is not. For every peg manufactured, there are at least two holes where it doesn't fit. Somewhere between the assembly line where the human data are produced and the knowledge foundry where the facts are processed into information the quality control becomes a little slipshod. About all you can say for human nature nowadays is that the product doesn't seem to be working as well as it did in the good old days.

Chapter Three

Blessings on thee, little man.
Barefoot boy, with cheek of tan!
With thy turned-up pantaloons,
And thy merry whistled tunes;
With thy red lip, redder still
Kissed by strawberries on the hill . . .

So begins John Greenleaf Whittier's poem about nature—probably the most familiar American description of the subject. That barefoot boy with cheek of tan whistling across field and stream typifies a highly selective version of the past which is now widely known as the good old days. But whether or not those old days were good when Whittier wrote of them in 1855, his barefoot boy has come to personify nature and the natural life.

But the poem is now a collector's item. The nature it describes belongs to another, bygone age. Today it is hard to imagine many barefoot boys knowing what Whittier's boy knew—

Of the wild bee's morning chase,
Of the wild flower's time and place,
Flight of fowl and habitude
Of the tenants of the wood . . .

The morning chase is no longer the bee's; nowadays it is the commuter's automobile. Time is no longer measured by the arrival of wild flowers. They can arrive at any hour, given the proper lighting and a twenty-four-hour florist. Today, time is a function of the countdown to blast-off and the distance from re-entry. Moreover, with another new dwelling unit going up every twenty-seven seconds to keep pace with population pressure in the United States, there is very little habitude left for the tenants of either wood or village. And anyway, that is no longer a matter of nature but a problem of ecology. In fact, what with pollution, additives and waste, it is hard to imagine many boys being allowed to go barefoot anywhere.

There are still a few streams and fields and all that, of course. And they can be seen in panorama for a ten-dollar ticket good for one year in any national park, or free, close-up, in color and without bugs on television if you don't care about the radiation hazard from your TV set.

Now, this is not to say that Whittier's poem is completely obsolete. Strawberries are not yet extinct, although you don't look for them on the hill anymore. Instead, you look under the sliced peaches in the compartment next to the dairy substitute products. And certainly sun-tanned cheeks are still available if you don't care about the radiation hazard from the sun. But the rest of the verse needs to be recycled and reconstituted. That business about the merry whistled tunes has to go. Almost any first-generation computer can whistle "Dixie" better, and stereophonically as well. In fact, fi is now so hi that only another machine can listen to it with true appreciation. And as for that couplet in the second stanza:

O for boyhood's painless play,
Sleep that wakes in laughing day . . .

well, everybody knows better than that today. There is nothing painless about boyhood's play. The traumas sustained in the sandbox of the unconscious will fester and burst on the playing fields of My Lai and Buchenwald. And as for laughing day, there are very few jokes to be found in field and stream. On the contrary, it is a very serious business—a mindless, grim, lonely fight for survival.

* *

Fortunately, however, the major repairs on the poem can be managed quite easily to make it conform with the true facts. All you need are a couple of items found around any modern barn (or garage): a tube of quick-setting epoxy tinted in Rustic Verdure; and an aerosol spray deodorizer scented with a drop or two of Steaming Pasture.

Today, as everybody knows, John Greenleaf Whittier's poem would go something like this:

Dressings on thee, little man
(Anointed for a safer tan),
With thine ever turned-up sleeve
(Anti-toxins to receive).
Lip and cheek strawberry-kissed
("Quite common," says the allergist),
But safe from flower, fowl and bee
(The benefits of DDT).
Ah summer! Season to be prized
When little men are immunized.

Each carefree dream can be pursued
(If it match thy aptitude).
Up into the cherry tree
(To commune with botany),
Up the river and o'er the lea
(For ninety minutes of therapy)
Lists of nature's recreations
(On thy college applications)
Can make of boyhood's innocence
Negotiable experience.

So there is half of the difficulty in trying to find out what makes people people rather than pigeons or chimpanzees. It is very hard to inquire into human nature nowadays as there is very little nature around.

The other half of the difficulty in the inquiry, as everybody knows, is that there are very few people around, either. A brief look at the distribution department of the human nature industry certainly indicates that the market in people is quite soft.

Railroad tracks, highways and/or air lanes still connect most places in the nation. At least the maps say so. But in real life it becomes harder every day to get there by public transportation unless you're willing to go via parcel post or railway express. Psychotherapy, once the "talking cure" between patient and doctor, has become largely chemotherapy. As many psychiatrists explain, medications provide faster relief from symptoms, so you can treat more patients than you could by the old method of conversation. Mass-circulation magazines have become very careful about whom they ask to subscribe. Sheer numbers of audience are not attractive to advertisers; they want specific kinds of humans with specific kinds of incomes, age ranges, interests and buying habits. A subscription list of just anybody is not profitable. Television, of course, cannot be that selective about the receiving end. The audience is faceless. But on the transmitting end, even though there are now well over two hundred million people in the United States, somehow the same few faces keep appearing again and again on the home screen. In one three-month period, twenty-one celebrities made at least three appearances each on the talk shows. And even in the blue-chip people market, trading is sluggish. The Metropolitan Museum of Art recently ran a thirty-year retrospective exhibition of works created between 1940 and 1970. Of the 413 canvases, sculptures and other creations on display, only twenty-seven were attempts at representing the human form.

People, it appears have become too expensive, too time consuming and too uninteresting to be feasible.

It also appears that people have become impractical.

As everybody knows, the astronauts didn't really go to the moon. They were put there by a triumph of hardware and a team of three thousand technologists. Today, hardly anybody can remember the names of the men who first walked on the moon, or the date of the event. Not only are people becoming indistinguishable from hardware, but it also begins to look as though people are hardware when you wander through the stock rooms of the human nature industry. Many internal organs are now interchangeable, and many experts look forward to the day when there will be spare parts for everything. Viviparous birth may be obsolete once the day of the test-tube baby arrives. Laboratories have already grown the fertilized egg of small animals to heartbeating stage. And if everything works out, there may eventually be no need for the sperm to fertilize the egg—nor any need for the egg, either. In theory, a recipe of the proper protoplasm implanted with a cell of the proper genetic coding, a cell from the cheek lining for example, should grow into a person.

The person himself, however, is a rather poor sample for serious study in many parts of the human nature industry. He is a datum that often interferes with the information about human nature.

For some time now, experimental psychology has been trying to find a way to get the human experimenter out of the experiment because his presence frequently pollutes the atmosphere and spoils the pure results. So far, no sure way has been found to filter off this contaminant. Using sensing devices and computers instead of humans to conduct such experiments does not seem to help matters, either. In the knowledge foundry of the human nature industry, where human data are processed into information, one psychologist threw up her hands in anger and disgust at the results of her research into human reaction to stress. "You simply can't get a straight input-output line from people, no matter what you do. The input goes in all right. But something happens inside them before the output comes out, and it happens differently in each subject. It throws all of your results off. I've had just enough of that kind of stress. I don't think I can take much more."

People do not seem to make very good subjects in other kinds of human experiments as well. Or at least the human data they produce for the research is not very informative of their nature. A team of experimenters working on methods to condition people say that they will not take subjects who know they are going to be conditioned. The knowledge of the process and the goal, it seems, obstructs the achievement of positive results. Only if the human subject can be kept in the dark like a machine can he be programmed to behave like one.

That view is not held in every sector of the human nature industry. The input-output theory of human behavior has many devoted, if surprised, followers. During a power failure that blacked out the entire northeastern United States some years ago, a lot of humans there discovered that they were quite similar to their immobilized everyday appliances. Moreover, there is a firm conviction in many parts of the human nature industry that conditioning of people is more possible and more feasible when people are aware of being treated like machines. At a computer-mating service, a twenty-eight-year-old fellow explained why he was looking for a wife by means of electronic scanning and matching:

"How can you really know how you feel—I mean, how you feel basically—about anything or anyone? What you think you feel today may not actually be true. You could think you feel differently tomorrow. But this system looks at you objectively. It makes your decision scientifically."

No matter which way you slice him these days, a person is a pretty poor specimen of human nature. Genetically, he is not comparable with the purity of the white mouse or fruit fly. Physiologically, he is not nearly as orderly as the crayfish or the frog. People respond more than they react, and so cannot be considered in the same high class of experimental subjects as the clam or the computer. And economically, people are just too expensive for the budget—any budget.

Now, this is not to say that people have disappeared. Doubtless they are still there somewhere. It's just that they aren't as visible to the human eye as they were in the days of John Greenleaf Whittier. In that bygone time, the big problem was how to tell the difference between man and animals. And while that problem was never actually solved, it is no longer a problem. These days, the big problem seems to be how to find the similarities between machines and small laboratory animals. And as for people—well, there is basically no need for that hypothesis in order to explain the facts.

2

Exactly when and where that depression hit the human nature industry is hard to pinpoint. There are different estimates about the time and place of the event. Some say it happened on Sigmund Freud's couch in 1895; others say it was in Henry Ford's garage in 1897; or at Kitty Hawk, North Carolina, in 1903. Then, there are those who say that it happened in two stages. First, nature came to an end—either in the laboratory of Niels Bohr in 1912 or in the mind of Albert Einstein in 1904. And then the people market collapsed. Some say that happened in the saddle of Kaiser Wilhelm's horse in 1913; others say that was the year all right, but that the human nature market actually fell in the Armory of the 69th Infantry in New York with the first modern art show in America. In any case, the event is usually located someplace between 1890 and Sarajevo.

At that time, of course, readers and other consumers in the human nature industry did not know it had happened. In those days, the old industry was still flourishing in the old shop, and the product was still being distributed by its traditional retailers: storytellers, poets, minstrels, journalists and riders of the lecture circuit. The preserve of Homer, Thucydides and Virgil had passed through the hands of Pope, Fielding and De Tocqueville, and was now in the keeping of Mark Twain, Lincoln Steffens and Edgar Guest among others of that not-so-distant time.

Some of those others, as many grandparents will recall, were Russell Conwell, Elbert Hubbard, Booth Tarkington, Upton Sinclair, Thorstein Veblen, Edward Westcott, Samuel Smiles, Orison Swett Marden, Arthur Conan Doyle, Gene Stratton Porter and William Graham Sumner. And some of the books: *Acres of Diamonds, The Shame of the Cities, Self-Help, Pushing to the Front, Health and Wealth, Tom Swift, Horatio Alger, David Harum, Rebecca of Sunnybrook Farm, Mrs. Wiggs of the Cabbage Patch, The Girl of the Limberlost, Black Beauty* and *A Heap o' Livin'.*

A typical story—as the product of the human nature industry was retailed in those days—went something like this:

A foundling, discovered in a barn, is reared by the kind farmer and his wife. The baby, named Walter because he is a boy, is a sturdy, cheerful, helpful, courteous child obviously of good stock. He is on excellent terms with all of the animals on the farm, but develops a very close friendship with a crow whose life he has saved. Walter and the grateful crow, Jango, form a business partnership to help the farm community guard against poachers. Jango refuses the money, so Walter saves it all to go to college. While there, Walter makes friends with everyone,

64

helping many with their homework, but not neglecting his own serious study of birds. Jango lives on the roof of the biology building where he narrowly escapes death at the hands of a city boy, Bert. Jango tells Walter about it, and together they invite Bert to the farm for a vacation in order to teach him the laws of nature.

While at the farm, Bert becomes gravely ill. And Walter, helping to nurse him back to health and strength, makes a discovery about nutrition. He vows that he will devote his life to developing a new strain of worm. It will be good for the birds, good for the soil, good for farmers and good for the economy of the great nation. On graduation, Bert takes Walter and Jango back to his home in the city to discuss the idea with his father who knows about these things. During the visit, two important events occur. First, Walter discovers that he and Bert are actually first cousins by blood. And second, Jango discovers a runaway horse and carriage. Walter manages to stop the horse, but Jango is killed during the chase through misjudging the height of the buildings and crashing into a seven-story skyscraper. The occupant of the carriage is a girl, Sarah or Grace, whose father is a tycoon, Mr. Vreeland. He is naturally delighted that his daughter has been saved, but saddened that Jango was killed. Consequently, he gives Walter a laboratory, called the Jango Institute, to develop a new strain of worm for science, mankind and prosperity. And in addition, he gives his daughter to be Walter's bride.

Unbeknownst to everybody, the Walter-Vreeland nuptials are solemnized on the day before the *Lusitania* is sunk. But that is after the fact, although it is hard to forget that. When you look back to those days now, it all seems to have been quite simple: you were born; you grew up; you asserted your natural self; and with a bit of perseverance and a fortuitous meeting or two, you succeeded. Any difficulties along the way—political corruption,

65

say, or epidemic or even poverty—required merely a little more enlightened self-assertion. As every worker in the human nature industry knew, if you give light, then the people will find their way.

After the First World War, however, there was serious question about that. In those days, for the first time, a part of the retail distribution from the human nature industry was being handled by social scientists and observers such as Margaret Mead, James and Mary Beard, James Harvey Robinson, Émile Coué, Earnest Hooton, Bruce Barton, Robert and Helen Lynd, Sigmund Freud, Bronislaw Malinowski. Some of the widely read books of that kind were: *Coming of Age in Samoa, Up from the Ape, The Mind in the Making, Sex and Repression in Savage Society, Civilization and its Discontents, Middletown, The Man Nobody Knows, Self-Mastery Through Conscious Autosuggestion.*

For the most part, however, the journalists, lecturers, broadcasters, other storytellers and poets still purveyed human nature at retail. But, to look at only the best-seller list, there were such names as John Dos Passos, Ernest Hemingway, Theodore Dreiser, Sherwood Anderson, Edna St. Vincent Millay, Sinclair Lewis, Floyd Dell, Dorothy Parker, Carl Sandburg, F. Scott Fitzgerald, Heywood Broun, Ring Lardner, H. L. Mencken, William Bolitho.

A popular kind of story of that time might have gone along lines like these:

Nick, a boy from a Midwestern town, grows up with the ambition to be a biologist like his father and develop a new strain of worm to benefit mankind and birdkind. To this end, he goes east to an Ivy League college, becomes the school's boxing champion, meets some Jews, and falls in love with Kathrine. During a school vacation, he visits Kathrine at her home, a beautiful estate near Phaeton, Long Island. Here, Nick meets Kathrine's brother, Bert, an optometrist who has lost a leg during the Great War. Each night, Bert limps out of the mansion and stands on the steps of the gazebo, looking out across the water to Portugal. One night, after a long evening of merrymaking at three speakeasies and a country club dance during which two people are drowned, Bert confesses to Nick that he lives only for the day when he can return to Lisbon and live near the grave of the only woman he ever loved.

Nick is saddened to hear this story, but glad to know that at least Bert has purpose in life. Nick is no longer sure of his. All he knows for certain is that he must get away—away from Kathrine, from her brother, from her country club and from her father, Charley, the inventor of the double-head spark plug.

But Paris provides no lasting answer for Nick. One afternoon, at a picnic with a retired army nurse during which a bullfighter is killed, Nick falls into a deep and feverish sleep. He dreams a vivid sequence concerning a stallion, a capon and a pair of white ducks. On waking, he finds that several things have become quite clear. He now realizes that Kathrine was the symbol of his grandfather. He sees, too, that it was no accident—and certainly no humanitarian spirit—that made his father interested in worms. And most important, he knows that he must go back.

In New York, he takes various jobs as a newspaper reporter, an ambulance driver, an advertising copywriter and, by a stroke of good luck, as a factory hand. He eats, he sleeps, he works, he sweats, and it is good. Then one evening on a visit to the Bronx Zoo during which an automobile dealer is killed, Nick meets Caroline, a dental technician. He takes her back to his small, bare, but clean room where they make love and it is good.

Caroline becomes pregnant and Nick, delirious with joy at a new life in the making, promises to give up his career at the factory and take his woman and child back to his home town where he will get a job as a biologist in his father's institute. But

Caroline senses that such a move would be a denial of all that Nick has suffered to achieve. As soon as her labor pains start, she goes to the waterfront, hires a small boat and rows across the Hudson to Weehawken where she and the baby die. Nick vows that her death will not have been in vain. He takes the ferry back in the rain, resolved to become a psychiatrist and help others to find freedom, too.

If it is humanly possible to do it, Nick will do it—as everybody at the time knew.

But, as everybody knows now, they don't turn out a product like that in the human nature industry anymore.

In the generation after World War I, as in the generation before it, you could still assert yourself and, with perseverance, you could succeed. The only difference after the war was that you had to discover your self first before you could assert it. And that generally meant escaping from the marble forest of materialism and then burrowing through the barren silt of civilization, layer under layer, until the true person was revealed and ready to create and live. He was there all along, of course, but he had to be realized before he could breathe.

But before the Great Depression was over, both that diagnosis and that remedy were suspect. By the end of the post World War II period, the ailment had been redefined. And so had the medicine to cure it. The human nature industry was moving into modern times.

Between the mid-1930s and the mid-1950s, there were still plenty of storytellers: John Steinbeck, Erich Remarque, John O'Hara, Lillian Smith, Richard Wright, Herman Wouk, J. D. Salinger, Irwin Shaw, James Jones, Norman Mailer, Margaret Mitchell. And there were poets as well, such as Norman Corwin and Archibald MacLeish. Most certainly there were journalists, as worried war watchers knew. But it began to appear quite plainly that the exclusive retail franchise for human nature industry was no longer theirs as it had been. Where a Margaret Mead or an Émile Coué or a Bruce Barton had been an occasional social thinker among the artists, writers, speakers and other retailers, the advertising and distribution system of the industry now included Norman Vincent Peale, Karen Horney, Dale Carnegie, Walter Pitkin, Erich Fromm, Harry Emerson Fosdick, Joshua Loth Liebman, LeComte DuNöuy, Dorothea Brande and so on.

It may have been partly because of the Depression when self-assertion was not enough—even if you could discover and realize yourself. And it may have been partly because of the German genocide of the Jews that called for a shocking reappraisal of the words "human" and "inhuman." But whatever the complete list of factors, the titles everybody knew were: *The Neurotic Personality of Our Time, How to Stop Worrying and Start Living, Peace of Mind, Human Destiny, Wake Up and Live, Take It Easy, A Guide to Confident Living, A Study of History, Escape from Freedom, Man for Himself, On Being a Real Person* and the like.

A table of contents of the time might have included chapter headings like these:

  I. *You're Anxious and You Don't Know It*
  II. *What 10,000 Ink Blot Tests Say About Us*
  III. *You Can't Commute to Life*
  IV. *Marriage—Love or Exploitation?*
  V. *What Our Schools Give Kids—and Take Away*
  VI. *Piecemeal Economy, Piecemeal Lives*
  VII. *The Sioux, the Balinese, the Helvetii*
  VIII. *The Arrow-Maker vs. the Riveter*
  IX. *The Drive Toward Wholeness*
  X. *Learn to Love Yourself Spontaneously*
  XI. *Who Makes the Laws Around Here?*
  XII. *Society in the Image of Man*

By the mid-1950s, it was becoming clear to human nature consumers that you could not hope to find yourself waiting to be realized somewhere in the rubble of the unconscious or in the shower after a hard day's work. In fact, you could not expect to find yourself in any one place. On the contrary, you were fragmented into dozens of little pieces that had been scattered across the past and present countryside. And you were alienated from what remained by the forces of industrialization, economics, government, education; everything conspired to teach you to hate yourself. So, before you could assert yourself, you had to reclaim the shards of your self, reassemble them, and then cherish the whole as the worthwhile entity it really was. But that was not so easily done. It required first an enormous engineering project to rebuild society on a human scale, based on human values, rewarding human achievement and fulfilling human needs.

Whether it was possible to engineer and build that new structure is not known because the human nature industry went out of that business between the mid-1950s and the 1970s. What with improved production methods and so on, it was no longer necessary to reclaim and reassemble the fragments of the product. Besides, as some industry people were saying, there weren't any pieces to begin with, so there weren't any to salvage.

During that period, some of the retail outlets of the human nature industry were still held by storytellers: John Updike, Saul Bellow, Philip Roth, Ross Macdonald, Bernard Malamud, Kurt Vonnegut, Jr., Harold Robbins and some others. There were also several poets and journalists at their traditional stands, but their names and works do not come as readily to mind as do those of advertising agencies and disc jockeys. So, a typical story of the time is rather hazy. It is hard to remember who was murdered or otherwise disposed of, or what agent explained it, and who his employer really was.

For the most part, the industrial park had become the preserve of social observers, social scientists and scientists who turned to social observation. Some of them were: David Riesman, Norbert Wiener, A. C. Spectorsky, Vance Packard, Russell Lynes, B. F. Skinner, John Kenneth Galbraith, Herman Kahn, Robert Ardrey, Konrad Lorenz, Desmond Morris, Rollo May, Eric Berne, Erik Erikson, R. D. Laing, William H. Whyte, Theodore White, Peter Berger, Erving Goffman, Edward T. Hall, Masters, Johnson, Kinsey, Martin and Pomeroy.

The bookshelf, as everybody knew, was divided into two general categories. On the one side were titles such as *The Organization Man, The Lonely Crowd, The Taste Makers, The Hidden Persuaders, The Making of the President, The Affluent Society, The Unprepared Society, The Unfinished Society, The Temporary Society, The Abstract Society* and *Walden Two*. This tireless analysis of the group and how it works (and how it ought to work) shares the human nature library with another kind of analysis. Some of the titles on that side of the partition are:

The Search for Identity, Identity and Anxiety, Shame and the Search for Identity, The Collective Search for Identity, Identity: Youth and Crisis, The Presentation of Self in Everyday Life, The Divided Self, The Dying Self, Games People Play, The Silent Language, Body Language, Sexual Behavior in the Human Male and Female, The Territorial Imperative and *The Search for Bridey Murphy*.

No other time has ever applied so much specialized technique and training to searching out and disseminating the basic information in everything from the voting pattern to the orgasm. No pause has gone unmeasured, no condolence left uncompared and uncontrasted. Here is a detailed study of twenty-two kinds of wink. There is a description in depth of the hello, the shrug and the smile. What once might have been a look at friendship patterns was now a close scrutiny of male-male valences, fol-

71

lowed by later and improved studies of male-female, female-male and female-female interaction. As everybody knows, you cannot open a popular magazine without reading a regularly scheduled report on the latest findings regarding human behavior. You cannot look at a bus station bookrack or evening television schedule without seeing a public communication about brain waves, comparative health practices, the circuitry of passion, the ritual transaction of greeting and farewell among chimpanzees and Chicagoans. No secretion, gesture, shiver or spoor is without a team of skilled investigators to take it apart, and a corps of professional communicators to hand down the results to the waiting audience.

In this era of output analysis, the typical title would probably be *The Effluent Society*. But it's not a book. In keeping with basic interaction, ritual and the other tools of the behavioral sciences, the ideal synopsis is of a play—the sort of theater so popular at that time:

The scene is the inside of a motorman's glove. Standing in the thumb is GEORGE WASHINGTON. *He is looking at his face in a small mirror, examining the moles and blemishes. Out of his sight, in the pinky, is* ROBERT FULTON. *He is dressed in overalls. In one hand he has a shovel. In the other he has a pick. Lying on the ground at his feet is a* SMALL BOY.

GEORGE (*Squeezing a pimple*): How are things?

FULTON (*Listening to his heart with a stethoscope*): Not so good.

GEORGE (*Examining his eyes in the mirror*): Glad to hear it. And how are things?

FULTON (*Sticking tongue depressor into his mouth*): Not so good.

GEORGE (*Tweezering a hair from his eyebrow*): Glad to hear it.

FULTON (*Putting a jeweler's loupe in his eye*): I don't like the looks of it at all.

72

GEORGE (*Examining his teeth and gums in the mirror*): Of course. This is the land of opportunity. Let us begin.

FULTON (*Begins to shovel out the young boy*): It's not coming so well.

GEORGE: How is it coming? (*His teeth fall out of his mouth, revealing themselves to be a yo-yo*)

FULTON: There's an awful lot of crap here.

GEORGE (*Playing with his yo-yo*): That's the puritan ethic. Can you see Buffalo yet?

FULTON: No. (*He shovels some more out of the boy*) Yes. No, no . . . I can't see Buffalo. But how about a couple of grouse and quail? (*He pulls them out of the boy*)

GEORGE: Grouse and quail? Didn't they play the old RKO circuit?

FULTON (*Shoveling*): There's an awful lot of wax here.

GEORGE (*Still playing with his yo-yo*): Wax? Are you sure you're digging the Erie Canal?

FULTON: The Erie Canal? I thought you told me to dig the ear canal.

THE BOY (*Gets up, realizing he has become POCAHONTAS in the course of the expedition*): I'm not a boy any longer!

GEORGE: Of course not. And you can't work for boy's wages. (*His yo-yo breaks, the false teeth falling on his foot*) Something just hit me.

POCAHONTAS (*Looking down on her large bosom*): What's that?

GEORGE: To hell with the canal. Who wants to go to Buffalo anyway? (*He studies the false teeth in a new light*) We'll build a bridge instead.

POCAHONTAS: I'm a woman!

GEORGE: Certainly. This is the land of opportunity.

As everybody knows, a boy can grow up to be anything he wants to be nowadays. And if he doesn't like it when he gets there, he can have it changed.

The difference between the sexes appears to be unnecessary for reproduction, according to basic research on turkeys and frogs. The difference between people appears to be only a matter of sugars and phosphates which may be controllable in time, according to basic research in genetics. Life and death are not yet interchangeable, but the vital organs soon may be if basic research in physiology works out. It also appears that the social contract can be rewritten at will, according to basic work done on college campuses, in public schools and at the breakfast table. And as for the rest of what appears to be reality—such as hopes and joys and achievements—all of that seems to be basically a local ailment that depends on the pressures of society and the rewards and punishments of personal experience.

All in all, it might seem to the consumer that today's human nature industry is manufacturing, distributing and advertising a much more *viable* product than it used to.

You no longer have to worry about asserting yourself, or discovering yourself or reassembling yourself. Beneath the learned role of the moment is another learned role, and under that one yet another. And at the very bottom there is basically nothing but a conditioned response. So, really, there is nothing to grow into, nothing to get back to, nothing to collect and mend. And consequently there is no need to rebuild society along human lines and based on human values. By getting down to basics, you can build a society to produce the kind of human lines and values you want.

The old stumbling blocks of people and their nature are gone. There is nothing to unwrap and assemble, and nothing to break and repair. Life is no longer a struggle, or a hardship, or even a mystery that unfolds. Basically, as everybody knows, life is now a *problem*. But it is a problem that can't be solved, so all you have to do is to *cope*. Under the circumstances, one does not have to be in love anymore. Basically, one is merely *involved*. You do not have to speak your mind anymore, either, or act on your convictions. Basically, there are none. Instead, you *act out*,

74

or you *interact,* or else you have a *dialogue,* an *encounter* or a *confrontation.* People are no longer eccentric, mad, unlikable or mean. It's just that they don't *relate* well. And that is because they are suffering from *hang-ups* or incomplete *communication.* Nothing is more or less important than anything else. It is only another lateral stop on the local *spectrum* of values, and thus either *relevant* or not. There is neither tragedy nor comedy. There are only *value judgments,* behavioral *adjustments* and politics.

This catalogue could go on at considerable length. Suffice it to say, however, that nobody talks about human nature. The closest you can come to the topic is the *images of man.* So, if you feel the need for your self, you have to go out and find one —trying on this self or that until you're *into* one that is *viable.*

3

In other words:

It appears that the human nature industry hasn't been distributing that product for quite a while.

As Alfred Kroeber put it a generation ago: "Psychologists have become very unwilling to discuss the inherent psychic nature of man. It is definitely unfashionable to do so. When the subject is faced at all, it is usually only to explain human nature away as fast as possible, and to pass on to less uneasy and more specific topics. Human nature is going the way the human mind has gone." And as Orrin Klapp says, "My father lacked many things, but one thing he did not lack was a definite conception of himself. I am sure it never occurred to him (nor, perhaps, did it to your father, since we are dealing with a generational difference) to ask 'who he was'; and he would have thought it odd, to say the least, that anyone should be concerned with such a problem."

Between that time two generations ago and today, the industry stopped talking about human nature. And it's not hard to see why.

For one thing, "a human nature" implies that it is a unity, as Professor Abraham Edel pointed out, and that sense of a unity gives it a moralistic, religious flavor. In earlier times, people used to ponder that unity, speculating about Natural Man, the Noble Savage and what would happen if people followed their inclinations. But, as Professor Edel added, those questions aren't asked today. The concept has changed. And it has changed, as Dr. John R. Everett suggests, "because social science didn't begin to make progress until the unity of the concept 'human nature' was broken up and examined." So that makes it very hard to talk about human nature in many sectors of the industry when so many researchers are doing what F. Champion Ward calls piecework.

That opens up the second reason why the industry no longer seems to be distributing human nature: the human's nature is very hard to do piecework on. In the words of one physicist-biologist engaged in research into cancer in clams: "I feel sorry for the scientists who have to work with human subjects," he said, asking that his name be withheld. "My subjects don't argue with me. Clams don't worry about what I'm doing or what they're supposed to do about it. And they all react just about the same way. Using people as subjects of any scientific study has built-in failure."

Microbiologist René Dubos smiles in agreement. "People do not only react. The human is much more likely to respond than to react. And that may make some scientific observers uneasy. Studying people under controlled conditions may not tell you what you want to know because people may respond dif-

76

ferently depending on the time of day, the season of the year, the place they're in—and more importantly their aspirations for the future."

That, in turn, leads to another reason—a third obstruction in the distribution of human nature. No matter how scientific human observers are, they seem to pollute their observed data and thus warp the information when studying other humans. Or even when studying animals, as Bertrand Russell remarks in an exaggeration to illustrate the difficulties in human perception: "Animals studied by Americans rush about frantically with an incredible display of hustle and pep, and at last achieve the desired result by chance. Animals observed by Germans sit still and think and at last evolve the solution out of their inner consciousness."

And, finally, human nature is not worth talking about for plain and simple reasons of conditions in both the human and nature markets. The world population as of this writing is 3.5 billion—double the number at the time of the barefoot boy with cheek of tan. Within a century, if present conditions in the people market continue, the earth population will approach twenty-five billion. As with any oversupply, the glut of people reduces the worth of the stock. And at the same time, nature appears to have become so rare that it's not even worth talking about anymore. If James Whitcomb Riley were alive today, he'd have to undergo extensive vocational retraining in order to get his old job in the human nature industry:

When Defrost is on the punkin
And Dilute is on the can
Of the concentrated turkey
Manyfactured in Japan . . .

A study of murders over a thirty-year span in Milwaukee shows that as the population increased, victims were more often unknown to their assailants. According to the report of that study in *Behavior Today*, as interaction among people increases in frequency, "violence increases and changes from directed to nondirected, purposeless violence (and) experience becomes more stereotyped and we are less able to perceive unique individuals." Between 1879 and 1940, the amount of personal description in obituaries declined from 75 per cent to 25 per cent. More recently, there has been a great decrease in what were once called family doctors. Many no longer make house calls at all. This change toward more impersonal medicine has been accompanied by a great increase in malpractice suits. In California, malpractice insurance can now cost a doctor $18,000 in premiums per year.

And your wimmern in the kitchern
Busy mixin chlorine through
The recirculated cider
Fore they pour a mug fer you . . .

To keep up with the population demand, a new housing unit must be built every eighteen seconds in the United States, and a new city the size of Philadelphia built every two years. "I don't know how much more welfare payments and aid to dependent children the economy can stand," said one former member of a mayoral commission studying his city's program. "And anyway, why should you spend part of your hard-earned wages to pay for the unwanted by-product of pleasure-making by a man and a woman you've never met."

They's somethin kinda harty-like
About the atmusfere
When the air condition's over
N'fore the snow machine is here . . .

In the past, says Robert Glasgow, the city has been many

things "and the generically attractive thing about the city was that it seemed to be an optimum center of choice." But no longer. "It is ironic that for all the current preoccupation with cities, no one has really developed a satisfactory theoretical concept of just what the city is supposed to be."

But it is difficult to figure out the nature of the city until you solve the problem beneath, namely, the concept of the nature of the human who makes cities and lives there. But the human nature industry seems to have stopped the distribution of that product for consideration. "Many scientists," says Hans Bethe, "think only of how to put the problem on the computer. They no longer think about the problem itself." And so the industry has not generally been working on what the city should be, but rather on a projection of what the city will become. And that is, according to a recent UN report, an epidemic culture of tuberculosis, parasitoses, skin diseases, diarrhea, malnutrition, venereal disease, psychosomatic illnesses, mental breakdowns, suicide attempts—the kinds of things that science and piecework have progressed so far against.

O, it's then's the times a feller
Knows that autumn clothes is worn
When yer girls go off to meetin
Dressed like ole September Morn . . .

"I always try to explain to my students," says a music teacher, "that making music is one of the things that distinguish the human from the animal." But it's hard to get that point across because most students seldom see animals. What they see more of are machines.

"I've been unsuccessful twice before," said a man who recently married a girl selected for him by computer. "The computer couldn't have any worse judgment than I did." Said another man mated by computer: "It seemed like a more logical method than trusting my emotions. . . . You lose a lot of time, money and effort that way."

The University of Washington's Adult Development Program has devised a curriculum in the "skills of living." Courses include relaxation, interpersonal relations, constructive communications and home management.

Yep, the fall's so appetizin
With the smog on street and tree—
It makes yer soul jump handsprings
To breathe air that you kin see . . .

"The trouble with sociological observation," says a sociologist, "is that you become a part of your study, and then your study becomes part of the data, so you have to do another study—and the whole thing starts all over again." After William H. Whyte, Jr., studied the "organization man," the organization was never again the same. And neither was the man. When his wife meets him in the station wagon with their 2.6 children and Yorkshire terrier, she must smile deprecatingly, Whyte found, and they both must be self-conscious about the length of time they have lived in their junior executive community.

Why, it looks jest like a cover
On the Satty Even'n Post,
When the frost is on the punkin
Cuz the punkin's on Defrost.

Even the antique products distributed by the human nature industry long ago and now decontaminated by time are not mentioned by name anymore.

In the "introduction to the work or bill of fare of the feast," says Henry Fielding, explaining what the reader will find in his *Tom Jones,* "the provision, then, which we have here made is no other than Human Nature." Now that is certainly plain enough.

80

But if the book is considered at all in the industry today, it is advertised as an item in something called "Origins of the English Novel."

"Ah love, let us be true to one another!" says Matthew Arnold in the concluding stanza of his poem "Dover Beach," "for the world, which seems to lie before us like a land of dreams . . . hath really neither joy, nor love nor light, nor certitude, nor peace, nor help for pain; and we are here as on a darkling plain swept with confused alarms of struggle and flight, where ignorant armies clash by night." Clearly, that is one model distributed by the old human nature industry. But nobody says so today. Instead, it is usually billed as part of "Nineteenth-Century Poetry."

"Why are you trying to fascinate me, Jack, if you don't want to marry me?" asks Ann in the last act of *Man and Superman.*

TANNER: The Life Force. I am in the grip of the Life Force.

ANN: I don't understand in the least; it sounds like the Life Guards.

TANNER (*Despairingly*): Oh, you are witty; at the supreme moment, the Life Force endows you with every quality . . .

ANN: Well, I made a mistake: you do not love me.

TANNER (*Seizing her in his arms*): It is false; I love you. The Life Force enchants me: I have the whole world in my arms when I clasp you. But I am fighting for my freedom, for my honor, for my self, one and indivisible . . .

That play, naturally, is not advertised as a communication from the old human nature industry. It is referred to instead by today's human nature industry as part of *The Collected Works of George Bernard Shaw.*

All in all, it appears that the human nature industry has stopped distributing its stock-in-trade and, moreover, would like to forget that it ever was in that business. Instead, the industry prefers to advertise two new lines of products developed to replace the embarrassing old one. These two substitutes for human nature are called Science and the Humanities, and are packaged under such labels as Social Science, Communication Arts, Business Administration, Technology, Contemporary Civilization and so on. In each package are smaller containers: Reading, Writing, Biology, Psychology, Poetry, The Novel, Long Division and so on. All of those, of course, are the products and consequences of human nature. But the industry does not like to mention that. And as a result, many students and teachers at all levels in Science and the Humanities have forgotten what they are really studying and teaching in school or, for that matter, why they are there at all.

As one high school honor student said, echoing thousands of others, "I'm not going to apply for college admission now. And maybe never. I've had enough school. In school you're not a person. You're just a student." But as many sectors of the human nature industry seem to see it, a student is a person—a person who will go to school and want to learn more than the basic vocational skills; and furthermore, a person who will work hard to achieve good marks in Biology (by taking a crayfish apart for some unspecified reason) and two hours later for the same reason will work hard to achieve good marks in English (". . . what we are seeking/Is idle, biologically speaking."—Edna St. Vincent Millay, 1892–1950).

*   *

But just because the human nature industry does not label the product, that does not mean a human nature is no longer being produced, advertised, distributed and consumed.

At the basis of the social sciences, says Solomon Asch, "there must be a comprehensive conception of human nature."

A sign on the bus that reads "Children Under 5 Half Fare"

82

plainly bespeaks a basic difference between adult and child nature.

The question of "What constitutes human nature," says Paul Radin, is "perhaps at the core of all investigations of culture."

In a New England arboretum set up to preserve local trees and flowers in a wild-life setting, a number of placards say "Please Do Not Leave the Paths"—making it apparent that nature is basically natural but that human nature is not.

Analyzing "Sex and Politics in the Underground Press," John R. Everett describes the philosophy expressed there: "The true evil of the system is that it represses almost everyone, even those who do not feel repressed."

Man: A Course of Study is a social studies program put together in Cambridge, Massachusetts, by a psychologist and two anthropologists. This course, used in over one thousand classrooms, has as its "big goal" to get youngsters to "try to answer three basic questions: What is human about human beings? How did they get that way? How can they be made more so?"

"We've got to push aside the velvet portieres of Victorian morality," says a psychiatrist. "Many people use dictionary words in discussing sex instead of saying what they basically mean. Webster's Unabridged is a compendium of euphemisms."

Without a doubt, the industry is still producing a human nature. You cannot run a bus line without it; or publish an underground press; or talk about Man; or criticize a dictionary of words. If the human nature industry were not making, distributing and advertising its stock-in-trade, you could not rear children or wildlife; you could not condemn pleasure-making and its unwanted by-products; you could not think about overpopulation, malpractice, students, persons, former unity or former Noble Savages. Without the model produced and consumed by the industry you could not get through the day, the week, the year and the lifetime. Nor could you talk about getting through them because they, like Science, Humanities, Long Division and the Origins of the Novel, are consequences of human nature.

You need a pretty fair notion of what human nature is before you can explain human nature away as fast as possible; or teach biology and chemistry as science, or poetry and technology as culture, or human nature as myth. Unless you are the owner of the latest model produced by the human nature industry, you cannot sit there laughing and scratching indulgently at a book that talks about some fictitious human nature industry somewhere and the recent model it has produced, advertised and distributed.

Oh yes, there certainly is a basic, unified conception of human nature. This basic model produced by the industry is not always so clearly rendered. Sometimes it comes in magazine articles, sometimes in mystery stories, sometimes in the want-ads, sometimes in research reports or in the critiques of them. But the basic message is there nonetheless, to wit: you've got to get down to the basics.

On the same day on the same newsstand three popular magazines billed these articles: "The Disguises of Intimacy" (*McCall's*); "How to Make Your Dreams Work for You" (*House & Garden*); and "Women and the Love Myth" and "How Report Cards Can Harm Children and Mislead Parents" (*Ladies' Home Journal*).

"I had to admit to myself," says a typical spokesman in a typical story by Ross Macdonald who is called an important novelist by many important people in the human nature industry, "that I lived for nights like these, moving across the city's broken body, making connections among its millions of cells. I had a crazy wish or fantasy that some day before I died, if I made all the right neural connections, the city would come all the way alive. Like the Bride of Frankenstein. . . . If I had liked the man I might have shot to kill. I shot him in the right leg. He fell at his mother's feet, clutching his knee and moaning. She didn't reach out to touch him or comfort him. . . ."

"Disadvantaged children," said Dr. Julius Richmond, dean of the College of Medicine at the State University of New York, "have compelled us to learn that we should not try to solve predominantly humanitarian issues on a scientific basis." The first step to that end, it seems, is to separate humanism from science. Meanwhile, according to a news magazine dispatch, the National Science Foundation has been undergoing a basic reorganization to place much greater emphasis on attacking the problems of society.

In Britain, some psychologists are trying to cure homosexuality by giving electric shocks to patients as they view photos of nude members of their own sex, but no shock when they view similar photos of the opposite sex. In the United States, some experimenters are trying electric shock treatment on gamblers. Meanwhile, a biologist at Carnegie-Mellon University has examined two hundred alcoholic patients and found that all were missing entire sets or parts of chromosomes. The genetic defects, he said, result in enzymatic deficiencies that make it impossible for alcoholics to handle alcohol normally or to control their drinking.

But in either case, the nature of the problem is very basic. And so, it appears, is the nature of human nature according to the latest model turned out by the industry. As Kenneth Oakley said a generation ago, despite the fact that man "has been described as the reasoning animal, the religious animal, the talking animal, the tool-making animal and so on, we are still in need of a working definition of man." Or, to put it in the language of Rollo May—a language more popular in the human nature industry today—every age has its myth and this age has the myth of mythlessness.

Well, the definition of man may not yet be basic enough. The myth may still be getting in the way of clear sight. But at least things are a lot more basic than they were two generations ago when many biologists were still talking in terms of the "vital principle" of an older model of human nature—what Driesch called "entelechy," what Bernard Shaw called the "Life Force," what Victor Herbert called the "Ah sweet mystery of life." Today we're past all that. Human nature is no longer a mystery. Now it is a problem—to be solved by basic research.

And that appears to be just what everybody is doing. You cannot turn around these days without bumping into somebody who is hurrying back to the basics. As a professor of ancient history says, "Before today's students will let you tell them who Plato was, you have to tell them who you are."

In the basics of mate-swapping sex, as one swinger said, you can see people "without the masks they have to wear most of the time."

Even the unaided eye can see the activity down there at the basics. The woods are filled with communes, primatologists and druids. The cities are filled with nuclear families, nuclear neighborhoods and nuclear schools. The air is filled with earthy language, bare breasts and testicles, and basic recipes for making bread, sex, brain waves and trips into the unconscious. The sky is filled with astrological cusps and the God of the fundamentalists. In New York and California, you can find a Central Premonitions Registry. In Chicago, the Jesus People fight it out with the Satan worshipers. In Washington, a senator talking about the unclassified Vietnam war papers weeps as he addresses the Senate, and a colleague explains to a reporter: "Well, he is a Taurus, and that explains a lot." In Cambridge, a Harvard graduate gets down to the nitty-gritty of life by driving a cab. In a swanky hotel in Colorado, a group of businessmen, who have traveled hundreds of miles for the privilege, get together in a group for some basic soul-searching, crying and touching.

These days, you can go around asking perfect—or at least eminent—strangers almost any question about any thing or any body. The only topics not allowed in polite society, it appears, are those relating to good taste and human nature.

But for all of that basic research and basic living, as everybody knows, things haven't worked out as well as they were supposed to. Instead, there has been a noticeable increase of uneasiness, discomfort and downright brutality and chaos. It's not surprising, of course, human nature being what it is.

Chapter Four

About this basic girl striding down Fifth Avenue in the news picture: that is a pretty good illustration of the risks you run in getting back to the basics in order to create yourself.

For one thing, if you are trying to get back to the basics you may have to walk the whole way. In the basics there are no pockets and consequently no place to carry carfare. That can make the expedition quite a hardship. At every transfer, you must keep borrowing small change from people with pockets. Otherwise, you can catch a bad cold and have to take tetracyclines or other antibiotics. In either case, that is one big trouble with getting back to the basics—it requires a lot of complicated technology to stay there.

For another thing, it is very possible that many people will mistake your basic meaning and use you inappropriately. They may think you are sick, or advertising something, or making a protest, or conducting an experiment of some sort. And having made the assessment that you are not quite human, they are likely to act on it. When you are stripped to the basics, you may be a natural member of the species *Homo sapiens* (as long as the climate is above 70 degrees Fahrenheit), but you're not much more than that. The really important statements have been censored, such as who you are, and where you're going and how you aim to get there. That kind of imformation requires the addition of a nose ring, say, or a tattoo, or an elk's tooth or a pair of chaps. So, that's the second difficulty in getting back to the basics. Basically, the basics aren't the best materials for creating yourself.

There is also considerable disagreement about whether the basics are to be found in the nude. Depending on whom you ask and when, the basics are more likely to be found in the drugstore, in the psychoanalyst's office, in the penitentiary, in the church, in slums and/or in the nursery. Also in college, in two years of college, in one year of college, in two different colleges, in no college at all.

Other people claim that the basics are more likely to be found in Europe, in alcohol, in meditation, in the stars, in organic vegetables, in leathercrafting, in other people's property, and/or in relationships with members of the opposite sex. Also in the camera's eye, in the vein, in herbs and berries, in grass, in low-status employment, or *in extremis*. In that regard, a man who escaped from Nazi Germany in 1939 says, "If you want to see the basics of human nature, you have only to look in a concentration camp. There you find people stripped to basic greed, cowardice, treachery, cringing obsequiousness, selfishness, childishness, envy and the rest of man's beautiful basic nature."

A number of people say that the basics are to be found at the end of the rainbow, at the end of the trail, at the end of the journey and/or at the end of a perfect day. Still others say that the basics can be found only in the group. But there is a wide disagreement about which group—chimpanzees, jackdaws, swingers, halibut, wolves, graylag geese, Trobriand Islanders, psychotherapy communicants, autistic children, lower-middle-class urban blacks, Yale sophomores, or Mexican semirural truck gardeners.

There is also the possibility, as many say, that the basics are not to be found in any one of these places, but are everywhere. In that case, you must get into the drug thing, the astrology thing, the chimpanzee thing, the perfect day thing and so on, until you get it all together.

But others say that is a step in the wrong direction. These people say the only sure route to the basics is to take it all apart. That is a very popular diagnosis and prescription, and can usually be traced to a generalized faith in what the advertisements call laboratory science and basic research. The public theory seems to be that just about any miracle is possible in the laboratory, and that researchers are already on the brink of discovering the basics that can be combined and recombined to make anything—avocados, rattlesnakes, people, the lot. With basics like those, you can not only create yourself but also, if you don't like the way the product turns out, you can re-create yourself and see how it fits.

Now, that is very basic stuff if out of it you can make a person or a pigeon or an avocado or an automobile, even theoretically. It is also very discouraging stuff. And so is the theory behind it, the notion of unlimited miracles. When you get down to that category of basics, no statement about anything is valid—not about snakes, not about pigeons, not about automobiles or people. In those basics, the proper study of mankind and everything else becomes the study of the electron and its component parts. And as one electron is pretty much like any other electron, basically, all the items of the universe are the same. Basically, the living and the non-living are identical, give or take a carbon atom or two. And so are the human, the inhuman and the non-human, except for a phosphate or sugar here or there.

That may be overstating the details a bit. But it doesn't alter the general proposition, namely, that getting back to the basics is rather difficult. And even if you get there, you are very likely to get hopelessly lost forever. Deep down, at the basic basics, everything is the same: a chaotic rubble of undifferentiated and unorganized data. At the basic basics there is no information whatsoever, even about such simple matters as where you are, what to eat, what time it is or what to do next. Down there at basics, nothing can live. The important differences are a lot closer to the surface.

2

That is where a nature is, a lot closer to the surface. And that is what a nature does—it pulls the undifferentiated basics into order. A nature turns the rubble into an arrangement. A nature redds up the world. In other words, a nature organizes chaos into information.

A nature knows which data to pay attention to in the rubble. Left to its own nature, an avocado pit on the ground will send roots down to look for the datum **WATER** and will send leaves up to look for the data **AIR** and **SUNLIGHT.**

A nature makes information regarding what TIME it is. Left to its own nature the slime mold receives the news about when to stop migrating and settle down to become a stalk of spores.

A nature organizes facts into information about what it SHOULD DO NEXT. When the informed data say a storm is building, the sea gull flies inland.

A nature arranges information about HOW TO DO IT—whatever it is. A rattlesnake classifies the rubble of the basics into EDIBLES, NEUTRALS and ENEMIES, and strikes out according to that information.

A nature informs itself out of the random chaos of world data. An avocado nature makes an AVOCADO of the data **EARTH, AIR, SUNLIGHT** and **WATER.** Rose nature takes the same data and makes a ROSE of them.

A nature knows which data to ignore. Left to their own natures, a stalk of corn in Indiana and a tomato plant in New Jersey will continue to organize world data into CORN and TO-

MATOES regardless of price data from the commodity market.

And so forth, demonstrating everywhere that a nature is an organizing capacity which knows which data to pay attention to. That is true of rock nature, hematite having organized IRON and OXYGEN data into one arrangement of information, and magnetite having classified the same basic data into another. And the same is also true of Nature nature, which is the selection and arrangement of world data by God or evolution or accident—depending on the way you organize the organization.

Naturally, the same is true of human nature. It is a nature, too: an organizing capacity containing the knowledge of which data to pay attention to.

Human nature selects data from the chaos and organizes them into an arrangement of information. People organize PAST data and FUTURE data. People organize the PRESENT and the MISSING. Also the NON-LIVING and the UN-DEAD. People arrange the random rubble into categories such as SKY, EARTH, WATER, FISH, ANIMALS, PLANTS, ROCKS. Human nature has made information about DREAMS, WEATHER, GOALS, ODORS, SOUNDS, UN-CONCEIVED BABIES, INCONCEIVABLE MONSTERS. Data of every shape, size, height, age, sex, weight, family, whorl, occupation, inseam, intelligence, earlobe, ailment, income, cheek and jowl have all been organized into information.

At first look, it would appear that all of that data collecting and organizing are so difficult as to be UNNATURAL or INHUMAN. Some people seem unable to manage it at all and go to pieces, fall apart, break down or suffer from similar disorders. But as it turns out, DISORDERS are also an order of things, especially when they are similar disorders. Some people seem able to organize only a small collection of data. But they are organized in such informative arrangements as RECLUSES, MONOMANIACS, FANATICS or other fixated, rigid, disoriented types. Then, too, some people seem to choose only one portion of data from the chaos. But such people are organized, too—in a religious order, a military uniform, a demanding discipline, an ivory tower, an office regimen, a total dedication, a relentless pursuit or complete control of their mates and children, peers or subjects.

Some people, it appears, can only organize the rubble of world data for short periods of time. In between, they frequently have to turn off, turn on, turn in, cop out, drop out, fall off the wagon, take off, go on toots and benders and trips and binges. But as all of these people are part of the world data, too, there are ORGANIZATIONS for them.

Most people seem able to organize the chaos of random data most of the time, but now and then must get away from it all—to the beach, to the library, to the movies, to sleep, to the mountains, to concerts, to the bridge table, the kiln, the golf course, the stadium, the bowling alley, to grandmother's house, to picnics, parties and balls. But as the RECESS is another way of organizing, it comes to the same thing—arranging the rubble of world data into information about WHAT TO DO NEXT.

Some people seem unable to get away from one particular way of organizing the rubble. Such people frequently have to go on diets, tranquilizers, committees, antacids, the campaign trail and/or the psychiatric couch. But OVERORGANIZED, like UNDERORGANIZED, is still an organized form of organizing.

For all that it appears hard to organize the vast chaos of random data, it is usually a lot harder for human nature to leave it unorganized.

A mountain climber will come back from a death-defying hike and say that he climbed the **MOUNTAIN** because it was there: a datum that had to be observed, surveyed, conquered—in short, organized. A practitioner of the higher anthropology will come back boasting that he has been adopted as a member of the tribe he was studying. But not, it turns out, because he was particularly irresistible. As later research often reveals, nobody in the tribe knew how to deal with the visiting datum until HE was organized and placed as a MEMBER.

A practitioner of the higher journalism, coming back from a hazardous human nature expedition into the academic community, finds that he must be organized by the experts before he can be answered. To his queries regarding human nature, he finds, there are often prefatory replies such as: "Where did you get your Ph.D.?" or "Why did you come to me?" or "Whom do you know in this university?" These, of course, serve to locate the height of the higher journalist, fix a point for beginning the discussion and a level for conducting it, and establish a structure for this particular interview.

A practitioner of the lower journalism, coming back to the newsroom with a story, will frequently face both a deadline and a notebook full of seemingly chaotic data. But somehow everything usually gets put together on time. And hardly anybody appears to mind that a paragraph somewhere in the dispatch may report: "Born in Nebraska, Mr. Smith is married and stands six feet tall." Hardly anybody wonders why a report on CRIME rates or a MARRIAGE ceremony is placed next to a report on potato CONSUMPTION, which in turn is placed next to a COMMERCIAL sales spiel about floor wax or hair wax. It is placed. That is the important part of it. Whatever the reasons for the arrangement, it is all arranged. It is surveyed, initiated, conquered. It is put together. It is redded up. It is incorporated. It is ordered. It is data organized into information. It is—well, all right, it is human nature.

No matter how hard it may appear to organize the chaos of random world data into information, it's a lot harder for human nature not to do so. And for very practical reasons.

Without an organization of the rubble, you could never sense intuitively that it was 5 P.M. and thus time for a drink. Without classified information, you could never tell what day it was and thus would never feel the relief that comes with saying, "Thank God it's Friday," nor recognize the hope and resolution of being able to shout, "Whoopee! Happy New Year!" Without an arrangement of random data, you could never tell in your bones when it was time to rise and shine, and when it was time to retire. So, everything considered, a wholesale organization of the chaos is quite useful. It gets a body through the DAY, through the WEEK, through the YEAR, through the LIFETIME.

3

Compared with the fern and the cockroach, the human is a rather recent invention. But two and one-half million years on earth (give or take a half million) are still a pretty long run. So, human nature has been around for quite a while. Whether you would want a Neanderthal man to marry your sister is another matter, what with image having become so important these days. However, if a Cro-Magnon man of about forty thousand years ago was unearthed today and somehow brought back to life, he would look just about like anybody else. And given some education and a little psychiatric counseling, he could be as modern as any modern man—complete with both a daughter who walks nude down Fifth Avenue and the distinct feeling that SOMETHING is very WRONG and had better be fixed as soon as possible.

In any case, humans have been collecting data about each other and organizing it into information for some time now. And moreover, they have been passing along this information to their children with what appears to be beneficial results. As of this writing, the species has not only survived but has also multiplied. True, that may be only a temporary condition; two million years are not eternity. The information passed along from generation to generation may not really be eternal verities; they may only have been useful verities.

On the other hand, two million years of observation and collection are long enough for a lot of data to have been organized into information. Some of that public information is:

YOU CAN'T CHANGE HUMAN NATURE.

AS THE TWIG IS BENT, SO'S THE TREE INCLINED.

HONOR THY FATHER AND THY MOTHER.

THE CHILD IS FATHER TO THE MAN.

HASTE MAKES WASTE.

A STITCH IN TIME SAVES NINE.

THERE IS NOTHING NEW UNDER THE SUN.

A NEW BROOM SWEEPS CLEAN.

THE LOVE OF MONEY IS THE ROOT OF ALL EVIL.

NOTHING SUCCEEDS LIKE SUCCESS.

THERE'S NO ACCOUNTING FOR TASTES.

BLOOD IS THICKER THAN WATER.

WHAT YOU ARE SPEAKS SO LOUD I CAN'T HEAR WHAT YOU SAY.

HE'S NOT HIMSELF.

OUT OF THE MOUTHS OF BABES.

TOO SOON WE GROW OLD, TOO LATE WE GROW SMART.

BIRDS OF A FEATHER FLOCK TOGETHER.

I DON'T KNOW WHY I LOVE YOU LIKE I DO.

WHEN A MAN MARRIES HIS TROUBLE BEGINS.

A DOG IN THE MANGER.

MY DOG THINKS HE'S PEOPLE.

PEOPLE ARE PEOPLE.

IT'S DOG EAT DOG.

THE PEOPLE THERE ARE MORE HUMAN.

YOU CAN'T MAKE A SILK PURSE OUT OF A SOW'S EAR.

WHERE THERE'S A WILL THERE'S A WAY.

A recitation of this kind of information could go on and on. And it frequently does among dull conversationalists—ranging back and forth across the generations and continents without stopping for breath, now citing an information from Ecclesiastes, now one from St. Francis, now from Benjamin Franklin, from Confucius, now an information from Edgar Guest. At least that is the case in this part of the planet. In other parts, information of a similar sort comes from other sources. But the principle remains the same: everybody everywhere has a complete set of information about HUMAN NATURE suitable for almost every occasion.

Some of that information, however, is not exclusive to people's nature, but also applies to **BIRDS** of a feather, great **OAKS**, the **SALT** of the earth and other aspects of NATURE. So, people have compiled also quite a bit of information about what is unique to humans. Everybody has a long list of that kind, too, which can be summoned to mind as the situation demands. Here, for example, is a small part of such a list about HUMAN NATURE compiled by a high school graduate in less than ten minutes:

ONLY MAN DELIBERATELY RISKS LIFE AND LIMB FOR AMUSEMENT.

ONLY MAN KNOWINGLY AND WILLFULLY COMMITS SUICIDE.

ONLY MAN SENDS HIS CLOTHES OUT TO THE CLEANERS.

ONLY MAN HAS RELIGIONS.

ONLY MAN COOKS HIS FOOD.

ONLY MAN HAS JAILS, CEMETERIES, HOSPITALS, MENTAL INSTITUTIONS.

ONLY MAN PERMITS HIS CHILDREN TO ORDER HIM AROUND.

ONLY MAN KEEPS ANIMALS AS PETS.

ONLY MAN LAUGHS, MAKES MUSIC AND HUNTS FOR PLEASURE.

ONLY MAN GAMBLES AND TAKES OUT INSURANCE POLICIES.

ONLY MAN GOES TO CHURCH WHEN HE'D RATHER DO SOMETHING ELSE.

Now, that list is not true in every instance about everybody everywhere. The Bantu do not send their clothes out to the cleaners. Many gypsies cannot get insurance policies. But that is neither here nor there. The nub of it is true: everybody everywhere has a full supply of organized data to support the proposition that people are different from chickens, chimpanzees or oak trees. Among the Bantu-speaking peoples of Africa, the words Ba-ntu mean more-than-one human being. In the language of the American Indian tribe who call themselves Kiowa, the word Kiowa means human being. The gypsy word for the gypsy language is Romany; the word for human is *Rom*. In German the word is *Mensch*. In English, of course, the word is human—with all its accessories from humane to inhuman. And so forth everywhere in the peopled world.

Whether animals and plants observe much data about NATURE in general or THEIR OWN NATURES in particular is very hard to find out. But there is no reason why they should organize such information. Great oaks from little acorns grow without a moment's doubt or identity crisis of any kind. Some dogs may think they are people. But they still get acquainted with one another by nose and orifice, and without any concern whatsoever as to whether they feel the same way about Bach and anchovy pizza.

Only MAN has made it his business to organize all of this information about **HIMSELF.** Only man has seen to it that the word gets passed along from generation to generation. Great oaks, birds of a feather and the salt of the earth are free of that worry. They do not have to pay attention to their own **NATURES.** But people must do so. When it comes to human nature, **HUMAN NATURE** is additional data in the chaos that must be organized into information. That is to say, only man has to figure out what HUMAN NATURE is before he can live.

So, that's one thing that distinguishes human nature from pigeon nature, say, or atom, avocado, chimpanzee or computer nature. People have to observe and collect the data of their own nature, make them into facts by organizing the lot into information.

As for observing and collecting the data of human nature, there are several kinds of ways to do that. And as there are kinds of ways, observing and collecting are organized. Most often, the job begins with lists. Each list of data has a heading of some sort. And as there are sorts of headings, even organizing is organized.

In any case (cases are also organized), the datum **LOVE** could be listed under the heading MOON, or the heading LIBIDO, or EROS or the suit of DIAMONDS. Similarly, the datum **DEATH** could be listed under various headings such as OSIRIS, PLUTO, ENTROPY, SPADES and the like. Items about birth could be assigned to a list called CYBELE, or ISIS, VITAL STATISTICS, DIANA, DEDUCTIONS, DEMOGRAPHY, GYNECOLOGY, ACCIDENT and so on. You can also assign the data of human nature to an atlas of the palm, the skull or the earth. For example, the datum **TEMPERAMENT** is sometimes listed under the heading MEDITER-RANEAN PEOPLES, or under the heading OCCIPITAL PLATEAU, or in the MOUND between the pinky and the ring finger. It is also possible to discard those list headings entirely in favor of others. You can simply render unto CAESAR the organized data which are Caesar's, and unto GOD the human nature information which is God's. Or you can list all of it ALPHABETICALLY.

Whatever the headings, lists are a great step forward in observing and collecting human nature data. Once you have list-headings, you know which data to pay attention to in the job of observing and collecting among the rubble. And once you have the data organized in some form, why, even alphabetical information can get a body through the day, if not the week, year or lifetime, as anybody knows who has ever used a dictionary. Regardless of the particular word you are seeking, there are at least eighteen others that will fix your attention en route. It is quite possible to make a morning's work out of looking up the meaning of taxonomy, and an afternoon's out of the proper spelling of practise.

Organizing the observed data of human nature in informative categories provides many other advantages in getting through the day, the week, the year and the lifetime. For one thing, this taxonomy lets you know at once where everything is or should be. That is a big help in knowing whether you feel out of sorts, or whether things are all right, okay, hunky-dory and generally in what the English-speaking world calls apple-pie order. (The German-speaking world calls it *in ordnung;* the Greek-speaking world calls it *en taxei.*) For another thing, lists of organized data are very practical for both routine matters and emergencies. You can figure out what must be done in the category called NOW or put off into the category of TOMORROW. Without the data of human nature arranged into information, you could never tell when to stop for a red light, when to announce your feelings about Bach and anchovy pizza and, in case of fire, whether to save the children or the record collection. Furthermore, a classification of human nature data is very handy for housekeeping. Only man can erect a shelter of four brick walls and a tile roof. But it requires a category of DWELLINGS to tell him whether it is fit for human occupancy and, if so, whether it is a jail, a hospital, a rooming house, a mansion, a disorderly establishment or a home. In addition, lists of information about human nature are important for knowing what is IN and what is OUT. For instance, salivation and digestion are normal and natural items to have on hand. But spit and feces are not.

When it comes to getting through the day, the week, the year and the lifetime, there are two additional advantages in collecting the data of human nature and organizing them into informative categories. The first advantage is that you can tell what is BUILT-IN to human nature and what is MOVABLE. Consequently, you know when to shrug and say, well, it's human nature, and when to get angry and with whom. It is a great saving of anguish to know what the stars compel and what they only impel; or what the gods have ordained and on what matters they can be appeased; or when to read the left palm and when to read the right palm; or—to put it in local, contemporary nomenclature— it is very handy to know what is GENETIC and what is ENVIRONMENTAL. The second advantage of making human nature data into facts and organizing them into informative lists is that you know the kinds of experts to start questioning when you embark on a research project into the subject of HUMAN NATURE.

On the other hand, there is one big difficulty in all of this organized, informative data about human nature, namely, there is always something on the other hand that messes up the organization. If it's not one thing, then it's another that upsets the observation, collection and arrangement of the rubble: the manufacturing of information about human nature—what is HUMAN and NATURAL.

Take the observed datum **DAD.** Depending on who observes it, **DAD** can be a father, a grandfather, a great-grandfather, a father-in-law, a stepfather, a former stepfather, a divorced father, a husband, any older man, any man your own age. In some parts of the world, the datum **FATHER** can mean a woman who has paid the fee required to start a family line bearing her name. In other places, a father often mothers a child.

The reason for this kind of mess is that an observed datum about human nature is not the nature itself—anymore than an avocado leaf's looking for sunlight is avocado nature, or a rattlesnake's identifying and striking an enemy is rattlesnake nature. Observed data about a nature are not a nature; they are the *consequence* of a nature. There is, for example, no evidence whatsoever that the human eye has changed physiologically in the past four thousand years. But Egyptians of four thousand years ago were able to look up at the stars in their courses and observe CONSTELLATIONS in the chaos—configurations that are invisible to most people today. The Greeks of three thousand years ago used the same word to describe both the colors **BLUE** and **GREEN** as they are observed and classified in the world's data rubble today. In much of the world a thousand years ago, poverty, misery, pestilence and disease were looked on as the NATURAL condition of man on earth. Until two hundred years ago, many people in this part of the planet saw nothing INHU-MAN about buying and selling other people; here, the human retina saw the datum **HUMAN** as white. Until about one hundred years ago, little children were generally observed as small adults and were frequently sent out to work a twelve-hour day.

Obviously such data as **EDDIE, BETTY, PAULINE, RALPH** and other given names are not a nature. But in many people's minds they are irrevocably welded to specific personality traits and characteristics. For such people, it would be almost impossible to organize the information that a great discovery had been made by someone named Eddie, or that someone named Ralph had misplaced his car keys. Many people would not be able to comprehend that kind of information. Or, if they grasped it at all, they would not be able to believe it was true.

And in the very same way, organized lists of information about human nature are not the nature itself, either. Otherwise the classifications would not be so flexible sometimes and so

103

rigid at other times. But the plain, observed datum about human nature information is that you can never be certain of whether you are getting the news, the commercial, an opinion or only static.

Items are forever being relocated from informative list to informative list. INTELLIGENCE, which used to be a fixed datum under the heading of BUILT-IN, now appears to be almost portable. There are several manuals available that explain how to improve your IQ scores, thus putting the matter in the MOVABLE list. HOMOSEXUALITY, on the other hand, used to be listed under ENVIRONMENT & SOCIETY. But now there are some experts who say that homosexuality may be an item for the list headed GENETIC & PHYSIOLOGICAL.

Or take the category of information called PATHOLOGY. Some observed, collected and arranged data stay there year after year —the VIRUS, say, and MENTAL CRUELTY. But many others seem to come like a mysterious fever and then go from the list the same way, burning at night and normal by dawn, unhealthy one day and satisfactory the next. CHILDHOOD used to be considered an ailment best gotten over with when you were young. But recently that item has been taken off the sick list along with many others. Some other former diseases are crime, mother, torpor, hallucination. On the other hand, old age used to be a healthy achievement. Recently, it is treated like an epidemic along with many other items. Some newly discovered diseases are anxiety, city, extended family, fantasy, death, manipulation, hierarchy, structure, authority, class, role, status and private property.

Now and then, the index of list-headings changes its shape and size, too. For instance, the classification CHILDHOOD was erected about three hundred years ago; the heading CIVILIZATION about two hundred years ago; SOCIETY and CULTURE about one hundred years ago. The construction of the categories YOUTH, UNCONSCIOUS, TEEN and PRE-TEEN are much more recent. But

104

there is no guarantee how long any of them will remain intact as organized bins for information about human nature. For centuries there was a terribly bloody dispute over which data were to be rendered unto CAESAR'S list and which to GOD'S. But those list headings have blurred. On the other hand, there is still a fight, sometimes more bloody than at other times, over the items that properly should be assigned to the categories of LIFE, LIBERTY, PROPERTY and the PURSUIT OF HAPPINESS.

Avocados, rattlesnakes and pigeons do not have these difficulties because it is not in their natures to have to observe the data of their natures, sorting them out along with the rest of the world data. It is only human nature that has to make information of its own nature, too, in order to keep chaos from encroaching. Only man has to observe data and organize them in order to live a HUMAN and NATURAL life. It is his nature to do so. The rest of it—the observed data, their arrangement and organization into information—is a *consequence* of his nature.

5

So, if data are at all observable and arrangeable, then they are the consequence of a nature—an organizing capacity containing the knowledge of which data to pay attention to, and what questions to ask those data in order to classify them into information. Take a list of cake ingredients. Those data are the consequence of the nature of the CAKE. And in turn, that datum **CAKE** is a consequence of the nature of a BAKER whose organizing capacity contains the knowledge of a cake. And in turn, that datum **BAKER** is the consequence of a human nature—an organizing capacity which contains the knowledge that baking such data as flour, milk, sugar and eggs together is both HUMAN AND NATURAL.

In the same way, before you can distinguish the data **PLANETS** from the celestial chaos and begin an informative chart of their courses, your body of knowledge must contain a notion, no matter how tentative, of a system at work up there. Similarly, before you can distinguish and observe the data **PEOPLE** amid the terrestrial chaos, you must have an organizing notion or abstract idea of human. And before you can arrange those observed human data into useful information, you must have an organizing idea of what a NATURE is.

Without those concepts of human and natural, human data cannot be attended to, nor ordered into informative answers to such simple questions as *What time is it?* or *What should I do next?* or *Where am I?* or *What do you want to be when you grow up?* Without an organizing idea of human nature, it becomes almost impossible for people to live at all. But if it is your nature to have that idea—if your body of knowledge must pay attention to the data of human nature—then the information necessary for living a human and natural life begins to fall into ordered form and to grow.

For example, it is observable data of human nature everywhere that people are **BORN** and people **DIE.** And in between those two occurrences, people **EAT** and **SLEEP** and **ELIMINATE** and **GIVE BIRTH** to **HELPLESS INFANTS.** Naturally these human nature data have to be paid attention to and arranged for if human life is to continue. And so the local landscape is marked with such information as CAUTION CHILDREN; SWEET AFTON MEMORIAL GROVE; EATS; ROOM TO LET; REST ROOMS.

Now, properly speaking, those signs announce a whole lot more than basic data about eating and sleeping and so on. In each is announced a vast, organized idea of human nature—a full concept about how to be human and natural.

A complete book of etiquette lies open in EATS. A way of life speaks out in ROOM TO LET. A whole philosophy of law

106

regarding child rearing and welfare stands behind CAUTION CHILDREN. The heavens are mapped and angels sing at the gates of the SWEET AFTON MEMORIAL cemetery. And moreover, there appears to be no way at all to strip away that kind of organizing idea of what is human and natural and free human nature from having to observe the data about itself and construct an informative body of knowledge from the collection.

Take the matter of MEN'S ROOM and LADIE'S LOUNGE. A local world of propriety and aspiration is to be seen in those signs. They are far more genteel and euphemistic than is required by basic practicality. And placing the apostrophe in a more conventional place so that the sign reads LADIES' LOUNGE only reinforces the local notion of what is acceptable. But just because the information is local does not alter the general proposition, namely that **ELIMINATION** is a datum about human nature and so it must be observed and organized into an informative body of knowledge in order for people to be HUMAN AND NATURAL.

To combine the two—Men's Room and Ladies' Lounge—into one neuter-gender LAVATORY still bespeaks an organized information regarding its use—privacy, cleanliness and the like. To give the place a directly functional label instead, EVACUATION CENTER, say, still constructs an informative body of knowledge that answers the questions of decorum, protocol, convention and agreement. An Evacuation Center bespeaks an organizing idea as much as does a Ladies' Lounge.

To give the place a less directly functional name and call it a LIVING ROOM, for example, does not improve the situation at all, and furthermore may lead to considerable chaos around the house. But to move the center out of the building entirely and into the back yard only puts the decorum, protocol and other fully organized information about it somewhere else. And moreover, it announces in unmistakable terms what everybody knows

107

anyway: the people in that place are completely housebroken.

There is one other possibility, of course, and that is to get rid of the center entirely and put it nowhere in particular and everywhere—to disregard the observed human need to eliminate and consequently the necessity to organize that datum into information. But as everybody knows, that simply isn't done. Not anywhere. People everywhere are housebroken. It's human nature.

And inasmuch as t----t training has been observed everywhere by the n---d eye, that makes **ELIMINATION ETIQUETTE** another observable datum of people's nature which must be arranged into information.

Exactly how that information is organized, of course, is a matter of local propriety like Men's Room and Ladie's Lounge. The observed human data of elimination protocols can be listed, for example, under the information heading of OBSESSIVE BEHAVIOR or AGGRESSIVE or NORMAL or PRUDERY or TERRITORIALITY . . . just as long as the data are placed somewhere in the body of knowledge about what is human and natural.

That is how a nature works, with its organizing capacity containing a body of knowledge that knows what data to pay attention to, and what questions to ask those data in order to organize them into information. When it comes to human nature, it is part of the human body of knowledge to pay attention to the data of human nature in order to organize them into accessible information about what is human and natural. That is to say, one thing human nature seems to be is a concept, an abstraction. Looked at that way, human nature is an organizing idea which becomes an organized idea—an informative body of knowledge called HUMAN NATURE that knows where everything human and natural belongs, and how and when and why it belongs there.

It is a very powerful body of knowledge, this organized idea of human nature. And when it changes—well, until quite recently the idea of running the mile in less than four minutes was unheard of. But then that idea was reorganized. And at last observation, the human race was clocked in at three minutes and fifty-one seconds.

Chapter Five

In other words:

There is no way to get people back to the basics. There is no way to separate human nature into ingredients, reducing it to one part biological organizing capacity and one part knowledge which that capacity contains.

As biologist Edmund Sinnott makes clear, you can talk about those two parts of the nature of living things, but you cannot divide them. On the one hand, "Every living thing is an organized system, well named an 'organism,'" developing in an orderly fashion "toward the growth of the mature individual, as if to a 'goal.'" And on the other hand, the biologist points out, "Around a living creature is its unorganized material environment, a random mixture of many things." Certain of these things, food for example, "are continually being pulled into the organism, where at once they lose their random character and are built into the organized structure of a living system. Every plant and animal thus acts as an incorporating center which brings organic order out of environmental disorder."

That is to say, the nature is indivisible. Only together do the biological organizing capacity and the body of knowledge it contains know what data to pay attention to in the world rubble, and what questions to ask those data in order to organize them into information.

But biologist Sinnott does not leave it at that. He goes on to quote a historian of science, humanist Herbert J. Muller:

"For the fundamental fact in biology, the necessary point of departure, is the organism. The cell is a chemical compound but more significantly a type of biological organization; the whole organism is not a mere aggregate but an architecture; the vital functions of growth, adaptation, reproduction—the final function of death—are not merely cellular but organic phenomena. Although parts and processes may be isolated for analytical purposes, they cannot be understood without reference to the dynamic, unified whole that is more than their sum. To say, for example, that a man is made up of certain chemical elements is a satisfactory description only for those who intend to use him as a fertilizer."

That example of the fertilizer, borrowed from a humanist by a biologist, may be acceptable in many sectors of the human nature industry. But that little notion about the unified whole of the organism being more than the sum of its parts—that is not so popular in much of the industry, and may explain in part why there are so few biologists around and so many biochemists, biophysicists, geneticists and neurophysiologists. It may also explain in part why a higher journalistic inquiry into human nature is not greeted with welcoming smiles and invitations to a hot meal.

As you would expect from any basic industry, there is a lot of work being done in the human nature industry to get down to fundamentals, particularly in the knowledge foundry where human data are processed into information. This basic research follows two main lines of endeavor.

One major thrust in the human nature industry is aimed at uncoupling the organizing capacity from the product, and then reducing what is left—the body of knowledge—into its ingredients. This kind of enterprise can be seen frequently. For example: "Man is by nature a classifying animal," reports an article in one trade journal of the knowledge foundry, *Science*. "His continued existence depends on his ability to recognize similarities and differences between objects and events in his physical universe and to make known these similarities and differences linguistically."

But to say that man is by nature a classifying animal is about the same as saying that a nature is by nature a nature. A nature classifies data: that is what makes it a nature. The differences between one nature and another lie in the kinds of data a nature pays attention to, and the kinds of questions it asks of those data in order to organize them into information. And as for having to communicate that classified information—linguistically or otherwise—in order to continue existence, that is true of many natures, not only of man, primates and mammals. As David McNeill points out, "Ants deposit chemicals to direct the aggregation and dispersion of the colony, mormyridae fishes of South America emit electrical impulses, fireflies flash light, and some male spiders use semaphore signals to indicate to the huge females of their species that they are mates, not food. In communication, as elsewhere in nature, evolution has been fertile. Human language is one highly specialized result of such evolution. . . . It should be viewed as one of the peculiar outcomes of natural selection, related to some systems of communication elsewhere, but not exactly the same as any of them."

That is not to say the statement is wrong. Man is by nature a classifying animal and he must communicate his information linguistically in order to survive. But as a basic definition it both includes and leaves out too many ingredients.

The other major thrust in the human nature industry is aimed at filtering off the body of knowledge from the product so as not to contaminate the biological organizing capacity and its fundamental ingredients. As one of the most famous geneticists in all of Christendom said, smiling benignly at the inquiry:

"You have to be very careful when you ask what human

113

nature is. Otherwise you will confuse human nature with attitudes toward human nature."

That is a very popular attitude in the human nature industry, both on the assembly line where the human data are produced and in the knowledge foundry where the data are processed into information. This widespread notion holds that the human animal's biological system stopped evolving at its present condition about forty thousand years ago with Cro-Magnon man. And thereupon, it began to dawn on him that he had the ability to make tools, communicate, paint pictures, organize families, have ideas and generally order the environment including himself. Those inventions, this popular attitude holds, are a contaminating cultural fungus obscuring and perhaps choking the pure human nature—civilized by-products of the evolved bio-neuro-physico-chemico-genetic capacity which distract the attention and pollute the real, basic data of human nature.

But that attitude toward human nature is not held everywhere in the industry. There are quite a few who say it is impossible to filter out the contaminating social and cultural attitudes and leave only the pure, basic product. There are many who are saying now that an attitude toward human nature is not a contaminant in people but a component of them; part of what makes people people is that they have an organized idea of human nature.

As Clifford Geertz puts it, the "innate, generic constitution of modern man (what used, in a simpler day, to be called 'human nature') now appears to be both a cultural and a biological" product. Moreover, well before the human nervous system was influenced by cultural forces, its evolution "was positively shaped by social ones." In the words of Sherwood Washburn, it is "probably more correct to think of much of our structure as a result of culture rather than to think of men anatomically like ourselves slowly discovering culture."

114

It does not appear that way, of course, if you look only at the statistics of the human enterprise on earth. People of sorts have been on the planet for some two million years, but for less than 1 per cent of that time have they lived as what common usage calls civilized men and women rather than as hunters and gatherers. That would make it look as though the animal's nervous system had evolved recently to a point where it could begin to apprehend the possibilities and advantages of domesticating animals, planting and harvesting crops, building permanent homes—and from those artificial landscapes apprehend the further possibilities of cities, power looms, barbed wire, aspirin and the rest. But despite what the numbers of millennia before civilization may indicate, it was not that kind of a leap from the precipice of advanced biology into the soft, decorative but superfluous cushion of culture. As Charles Darwin taught in a lesson which everybody knows but few seem to remember, people are continuous with the other animals; like the other species, the human species has evolved in *all of its characteristics,* not just in two or three such as his optic nerve and neocortex. The biological organizing capacity has evolved and, within it, the body of knowledge that organizes data into information has evolved apace over the past two million years or so.

Those millennia mark more than a bio-neuro-physico-chemical change in human nature. "This is not simply a study of biological evolution," say Lee and DeVore, "since zoologists have come to regard behavior as central to the adaptation and evolution of all species. The emergence of economic, social and ideological forms are as much a part of human evolution as are the developments in human anatomy and physiology."

That is certainly not the most prevalent attitude toward human nature in the industry, especially in the knowledge foundry. It is much more customary, as Margaret Mead points out, to say that "man is a culture-building animal"—meaning the

115

ability to build a system of communications, to make and use tools, and so on. In that statement, "the ability to build a culture" is treated as if it were a piece of behavior typical of the genus *Homo* and species *sapiens* but independent of learning, Mead says.

"It might be more useful to say that *Homo sapiens* is a species which can only survive in a man-made environment. . . . Such a statement combines the biologically given conditions of a prolonged infancy with complete dependence on adults, for whom no environmental substitute is adequate, and the genotypic capacities of brain, eye, hand and so on that make it possible to learn a culture and to act within it, to maintain, transform, and in some instances, transcend it. Man may then be said to be a *culture-living* creature."

2

It wasn't always that way, of course. The human body of knowledge that makes so much of human nature man made was shaped and nurtured originally by its container—the human biological organizing capacity.

Compared with the fern or the apple tree, man can run about fifteen miles per hour faster. So his biological organizing capacity equips his nature nicely for gathering stationary and slow-moving food. But when it comes to big-game hunting, the biological part of human nature is less than adequate. Even in two-hundred-yard spurts, man can accelerate to only about thirty miles per hour, whereas the cheetah can run for more than two hundred yards at seventy miles per hour, and the antelope can run at sixty miles per hour.

For a large animal, man moves poorly and can easily be outdistanced by even his small domestic dogs and cats, as J. B.

Birdsell remarks. "We walk flat on our feet, in plantigrade fashion, a mode which is also found in such relatively slow-moving animals as bears and raccoons," he says. Man is simply not anatomically designed for speed. "The calf of a man's leg is a complex mass of muscles which acts on the immediately attached foot. This weight is in the wrong place. . . ."

And as for the other aspects of biological human nature, they are not particularly marvelous, either. Man's eyesight is not so acute as the sea gull's; his sense of smell is not so good as the dog's; his hearing is not nearly so responsive as the bat's.

But for all that his muscular organizing capacity is poorly designed for speed and his sense organizing capacity is generalized, the human's nature survived and multiplied for more than a million years by hunting big game. As humans observed about their nature many years ago, the race is not necessarily to the swift, nor the battle to the strong. The victory of the race—or its survival at the very least—can depend largely on the body of knowledge enclosed within the organizing capacity.

Running no faster than about four miles per hour, a durable and versatile animal such as man can cover nearly one hundred miles in twenty-four hours if he is toughened by training. Naturally, it requires some remembering, anticipating and other thinking to begin training and keep at it. But with a body of knowledge contained in the organizing capacity it becomes possible to turn big game into an observable, collectible datum and arrange it into edible information. As William S. Laughlin explains: "Indians can run down horses and deer by keeping them moving, taking advantage of the tendency of many ungulates to move in an arc by traversing the chord . . ."

Clearly there is a body of knowledge contained in that organized expenditure of energy. It is a body of knowledge that knows which data to pay attention to regarding ungulate nature so as to organize those data into information—answering such

117

questions as what time is it? (*time for the deer to be tired*);
what should I do? (*gauge the deer's arc and traverse the chord*);
and what should I do next? (*as Laughlin says: "A man can run
down a horse in two or three days, and then decide whether to
eat it, ride it, pull a load with it, wear it or worship it"*).

That is only one example of the way in which the biological
organizing capacity shapes the body of knowledge it contains.
There are plenty of other illustrations of this matter.

Compared with the turtle, man has a much larger brain
for organizing the world's rubble of data. But that larger brain
is also a biological limitation. A newly-hatched turtle is off
foraging for edible data a few hours after birth. But the human, with its larger brain, cannot be born so well developed
and ready to begin organizing the chaos of its environment into
information for survival. The human infant's head is even too
large as it is for easy passage out of the womb and into the
world. It takes years before the human develops to a point where
its body of knowledge knows what data to pay attention to and
its biological capacity is capable of organizing those data into
information. Until that stage of development, the young human's world must be almost wholly organized for it by adults
who know which data to pay attention to and how to order
them into information. As a result, the human develops with
its biological organizing capacity filled largely with a body of
knowledge presented to it by parents, grandparents whose bodies
of knowledge had been filled in large part by *their* parents and
grandparents—and so on back through time before living
memory or written history.

For another example, the biological organizing capacity of
upright posture also shapes the body of knowledge that is an
integral part of human nature.

An animal that has to carry food and other data around in

its mouth, as Bernard Campbell points out, does not have a mouth free to develop a language. And as Robbins Burling puts it: "Since language is learned so early and since it is central to so much of our other learning, it is even tempting to wonder if our ability to learn a language does not somehow lie at the core of our other human abilities. Conceivably our very ability to perpetuate varying traditions in all aspects of our culture rests in part, at least, upon our ability to perpetuate varying traditions in that most human of all our abilities, our ability to speak."

Upright posture on two feet also frees the hands for tool carrying, food carrying and—because of that—for food sharing and other co-operative ventures. And while Jane Goodall reports that chimpanzees can walk upright on two feet and perform these acts of carrying, she also reports that they can carry a handful of objects for only very limited distances and even then they cannot move quickly.

This upright, bipedal biological organizing posture alters the shape of the body of knowledge in another way, namely, human vision. The view of an animal on all fours at about two feet above the horizon is one thing, says Anne Roe, but "to see it from five feet is something else, defensively useful, and presents a landscape quite different for the animal to organize." Under these circumstances, "to see ahead is not only a figure of speech," she says.

To stand upright, on two feet, with hands free and both eyes looking forward in three-dimensional vision provides what Campbell calls "the world view of the higher primates unique both in quality and in kind. Primates alone have come to know the structure of the environment in terms of both pattern and composition. They see the environment as a collection of objects rather than merely as a pattern. . . . The evolution of vision is one essential basis for the evolution of an animal that came to understand its environment so well that it could control it for its direct benefit."

Upright posture, freed hands, stereoscopic vision, an appetite for both plants and meat, an ability to speak, a long and dependent childhood in which to learn the accumulated information of the past—these kinds of organizing capacities in human nature had tremendous effects on their own evolution, leading to the perpetuation of the more upright, more manually dextrous, more articulate, larger-brained humans requiring an even longer time of childhood and its learning to reach maturity. At the same time, this sort of organizing capacity in human nature had tremendous effects on the shape of its contents: the body of knowledge. World view, hunting, the ability to communicate and manipulate, the need to learn in a completely organized world—such biological capacities gave humans a perception of the world's rubble different from the perception available to any other nature. People had the capacity not only to differentiate more discrete objects but also to observe more precise details of the data around them. As Campbell puts it: "Man's analytic perception, more than any other factor, opened the door to the development of conceptual thought and eventually to his remarkable culture."

So the human organizing capacity has had tremendous effects on its contents, the human body of knowledge. And in turn, the human body of knowledge has had tremendous effects on its container, the organizing capacity. That is because human nature is not two separate parts but is organic and indivisible. HUMAN NATURE is a datum like any other nature in the world rubble. But HUMAN NATURE is also an indispensable conceptual thought in the human mind—a notion that people have about their nature because it is their nature to have such notions.

3

A conceptual thought is an organizing idea that pulls random data into information. And organizing ideas of that sort are not an exclusive property of human nature. Creatures extremely low on the intellectual scale, says William James, may have conceptual thought. "All that is required is that they should recognize the same experience again. A polyp would be a conceptual thinker if a feeling of 'Hello! thingumbob again!' ever flitted through its mind."

But before a polyp can say "Hello *again!*" it must have an organizing idea of what to pay attention to—which data to abstract from the chaos—in order to recognize a thingumbob. As James explains, "Each act of conception results from our attention singling out some one part of the mass of matter for thought which the world presents, and holding fast to it, without confusion."

Looked at that way, a conceptual thought is an organizing idea that makes particular random data observable or abstractable from the chaos. That is to say, the conceptual thought comes first. Otherwise data could not be perceivable as information. As psychologist Jane Torrey puts it, a perception *is* an organization.

It is much more tempting to put it the other way around, and say that the data of the world are perceived first and then organized into information by the nature. But it doesn't appear to work that way. Quite the contrary, the world data abstracted from the chaos as information seem to be a consequence of the nature that has perceived the information. For example, it is tempting to say that the eyes produce pictures in the brain.

121

"This is absurd," says Richard L. Gregory in *Eye and Brain*. "What the eyes do is to feed the brain with information. . . . The seeing of objects involves many sources of information beyond those meeting the eye when we look at an object. It generally involves knowledge of the object derived from previous experience, and this experience is not limited to vision but may include the other senses: touch, taste, smell, hearing and perhaps also temperature or pain. Objects are far more than patterns of stimulation: objects have pasts and futures; when we know its past or can guess its future, an object transcends experience and becomes an embodiment of knowledge and expectation without which life of even the simplest kind is impossible."

This concept of sensory data—this idea of the way a nature's body of knowledge affects the shape of the organizing capacity—is quite new in many sectors of the human nature industry. And, in fact, it is still not an acceptable hypothesis in several parts of the knowledge foundry where human data are processed into information. Until recently, most schoolbooks dealing with visual perception rendered the eye in great detail: retina, cornea, iris, optic nerve and a little picture of the perceived object as it was received in miniature, upside down but accurate representation in the brain, and that was that. Naturally, all of that information about the eye and its perception of world data was not easily come by. Many researchers endured long hours, low pay and other hardships in order to find these data—dedicated people urged on despite physical privation by a conceptual thought or hypothesis about human nature.

And the same has been true in many sectors of the human nature industry regarding the ear and how it perceives sounds. Many music teachers still present the melody first and in great detail—its themes and phrases, its tensions and resolutions, and so on. And then, if there is time, a word is given to the harmony with the promise that more on that subject is available to interested parties. "But," says arranger and composer Frederick Marx, "the organization of tones which we call a melody does not come first. The melody is the child of the harmony. It is an organized melody because it grows out of an organized progression of harmonies in your head. You hear chords in your mind's ear and as a result you can write a melody: a horizontal succession of chordal tones and passing tones. Of course you can write a melody according to a mathematical formula based on the 12-tone scale or some other scale. But in that case, the formula comes before the melody. Either way, the organization produces the melody." When you hear an air whistled by someone who cannot carry a tune, it does not sound like a melody because your mind's ear cannot hear the progression of harmonies that would organize the whistled notes into a succession of chordal tones and passing tones. The whistler may hear a melody, but you hear noise and try to tune it out.

Even in so ordinary information-gathering as looking at yourself in the mirror or reading the newspaper, the data are selected and arranged by a conceptual thought or organizing idea.

As art curator Campbell Wyly suggests, just stand in front of a mirror as though you were getting ready to shave or apply make-up. Then, with a piece of soap, mark off the reflection of your face from chin to head top. When you measure that distance on the mirror, you find that what looks like a full-sized, accurate image is actually about one-half life-size. What you are seeing in the mirror is a scaled-down version, a sort of working model, of your face.

A newspaper photo seen through a magnifying glass is merely an arrangement of dots, some darker than others. But without that magnifying glass to disorganize the organizing idea, those dots become data ordered into meaningful information. Even when dots are equally spaced and of equal hue, says

Gregory, there is a tendency to organize them into columns and rows. "We can see in ourselves," he says, "the groping towards organizing the sensory data into objects." If we didn't, the cartoonist would have a hard time because he presents only a few lines to the eye and the eye sees a face complete with expression.

So, perceiving and thinking are not independent; "I see what you mean" is not a puerile pun, but indicates a connection which is very real, says Gregory. "The senses do not give us a picture of the world directly; rather they provide evidence for checking hypotheses about what lies before us. Indeed, we may say that a perceived object *is* a hypothesis, suggested and tested by sensory data. . . ."

In the wake of melodies organized by conceptual thought, people march in orderly fashion into war, into marriage, out of school and into careers. On the basis of black and white lines and dots arranged into information by organizing ideas, people get rich, get poor, get control, get ulcers, get ahead, get heart attacks, get bombed, get emancipated. In such ways the human body of knowledge has profound consequences in the human organizing capacity. Similarly, when the sensory data do not confirm the hypothesis or organized idea, people are said to be misled, misguided, disoriented, disorderly and otherwise mistaken—often at a great toll in health and life, to say nothing of time, energy and money. When the organized idea or working model of the data ignores those data, people are said to be suffering from hallucinations, illusions, delusions and other manias. Those people are frequently removed to some other, organized place where the data are arranged into information for them. In any case, the organizing idea affects the organizing capacity.

Between one kind of nature and another, there are differences in the conceptual thinking—the organizing ideas which make world data observable or abstractable from the chaos. Human nature and polyp nature both may be able to abstract the kind

124

of data called **THINGUMBOB** from the rubble. But only human nature may be able to organize the class of thingumbobs under a larger, more abstract information heading called POLYPS TAILS. That is to say, at one level of organizing idea, your tail becomes visible. But you have to move to another level of organizing idea in order to recognize tails in general—and to still another level to observe organizing ideas and their levels. At the human level of organizing ideas, says William James, conceptual thinking can conceive "realities supposed to be extra-mental, as steam engine; fictions, as mermaid; or mere *entia rationis*, like difference or nonentity."

High-level organizing of abstract data is everyday practice for human nature, even among the very young of the species. As Bernard Campbell spells it out:

"The concept 'bird,' for example, must be abstracted from the perception of, first, 'this flying object' and, later, 'that flying object.' The concept 'bird' does not apply to 'many birds' or 'all the birds I have seen' but all birds possible in space and time. Similarly, the concept 'food' applies not to 'this food' but to all possible and potential food—fruit not yet plucked, animals not yet hunted."

The ability to have spoken language may be transmitted genetically, Eric Lenneberg says. "The basic skills for the acquisition of language are as universal as bipedal gait," and may be due to "as yet unknown species specific biological capacities." But, he reports, the first things learned in language by the young child are not items but rather "principles of categorization and pattern perception. The first words refer to classes, not unique objects or events. The sounds of language and the configuration of words are at once perceived and reproduced according to principles; they are patterns in time, and they never function as randomly strung up items. From the beginning, very general principles of semantics and syntax are manifest."

125

It takes a very high level of organizing idea to abstract principles from the already abstract data of words. But children do it at a very young age. Susan Ervin reports that "children extended the regular past tense suffix where it could not have been imitated"—for example by saying "buyed, comed, doed." In some cases, these extensions of the past tense principle occurred "before the child had produced any other regular past tense forms. . . ." The regularity of extending the principle of the past tense, she reports, occurred "quite early and suggests that it takes relatively few instances and little practice to produce analogic extension." In other words, as David McNeill summarizes it, "Overgeneralizations apparently occurred before anything existed in speech to overgeneralize from."

Poetry, too, can be looked at as a high-level organizing idea at work, abstracting metrical arrangements of data from the symbols or abstract data which are called words. Eeny-meeny-miney-mo may have been suggested once by a physiological rhythm. But that kind of four-beat line idea organizes love lyrics, instructional nursery rhymes and sales commercials, says Robbins Burling. "If these patterns should prove universal [he has found them in English, Chinese, Benkulu and many other languages]; they must depend upon our common humanity. We may simply be the kind of animal that is predestined not only to speak but also, on certain occasions, to force our language into recurrent patterns of beats and lines."

To look on yourself as this "kind of animal" or that "kind of animal" makes you the kind of animal who pays attention to the similarities and differences in nature and among natures. It is a mistake to believe, as much of the human nature industry held for most of the past century, that only with Darwin in 1859 did people discover that the human animal was continuous with other animals. As William Laughlin suggests, primitive man and presumably ancient man a half-million years earlier ab-

126

stracted the principle that **PEOPLE** could be looked on as data in the ANIMAL KINGDOM.

Laughlin goes on to say that "we may consider the likelihood that man was always aware of his affinity with other animals and consequently did not need to 'discover' this obvious relationship any more than he discovered his stomach or eyeballs, or that the female of our species discovered that she was bearing the young."

4

If you can organize the data **SEXUAL INTERCOURSE** and **BABIES** in the same information category, you have an organizing idea which makes very abstract data visible and arrangeable. As far as anybody can tell, cats do not understand where **KITTENS** come from, nor that they are data belonging in the ANIMAL KINGDOM category of information. Only people appear to have evolved that kind of body of knowledge, and continue to evolve it through higher and higher levels of abstraction.

But exactly how human organizing ideas evolved through the past is hard to trace with certainty.

Two million years' worth of human nature and its working models of the world have vanished. All that remain evident along the path are a few consequences of that nature—some bones, some chipped stones, several pictures, pots and other meager shards of data abstracted from the rubble of the past. But because those few data are evident to the human eye, they must be organized into information. It is human nature to do so. It is a necessity that the human nature industry organize them into an idea of what human nature was, and how it came to be what it is. In particular, it is the responsibility of the knowledge foundry to process human data into information which answers such human questions as Where am I? and Where did I come from?

Much of the interpretation of those data along the path is still up for grabs. There is nothing final or definitive about the organized idea of where and how the human body of knowledge evolved. But there are some very plausible concepts or organized ideas about it.

For example, to refer to Campbell again, success in big-game hunting required cooperation among males. Catching and killing large animals required ingenuity and skill—observing their habits, making axes and so on, in order to cut up meat which people's teeth could not do. Planning the hunt and food sharing afterward brought the group together and may have encouraged the development of speech. Nursing and pregnant females could not endure the hunt, and so would have to be left at a home base. That, in turn, would have encouraged further division of labor between the sexes. And so on.

Furthermore, lactation generally prevents conception, and, as Adolph Schultz points out, the social and cultural custom of prolonged nursing therefore not only brings long and close contact between mother and young but also spaces the children so that injurious population density does not occur. Many groups of people have evolved a taboo against sexual intercourse during the nursing period, which may prove that old wives' tales are very, very old.

And then again, maybe not.

It is also very difficult to trace the development of any one person's body of knowledge, marking off the point where this organizing idea was formed or that hypothesis was arranged. You would have to go back to the moment of birth and then, as Margaret Mead says, follow the ways in which the baby was held, carried and sung to because those experiences—like every other—contribute to the individual's organization of world data into information. And even if you retraced all of those steps, it would still be almost impossible to map in detail the building of the body of knowledge that ignores certain world data, pays attention to others and knows what questions to ask those data in order to pull them together into systematic information.

Says Ulric Neisser, "One easily forgets the *occasions* on which one learned how the local streets are oriented, what the Civil War was about, how to shift gears or how to speak grammatically, but they leave a residue behind. Because these residues are organized in the sense that their parts have regular and controlling interrelations, the term 'cognitive structures' is appropriate for them." It is very possible that the form and organization of some cognitive structures, especially those for space, time and language, are determined genetically, he says.

On the other hand, it is also possible that many particular bodies of knowledge come only with the experience of having to develop into maturity in a world where the data are completely organized for the helpless infant. Sorting out these two kinds of knowledge only makes it harder to trace the growth of individual hypotheses or working models of the world.

What can be said with some certainty, however, is: The human biological organizing capacity has had tremendous effects on the shape of the human body of knowledge; and the body of knowledge has had tremendous effects on the biology of the creature. What can also be said with some certainty is that the evolved human body of knowledge makes a more abstract level of data observable and therefore organizable than those data available to other natures. In other words, people build more and more comprehensive working models of the world.

Chimpanzees, for example, can see implicit in a leafy twig a potential pole for termite fishing. Jane Goodall reports chimpanzees having stripped twigs—abstracting the datum "pole" from the chaos—in preparation for an expedition to a distant termite hill. Apes, too, have concepts of certain objects, Campbell says. They have organized ideas, bodies of knowledge about how to deal with those abstract data here and now, "objects they can see and the function of which is clear."

But, says Campbell, an ape cannot conceive the tool without seeing it. "He cannot see the stick in the plank or a hand-axe within a piece of rock. This man alone can do."

Now, if you can look at a rock and reorganize it in your mind's eye into a hand-axe, then you can probably do all sorts of other things as well. For one, you can make a tool that will very likely help you to survive better than the fellow who can't perceive the abstract datum **HAND-AXE**. In that regard, your group will probably survive better, too. And, if you pass your knowledge along to your children, they and the succeeding generations will probably tend to survive better. And by and by that organizing IDEA OF HAND-AXE will shape the body organizing capacity of the maker.

Moreover, if you can classify a stone too heavy to hurl under the information heading POTENTIAL TOOL, then eventually you may be able to classify the datum **DEER** under the information heading ARC-RUNNING ANIMAL. And if you can do that, then sooner or later you will probably be able to see implicit in a wild cow a domesticated animal. And with each step in the evolution of the human body of knowledge, the species will tend toward more efficient survival. If you can have an organizing idea that conceives a hand-axe in a rock, you may eventually have an organizing idea of an agrarian way of life, an urban, an industrial and a technological. With each of those organized ideas, V. Gordon Childe says, the population of the human species on the face of the earth leaped in numbers.

Clearly, the human body of knowledge is still evolving. And because human nature is organic, the human organizing capacity is evolving, too. Research into the conditions of stress and their consequences on the human body, says David A. Hamburg, suggests that the anticipation of personal difficulty—whether it be physical danger or psychological or social danger—the anticipation of danger "may lead to important changes not only in thought, feeling and action, but also in endocrine and autonomic processes, and hence in a wide variety of visceral functions."

In an urban-industrial organized way of life, there is great stress caused by physical poisons. They were created because of the evolved human body of knowledge, organizing ideas that have rearranged world data into usable information with noxious by-products. Those poisons, says Anthony F. C. Wallace, hold fearsome potential dangers of disorders in the human central nervous system. Consequently, he says, the most extraordinary measures must constantly be taken by hospitals, physicians, courts, police, jails and so on to "protect society" from people suffering from gross disorders of the central nervous system. "One must suspect, in fact, that it is on the almost invisible processes of neurologically relevant physiology that natural selection is currently at work most effectively . . ."

Now, that is not to say that if you build a better working model of a rock, the world will eventually poison your central nervous system. What it means is that people are the kind of people who are capable of organizing more and more abstract ideas; and if you keep organizing ideas of that sort, they will eventually organize you.

If you can look at a rock and conceive the abstract notion of a hand-axe then you have come up with an idea for a reorganized way of life. That may not happen overnight, nor by plan or choice. But the fact remains: if you can look at your way of life and think of an improvement on it—by protecting society from this menace or that, or by hunting deer in addition to hunting ferns and termites—then you probably have a pretty good idea of what is human and natural; you have an organized body of knowledge, a working model, of human nature.

It is not so hard to build that working model. Not if you have a nature which constructs analogies from the past tense before you can speak the language properly; a nature which can make an hypothesis capable of arranging black and white lines and dots into a course of action; a nature which can abstract general principles of human nature from both a picture of the eye and a lesson in music appreciation; a nature which sees organized information about itself in such random and unlikely data as chimpanzees, polyps, hand-axes and eeny-meeny-miney-mo.

5

As you can see, the human nature industry provides steady work and full employment. Almost everybody has an organized idea of human nature, and consequently everybody can produce human data from the world chaos. That is to say, everybody has a particular body of knowledge or working model which explains where everything human and natural belongs, and how and when and why it belongs there. Consequently almost everybody can process the data into the information required to get through the day, the week, the year and the lifetime. For examples:

When a monstrous birth occurs, the defining lines between HUMAN and the datum **ANIMAL** may be threatened says Mary Douglas. To keep a **MONSTROUS** datum in its assigned information category, the Nuer of the southern Sudan "treat monstrous births as baby hippopotamuses accidently born to humans and, with this labeling, the appropriate action is clear. They gently lay them in the river where they belong."

In New York in 1871, reports Vincent Fontana, a child

132

named Mary Ellen was being seriously maltreated by her adoptive parents who beat the little girl regularly and kept her malnourished. "Interested church workers were unable to convince local authorities to take legal action against the parents. The right of parents to chastise their own children was still sacred, and there was no law under which any agency could interfere, to protect a child like her. The church workers were not discouraged; rather, they appealed to the Society for the Prevention of Cruelty to Animals. They were able to have Mary Ellen removed from her parents on the grounds that SHE was a member of the ANIMAL KINGDOM and that therefore her case could be included under the laws against animal cruelty. As a direct result of this incident, the Society for the Prevention of Cruelty to Children was founded in New York. . . ."

So, sometimes human data are arranged under the information heading of Animal. And, naturally, sometimes animal data are arranged as Human information. It depends, of course, on your working model of human nature. Says John Lilly, after years of studying dolphins: "If what I believed about dolphins was true, that dolphins have intelligence equal to or superior to human beings, we have to be willing to adopt the perspective of the dolphin. I had no right to hold them in a concentration camp for my scientific convenience." And with that, Lilly stopped his experiment and turned the laboratory dolphins out to freedom in the seas.

A South American tribe, who would be classified here as going naked, classify themselves as the Botocudo tribe. They owe this name to large cylindrical plugs of light wood which they wear in their ear lobes and lower lips. One European visitor, Baron Von Nordenskiold, reports that he tried to buy those facial plugs from a Botocudo woman "who stood all unabashed in customary nudity" during the bargaining. Eventually the offer of goods grew too great to be refused, so she removed the wooden plugs and sold them. Without them, however, she was stripped to the basics—a datum removed from its proper information category—"and she fled in shame and confusion into the jungle."

In many armies, soldiers are granted leave on account of the death and funeral of their datum "mother." In Africa, reports Max Gluckman, a Barotse soldier overstayed his leave for that reason. But trouble for him threatened when the District Commissioner found out that it was not the datum "mother" who had died but the datum "mother's brother." Says Gluckman: "I explained that the Barotse call the mother's brother 'my male-mother,' or more simply even 'my mother.' The mother's brother was a very close relative whose funeral a man should attend." With that information, the District Commissioner wrote to the army in hopes of resolving the soldier's difficulty: "Please ask the soldier if his mother was a woman or a man. If he says his mother was a woman, he is lying; if he says his mother was a man, he is telling the truth."

In order to look out on the world data and observe an area of **LAND** as DESOLATE, you need an organized idea of human nature—a body of knowledge about what is human and natural. As Fred Eggan reports: "Some well-meaning groups of whites tried to move a group of Shoshone Indians out of a desolate valley, and the Shoshone answered, in effect: 'What? Leave all these wonderful mice around here?'" To which Peter Gardner adds, "I have wondered how the South Indian Paliyans managed to maintain a population density that must be nearly two persons per square mile. . . . It's because they catch mice, rats, bats . . . and let the big game go."

The German genocide of the Jews was prosecuted after World War II as a crime against humanity. And, in fact, says Anthony F. C. Wallace, the Germans had to reclassify the Jews as less than human—putting them into concentration camps and so on—

before the mass killings of six million people were carried out. The information categories called SATISFACTION and AFFLUENCE also depend for their construction on an organized body of knowledge about human nature. Wants are "easily satisfied," says Marshall H. Sahlins, "either by producing much or desiring little, and there are, accordingly, two possible roads to affluence. The Galbraithean course makes assumptions peculiarly appropriate to market economies, that man's wants are great, not to say infinite, whereas his means are limited, although improvable. . . . But there is also a Zen solution to scarcity and affluence, beginning from the premises opposite from our own, that human material ends are few and finite, and technical means unchanging but on the whole adequate. Adopting the Zen strategy, a people can enjoy unparalleled material plenty, though perhaps only in a low standard of living." That, Sahlins thinks, describes man the hunter.

It clearly takes an organized idea of human nature in order to classify the data CHILDREN as information called UNDEVELOPED HUMANS. "The most outstanding characteristic the child beaters share is their attitude toward children," says E. Davoren. "Understanding this attitude and what it means helps one to make sense of the behavior of these people. The severe beater of children is not capable of seeing the infant or child as an immature human being without capacity for adult perception and behavior patterns."

Ethologist Konrad Lorenz, discussing with a colleague the behavior of geese, says he was amused to hear her reply that she wasn't surprised at all because the geese were only human. On the other hand, in an upstate New York city, a zoo was broken into and small living animals were torn limb from limb. Police discovered that it had been done by youngsters, two of them the children of a policeman. He, however, was not especially upset inasmuch as only animals had been destroyed.

135

Meanwhile, among certain low-caste Indians it is not unusual for a mother to cripple a child carefully and painstakingly, making it into what John R. Everett calls "an artistic invalid so that it can earn money as a work of art."

And so on and on, from place to place and time to time—demonstrating from instance to instance that the more abstract your organized idea or body of knowledge about human nature becomes, the more data you can distinguish in the chaos and arrange into information. If, like the Swazi in South Africa, your human and natural means of exchange is cattle, then, says F. C. Bartlett, you "could remember cattle transactions . . . with astonishing accuracy," unlike the Europeans who lived in the same area and may have been involved in many of those transactions.

Consequently, with an organized idea or particular body of knowledge about human nature that pays attention to human and natural data, you can organize information not only about CATTLE TRANSACTIONS, but also information about the WAYS PEOPLE ORGANIZE information from observable human data. Once you have an organized idea of human nature, you can see the ways American abusive parents classify their children; and you can see the ways Sudanese Nuer parents classify monstrous births. And as a result, you know what is an outrage and what is a folkway. Once you have that body of knowledge or working model of human nature, you can see where every datum belongs and how and when and why it belongs there.

It is a very powerful idea, this evolved body of knowledge about being human and natural. It tells you which information categories are worth dying for—Nation, say, or God or Family or Money. Moreover, with a working model of human nature, you can tell the proper way to treat people who reclassify human data—whether to give them $15 for arranging a wedding, $1,500 for arranging a divorce, the electric chair for arranging for Russia to have the H-bomb, a Supreme Court trial for rearranging the Pentagon's Vietnam papers from CLASSIFIED to UNCLASSIFIED.

Those are not random data by any means. Quite the contrary, they are the organized consequences of an evolved nature that must build a body of knowledge about itself, a working model of its nature, in order to survive. As the philosopher should have put it, but didn't: "I was, therefore I thought; now I think, and therefore I am." But that thinking-and-therefore-being isn't hit-or-miss, either. It is a consequence of the entire human nature industry, a full-employment firm of model builders that produces, distributes and advertises human nature—the only product in the world capable of protecting people from the ultimate jeopardy of encroaching chaos.

That said, it remains only to look at the local models, noting their advantages, styling and other benefits.

Chapter Six

So, that's one thing human nature seems to be: an organized idea of human nature—a particular body of knowledge, a working model, like a planetarium or a recipe for bread or a concept of a hand-axe.

Exactly how much of that idea of a human nature is organized in the womb is difficult to find out. That is because babies are incubated for only nine months, so they are not quite done when delivered. You have to wait until they are in better working order to ask them what they know. And by then it is too late to distinguish the particulars they had at the outset from those they have picked up along the way about the social contract, say, or private property. It would take an additional five or six years of incubation at least to produce a newborn human who could be connected one way or the other with any innate knowledge about the Common Market, the Oedipus Complex, the Conservative Party or other parts of the working model of human nature. Those notions might be organized in the womb. But there is no way of finding out. And the possibility of doing so is rather remote because a six-year-old newborn human could be manufactured only in the laboratory. But as that place is the leading basic sector of the human nature industry, the basic interest there is in getting beneath what people know and under their ideas. So laboratory science is not especially concerned with producing test-tube children or test-tube adults, but is much more interested in making basic test-tube babies just like the kind you can make during your lunch hour—half-baked infants who cannot tell you what they know, and moreover must be reared to completion in a world where most of the data have to be abstracted from the chaos and organized into information for their survival.

At any rate, nobody can tell for sure how much of the idea of a human nature is organized before the human is born. But one thing is certain: the general outline of that idea is there—the organizing capacity with its body of knowledge that must pay attention to **HUMAN** data and arrange them into information about HUMAN NATURE. That is to say, the cognitive skeleton is there: the evolved framework for some working model that explains where every **HUMAN** and **NATURAL** datum belongs, and how it belongs, and why and when. And another thing is certain: that framework must be filled in; that working model must be built; that idea of a human nature must be organized or nobody would be able to cross the street or even think of a street at all, or in any other way get through the day, the week, the year and the lifetime.

But with that particular body of knowledge all sorts of data become abstractable from the world rubble, and all sorts of human and natural information are arrangeable. Not only are such data as cows and wheat visible in the chaos, but also the further data of milk and flour are abstractable, and the still more abstract data of cream and butter and whole wheat and white flour. And inasmuch as those data have been made visible by human nature, they must be arranged into human and natural information by the organizing idea of a human nature. And so they are arranged that way. With a working model of human nature that explains where everything belongs, you can easily locate all the data and see at once the difference between what is a sacred cow and what is grist for your mill.

In addition, you can also see that it is natural to reorganize those data of milk and butter and flour into a new datum called bread. Baked for about forty-five minutes within an organized idea of human nature, that datum **BREAD** is organizable into a golden-brown loaf of human and natural information about all sorts of things.

It can be located in the categories of Human Rights and Social Contracts. For example, people can ask as their part of the bargain: "Give us this day our daily bread."

Those combined data of flour, milk, butter, etc., can also be baked into information about law and justice. For example, people can tell who deserves a crust of bread and who is to get bread and water.

Organized by an idea of human nature, those data can provide information for the division of labor. People can tell whose song to sing by whose bread they eat. People can tell the difference between the baker and the butcher and the candlestick maker.

Then, too, the loaf of data can be arranged under the information heading Private Property. People can tell whether half a loaf is better than none and whether to break the bread or to cast it upon the waters.

Baked within a working model of human nature that explains where everything belongs and how and when and why it belongs there, the datum bread becomes informative of love and happiness. People can tell when to cut down to one slice of bread per day—and having done so, they can tell whether to set their sights on dough or on a loaf of bread, a jug of wine and thou. And having decided one way or the other, they can tell whether it is more fulfilling to buy bread from the store or to bake it at home.

With an organized idea of bread inside an organized idea of human nature, you can make human and natural information about staying healthy and well. You can tell that bread is the staff of life, but that man does not live by bread alone. And not only that, but you can also tell how and when and why to serve the accompaniments. You can see quite plainly who gets bread and milk, when to serve bread and peanut butter and

141

jelly, where to serve bread and wine and cheese, why to serve dry toast and tea or crackers and soup.

And so on and on, through good bread and ruined, breakfast rolls and tea sandwiches, ham and cheese on rye, Zwieback and communion wafers. In addition, there is information to be made about managing the body politic. You can tell whether it is wisest to throw your followers a few crumbs, or give them bread and circuses, or warn them to bake unleavened bread, or laugh and tell them to eat cake.

All in all, with a working model of human nature, you can tell which side your bread is buttered on.

That is what a working model or organized idea or particular body of knowledge about human nature can do for the abstracted data of flour, butter, milk and the rest. That is what any working model or organized idea of anything does. It explains where the data belong, and when and how and why they belong there. That is the great advantage in having a human nature industry of model builders. They turn facts into information. And consequently, you can tell what is the beginning and what is the end, which end is up, where things fit, and what things are not fit and proper. That is as true of a working model of human nature as it is of a working model or organized idea of bread or cake or the solar system.

Now, it is frequently possible to build more than one working model to make data visible, locatable and explainable. Take the following data for example:

BUTTER
FLOUR
SUGAR
EGGS
MILK
ORANGE EXTRACT

Depending on your idea at the outset, you can organize those facts into various categories of information—cake or soufflé or pie crust or crepes suzette. They are all comestibles, of course. But each has its own suitabilities and protocols. Cake is seldom served hot, for example. Soufflé is almost never served cold. Pie and crepes can be taken as main courses or as desserts, depending on what they are filled with. Hardly anybody ever puts birthday candles on a soufflé, and only the grossest sorts of people make a kidney or asparagus icing for a cake.

Or take the solar system. You could build several kinds of planetariums or working models to explain the stars in their courses and make information out of observed celestial data. Here, for instance, are some facts about the sun's rising and setting—the times of sunrise and sunset at Paterson, New Jersey, on New Year's Day of 1965, 1966, 1967 and 1968.

January 1	Sunrise	Sunset
1965	7:22 A.M.	4:45 P.M.
1966	7:22 A.M.	4:45 P.M.
1967	7:22 A.M.	4:45 P.M.
1968	7:22 A.M.	4:45 P.M.

With data of that sort for every day in the year and every year in the decade, you could build at least two working models to explain the facts of the moon and stars and planets. For one, you could set up a planetarium with the earth in the center, and around it the sun and the other heavenly bodies, rising and setting as they passed into view and out again. For the other working model, you could say that the sun does not rise and set at all, but remains fixed at the center while the earth with its moon and the other planets pass around the sun. With either model— earth at the center or sun at the center—you could figure out the power, speed and trajectory necessary to put a man on the moon. Moreover, you could explain such regular data as sunrises, sunsets, new moons and full with a working model of a flat earth like a tea tray and a flat sun like a red-hot pizza falling somewhere beyond Pompton Lakes, New Jersey, at 4:45 P.M. on New Year's Day, and skimming up again from somewhere beyond Hackensack on the following morning.

It is hard to say which model explains the facts in the best way. If you are building a house or hanging a picture on the wall, it is a good idea to have a flat earth rather than a rounded one. Otherwise nothing will be level and true, and you may lose your balance and your walls as well. If you are navigating a boat by the stars, it is wisest to use a working model of the heavens that puts the earth at the center of things. Otherwise you may not be able to get any reliable information out of the data as to where you are and how to get where you want to go. With a working model that puts both the earth and the North Star in motion at the same time, there is no point in trying to get your bearings by looking up from time to time.

And the same is true for the particular body of knowledge about human nature. There are at least three organized ideas that assemble observed data into categories of information—three working models of human nature that explain where the facts of life belong, and how to put them there, and when and why they fit there.

2

Now, it is traditional to name models of human nature in either Greek or Latin. So human is pronounced either *anthropos* or *homo*. And the nature is named for some distinguishing characteristic of the model. For example, a model of human nature could be named for the place where it was discovered such as *Homo Neanderthalensis*. Or it could be named for the time when it might have been operational. A model suspected to have been in use at the dawn of the modern era would be called *Eoanthropus*. Another might be named for its construction. For instance, an upright model could be called *Homo erectus*. Or a model of human nature could be named for one outstanding capability. A model capable of making tools and things might be called *Homo faber*. A model capable of knowing—of holding a body of knowledge or organized idea or model—could be called *Homo sapiens*.

In keeping with this protocol, the following catalogue of models employs names and labels that are meant to be evocative only. The entries listed below have no personal, professional or individual connection of any kind with other owners of the same names. These three working models of human nature are labeled abstractly and theoretically, the way a working model of an automobile might be called a seven-door, four hundred-horsepower Spengler.

I

GENUS: *Alva Edisonthropus*
SPECIES: *Homo Tinkerectus*
VARIETY: *Skinnerens Newtoni Freudensis*

Even a brief glance into the working model of *Edisonthropus Tinkerectus* reveals a human nature that runs like clockwork. Even a child can easily see what makes people tick.

You can observe the defense mechanisms in operation. You can watch the hunger drive, the sex drive, the sleep drive and the thirst drive pushing and pulling. You can watch the pistons and shafts projecting, rejecting, introjecting, regressing, withdrawing, recoiling, resisting and recovering. You can hear the whirr and clang of inner conflicts. You can smell the puffs of free-floating anxieties. You can feel the throb of family function, reflex actions, dream work and magical undoing. With a rudimentary understanding of mechanical principles you can see at once how the clockwork of *Edisonthropus Tinkerectus* runs in conformity with the Law of Self-Preservation, the Effect of Proximity, the Pleasure Principle, the Mechanism of Obsession-Repulsion, the Inferiority Complex and other assorted natural laws.

That makes it quite easy to keep the model of this machine in good running order. You can devise gauges to measure the build-up of group pressure, marital tension, urban stress. You can mark off yardsticks to determine the length of the attention span and the generation gap. You can compile tables, schedules and scales to list and weigh preferences, aptitudes, capabilities. You can test the tensile strength of inhibitions, stimuli and responses. With an ordinary pocket watch you can time delayed reactions. And in case of breakdown, you can frequently trace the cause back through the cogs and pulleys to a difficulty in ventilation, perhaps, or a malfunction in group dynamics, or an axle frozen at a point of early fixation, or even to a dysfunction of society. It takes little more than a carpenter's level to find out whether the mechanism of *Edisonthropus Tinkerectus* is out of line or unbalanced. But even with the naked eye you can often tell when the machinery of the mind is not properly engaged, or whether there is a screw loose somewhere.

By using this model of human nature, you can make information out of all kinds of random data. You can tell not only what is grist to your mill, but also how to make your mill perform better. You can ask not only for your daily bread, but also for the nutritious kind of bread that is the staff of life—the sort of fuel necessary to stoke the boiler of your engine properly. With *Edisonthropus Tinkerectus* as an organized idea of human nature, you can tell at once that haste makes waste and that you need a new broom to sweep it clean. With a working model that obeys natural laws and mechanical principles, you can understand clearly that as the twig is bent so is the tree inclined. And with the Law of Gravity being what it is, the apples don't fall far from the tree.

This model of human nature with its cogs and wheels also helps you to get information about other human activities. For example, you can understand the machinery of government and industry. And with perseverance and application, you can become a fairly large cog yourself. Once you are on the right track, you can discern what is relevant—an important key to unlocking the secrets of success. On the other hand, if you are on the wrong track, you can throw a monkey wrench into the works and thus cause troubles for yourself.

But with *Edisonthropus Tinkerectus,* the machinery is usually out of order only temporarily because everybody knows what makes the wheels go round. Generally it requires an adjustment or two at most in order to get things running smoothly once again. If you are wound up, you must unwind in order to perform your tasks smoothly. If your children are having difficulty in school, you must improve the tools of learning, redesign the school plant, or devise new audiovisual hardware. In cases of inequity or infringements of rights, you must set the wheels of justice in motion. And if they are inadequate, you can turn to the legislative machinery. That, of course, requires information about the political machine, and where to apply the grease if you want to pull strings.

Viewed from most angles, there is great hope and reassurance in a human nature that looks and runs like *Edisonthropus Tinkerectus.* It is a working model of man that offers the advantages of harmony and regularity. What with its mechanisms and reactions that follow natural laws, it is accurate, precise, measurable. This is a human nature you can count on. You have only to study the model closely and measure its behavior carefully in order to understand the principles and regulations which it obeys.

Furthermore, it is the model of a nicely manageable nature. You can take it apart and adjust it when something goes wrong. And, if need be, you can replace even the big wheels when they no longer function properly. For that reason an inauguration is a great occasion: first because it demonstrates that the parts are interchangeable—even the steering wheel; and second because it proves that the machine will operate smoothly once again as soon as the power is turned on.

This *Edisonthropus Tinkerectus* model of human nature has provided a long and durable idea of what people are, and where everything belongs, and when and how and why to put it there. As an organized idea or body of knowledge it has opened men's minds to great achievements and even greater possibilities. With this model, it is always just a matter of time, effort, research and development before people will be able to replace worn-out tickers and faulty drives such as freedom and dignity.

II

GENUS: *Tarzanthropus*
SPECIES: *Homo Inherens*
VARIETY: *Calvins Darwini Lorenzis*

It is not so easy to inspect the inner workings of this model of human nature. The naked eye is not enough, nor the naked nose nor naked ear. You need special training to observe the organization of *Tarzanthropus Inherens* as well as high-powered lenses and acutely sensitive hearing aids. Without them, this model is too vast and too small in its particulars to be apprehended. It would be like trying to look at the inside of a dust storm or a snowfall. Besides, there is no machinery at work in this model, so there is no point to asking what makes it tick.

Tarzanthropus Inherens is made of primordial slime, prehistoric vapor and unconscious soot, crystals and other precipitates—all trapped in an electromagnetic field. There are no cogs or drives, no wheels to turn or gears to engage, no strings to pull anywhere. *Tarzanthropus Inherens* is a solid state model with such components as a block of emotions, a helix of hereditary message units, a constellation of relationships, a band of communication wave lengths, zones of pleasure and pain, a bank of memories and so on.

Consequently, this model cannot get off the track, nor can you throw a monkey wrench into the works. There is no track. There are no works. Nor are there any locks, keys to them, or other moving parts. And so there is nothing to wear out and nothing to replace. It is all built in. The only motion is the flow of electrons between the points of signal input and signal output, filtered through an unconscious crystal here, impeded by a primordial electrolytic solution there, modulated by a prehistoric condenser somewhere else. So under the circumstances, good working order and adjustment in this model are usually only a matter of fine tuning in frequency response, volume control or rate of sedimentation.

Now, that is not to say that a difficulty in *Tarzanthropus Inherens* is easy to trace. For one thing, there is no clockwork to watch, feel, hear or smell—and so no pulleys, pistons and drives to tighten, loosen or realign. And for another thing, the components are built-in and tailored to fit each model—with just enough variation in size, scope and arrangement from case to case to require individual attention with very sophisticated divining equipment. For example, a problem with vertical hold in this model may need a careful audit of the memory bank and an isotope scan of the cortical circuitry in order to locate the trouble. And even then there is no guarantee that an adjustment in fine tuning can be made without irrevocably altering the entire model. Clearly this is no job for a tinkerer with a book of natural laws in his vest pocket and a box of spare parts downstairs in the cellar workshop. It takes another order of know-how than perseverance and hardware to put this model in good condition if something goes wrong. *Tarzanthropus Inherens* being a miracle of individually built-in sensors, adapters, capacitors and other hidden wonders as yet undiscovered, it takes a magician to tend this model; it requires a wizard who knows which precipitates to filter and which to mix, or which levels to depress and which to stimulate in order to achieve the proper wave length of the model and to restore its inherent, individual resonance.

But for all of its built-in complications, this model of human nature has quite a few built-in advantages over *Edisonthropus Tinkerectus* when it comes to making information out of random data. To begin with, *Tarzanthropus Inherens* has an inherent need of a loaf of daily bread. Jane, on the other hand, knows that a half a loaf is better for her, with her slower individual metabolism. The individual resonance of *Tarzanthropus Inherens* vibrates with self-fulfillment at the prospect of a loaf of bread and thou (but no jug of wine on account of allergies). Jane's resonance, however, requires cake from time to time and home-baked croissants rather than bread for self-fulfillment.

With *Tarzanthropus Inherens* as an organized idea of human nature, you can see at once that you can't change human nature, and that blood is thicker than water. With a working model where everything is built in, you can know that along with its fixed frequencies and inherent capacities it also has inalienable rights and intrinsic worth. Regardless of how well the model works or whether it pulls its own weight, *Tarzanthropus In-*

herens has built-in worthwhileness which cannot be replaced or exchanged. Moreover, these rights and privileges are not optional. Nor do they have to be earned. They are standard issue and come innately with each model.

As an organized idea of human nature, *Tarzanthropus Inherens* has another advantage in making information out of observed data. With its components built in to individual specifications, you can start immediately to classify birds of a feather and tell readily when a person is not himself. But built in, fixed, individual components being what they are, you cannot make a silk purse out of a sow's ear. It is all right to try doing so, however, if that is your preference inasmuch as there is no accounting for tastes.

As working models go, this one has an additional important benefit. With its components fixed and its electrolytes hermetically sealed, there is considerable protection against injury or spoilage. That's more than you can say for the previous model. In the hands of inept mechanics, *Edisonthropus Tinkerectus* could have turned out to be Mr. Hyde rather than Dr. Jekyll. But *Tarzanthropus Inherens,* tended by apes, angels or ants, would still have finished up as Lord Greystoke, as Edgar Rice Burroughs made very clear.

III

GENUS: *Pierpons Morganthropus*
SPECIES: *Homo Exchangenesis*
VARIETY: *Adamusmithicus Woodrowilsoni*

Of all the organized ideas of human nature in this part of the world, this working model is the easiest to observe. All you need is the ability to read and an ordinary magnifying glass in order to see the fine print. That is because *Morganthropus Exchangenesis* is a paper cutout—a collage, a paste-up of pieces of bond, parchment, foolscap, rice paper, newsprint, ledger sheets, vellum, letterhead, mimeo, sheepskin and social note stationery.

Even with the naked eye you can see certificates (of birth, of death, of education, of achievement, of marriage, of ownership, occupancy, health, wealth and condemnation).

You can also see licenses (to enter, to exit, to remain, to perform, to practice, to participate, to hunt, to fish, to mine, to teach, to sell, to buy, to kill and to plant).

In addition, *Morganthropus Exchangenesis* is composed of promissory notes and pledges (to pay, to redeem, to honor, to love, to obey, to defend, to attack, to lend, to borrow, to rear, to cure, to take, to give and to remain absolutely neutral).

Also posted on this working model of human nature are regulations and rules (of coming, of going, of addressing, of turning, backing up, proceeding, spelling, querying, demanding, as well as of plurals, singulars, subjectives and objecting). There are also declarations (of war, of love, of independence, of intent, of failure and of purchase). In addition, there are bills (of lading, of rights, of particulars, of divorce and of indebtedness).

In addition, *Morganthropus Exchangenesis* is made up of such pieces of paper as receipts for, notices about, warnings against, directions to, treaties regarding, writs of, clauses in the event of. And also options, warranties, vetoes, addenda and errata.

Made up of all these bits and pieces of paper, *Morganthropus Exchangenesis* has a ragged and rakish look, like an old kite with a tail. There is nothing substantial looking in this model of human nature as is the case with *Edisonthropus Tinkerectus* and its machined parts and meshed gears. Nor is there the built-in solidarity of *Tarzanthropus Inherens* with its matching components. On the contrary, *Morganthropus Exchangenesis* is only as good as the paper it is written on. Its bond is only as good as its word. There is nothing inherent, intrinsic or inalienable about these pieces of paper. Nobody is born with a license to practice dentistry or with an overdrawn checkbook. Infants do not come equipped with an American passport or an American Motors proxy vote. These certificates, notes, regulations and declarations have to be applied for, handed over, assigned and agreed to by people who have the written and signed certificates and notes allowing them to do so.

These permits, options and IOUs are not meshed like cogs and wheels. These bills, receipts and treaties do not operate on fixed frequencies with a natural resonance. Almost any two people can have a license to marry even if they do not have all of their buttons or are not on the same wave length. The only requirements for the marriage documents are other documents in exchange—birth certificates, health certificates, application forms, signed oaths and contracts, and a certificate redeemable at the bank.

That is the great advantage of *Morganthropus Exchangenesis* with its ragged, flimsy, yellowing appearance. These bits and scraps of paper are negotiable. You can barter with them. You can exchange them for equivalents in rights, privileges, places, times, work, light, air and the like. Or you can store this paper for use in later transactions.

As an organized idea of human nature, this model is very handy for making information out of observed data. You can ask for your daily bread and know beforehand whether to expect dough, a half a loaf or only crumbs. If you take bread without a redeemable certificate in exchange, you can know that you may get bread and water.

With a working model of human nature made of negotiable components, you can see at once what to save and what to

153

spend, what to hoard and what to discard. You can know that a stitch in time saves nine. You can identify a dog in the manger. You can recognize a misspent youth, a profitable experience, a squandered love. With a body of knowledge such as *Morganthropus Exchangenesis* you can transact an entire life. You can store up your anger, bank on your common sense, invest in your children's education, put your money where your mouth is, take stock of the situation, save your strength, waste your breath, put a down payment on the future and take a new lease on life.

That is more than you can say for the other two models of human nature. *Edisonthropus Tinkerectus* may tick along performing its tasks like clockwork. But it can't buy you a controlling interest in your destiny for love or money. *Tarzanthropus Inherens* may be a miracle of built-in components individually and inalienably tailored to suit. But it can't offer you a better deal than you've got, nor help you to profit by other people's mistakes. With the organized idea of *Tarzanthropus Inherens,* you can't make a silk purse out of a sow's ear. But with the negotiable paper model of *Morganthropus Exchangenesis,* you can see clearly that where there's a will there's a way. With the body of knowledge of *Edisonthropus Tinkerectus,* you may know that haste makes waste. But with *Morganthropus Exchangenesis* and its barters and transactions, you can see how waste will make hay while the sun shines.

All in all, *Morganthropus Exchangenesis* offers three very attractive selling points in organizing the chaos of observed data into information about human nature.

First, this model provides a ready and orderly measure of worth. You can tell quickly whether you have valuable information and how much to ask for it. You can see whether your marriage is a going concern. You can say who is a successful teacher and who is a failed writer. In that way you can always tell what the score is.

Second, this model is easily repaired if torn, mutilated or spindled. You need only a pair of scissors, a pot of glue and a pencil in order to rewrite the rules and regulations, or amend another clause or option. If that doesn't work and it is still a bad deal, you can change the name of the game.

And that is the third advantage of this model: it is plainly and clearly a game, what with its permissions and penalties, wins and losses, rules and regulations, and the way the ball bounces. It takes a mechanic to operate *Edisonthropus Tinkerectus*. It takes a wizard to tend *Tarzanthropus Inherens*. But anybody can understand *Morganthropus Exchangenesis*. Anybody can learn the order of play. Anybody can make the swaps and trades. Anybody can ask for a favor, owe one in return and repay it. Anybody can be in the market for a new spouse, say, or shop around for a marketable education. People can do all sorts of things if they're willing to pay the price, play their parts, go by the rules and make the best of a bad bargain.

There is also a bonus attraction in this model. Being a flat, paper-thin model of human nature, *Morganthropus Exchangenesis* is easy to see through and easy to rise above. There is great consolation in that. You can play the game without having to take it seriously all the time. And when it's over and the time has come to cash in your chips, it's very reassuring to know that you can't take it with you.

Chapter Seven

Once upon a time there was a balloonist who hired himself out as an attraction to fairs and lodge picnics. While thousands cheered, he would climb into the gondola basket, cast off the stays and drift high into the sky above the fairgrounds. After a half hour or so, he would let the gas escape slowly from his balloon and drop gently back to earth. Then he would collect a fee for his behavior, pack up his balloon and go home. That was the way he made his living.

One day, after he had cast off and was rising into the sky above a county fair, a very strong wind came up suddenly. It carried his balloon far across the countryside, over strange mountains and beyond forests and fields he had never seen before.

By and by the sun began to sink in the west, and the wind died down. As dusk approached, the balloonist saw far below him a farmer plowing a cornfield. Very carefully he let enough gas escape from the balloon until he was hovering above the farmer.

"Hello," the balloonist called down. "Where am I?"

"You?" the farmer called back. "You're up there."

Well, there is very little you can do for people like that. They give you observed data. They give you facts. But they do not give you information. And as a result it is quite difficult to tell where you are.

It requires an organized idea at the outset—a body of knowledge, a working model—to give form to observed data, to make information out of facts. Without a working model of human

157

nature to explain where the data belong and how and why and when to put them there, it is just about impossible to say where you are, or even whether you are lost and found. That is because you need a working model—a completely organized idea with a beginning, middle and end in order to know whether you are halfway there, on the wrong track or safely arrived. You have to know where you have come from and where you are going in order to know where you are.

Without a body of knowledge about these things at the outset, it is rather hard to say where you have come from. To begin with, there is that business of the sperm and the egg. Looked at without an organized idea of human nature, it appears a very chancy matter as to which single sperm of the tens of thousands will fertilize which egg: April's, January's, June's or July's. That is true not only about where babies come from, but it is also true about where their parents came from. And as for whose egg will be fertilized by whose sperm, that frequently appears to be a random coupling when looked at without an organized idea or working model of what people are, and where they're going, and how to get there. Many men and women have never met on account of differences of birth dates and birthplaces, and so they have never had babies together. On the other hand, many others have coincided for the same reasons and have become parents. Looked at without an organized idea of human nature, parentage and its offspring are a matter of random coincidence in the world rubble. But once you have a working model of human nature that explains where things fit, and why and how they fit there, you can see at once that a marriage was not a coincidence at all but was instead a mistake—or made in heaven, or on the rocks or any of the other things people say about the organization of data called marriage. Without an organized idea of human nature, you would have to say that random men and women of fertile condition get together and have children. And those random offspring grow to fertile condition and meet others of the same kind of origin and become your parents.

As to where you are going, that is also difficult to know without a body of knowledge about human nature at the outset. Nobody can say when and where everybody will die, or of what cause, or with what consequences to themselves and to others. Without a body of knowledge or organized idea of human nature to make human data observable and arrangeable into human and natural information, you would have to say that bedrooms, bathrooms and highways are as random arenas as battlefields when it comes to mortalities. Who lives and dies is quite chancy at every minute in every place, and generally comes as a surprise to both the quick and the dead. Many people who set out for a glass of beer or a head of lettuce discover that they have been shot to death, beaten to death, crushed to death or hit-and-run to death. Many people who have just come from a thorough physical examination with a completely clean bill of health suddenly find a fatal error in the addition. Many people with a full calendar of commitments for the weekend die on Friday night. Without an organized idea of what is human and natural, you would have to say that it is very dangerous to have a complete medical check-up. You would have to say that peacetime is as chaotic as wartime regarding mortal casualties. You would have to say that dissolution is where everybody is going.

So, all in all, without a working model of human nature you cannot really inquire as to where you are. There is no information on the subject. The only answer you can get to the question of where you are is a piece of observed data, to wit: you are somewhere between random and chaos.

That is also the case with the other information people are always requesting of each other, such as: What time is it? and What's the matter? and What should I do next? Without a body of knowledge about where everything fits and how and when and why it fits there, you would have to answer these questions with the uninformative fact, "I don't know." Here is a real-life example of this difficulty involving a bit of commonly requested information:

Q: What is your name?
A: I really don't know, but my
   parents call me Albert Schweitzer.

How they came to call him by that name is easy enough to see, of course. His mother always liked the name Albert and, in fact, called two dolls and an Easter rabbit by that name when she was a child. She resolved at that time to name her first-born son Albert. The second name, Schweitzer, belonged to her husband. He got it from his father who got it from his father—and so forth backwards, through This Schweitzer and That Schweitzer, Jr. Exactly when the name became attached to the family is hard to find out because nobody remembers any forebear who came from *Die Schweitz*—Switzerland—or any forebear who even vacationed there. But in any event, the name is probably not much more than a thousand years old. (The canton Schwyz is documented to A.D. 972.) Much more likely, the name was given to the family during the Napoleonic era for purposes of census and taxation.

So, there is Albert Schweitzer—named for an Easter rabbit in front and for a political real estate location behind in order to satisfy the demands of a French tax collector long since wholly and completely dissolved. But who Albert really is, why, he doesn't know that anymore than he knows where he is without an organized idea of human nature. And the same is true of anybody else named Albert Schweitzer, or any other name for that matter. Without a working model that explains where everything belongs and how and when and why it belongs there,

160

you cannot introduce your wife by name. Nor can she insist that being called by her maiden name is more human, more natural, more consistent with her rights.

The rest of the journey from random to chaos proceeds in similar fashion. Without an organized idea or working model of human nature, you would follow a route that appeared to be only a concatenation of accidents, coincidences, momentary sexual attractions, inexplicable arrivals and departures, mysterious associations, temporary careers. Without an organized idea or body of knowledge about human nature, there is almost no way for people to survive at all—almost no way to accomplish what many sectors of the human nature industry call adapting to the environment. The plain fact is that people do not survive by adapting to the environment. The human infant survives because the environment is adapted to it. The human infant survives because of a man-made organization of information which has been arranged by an idea, a body of knowledge, a working model of human nature. What people have to adapt to—if that is the right word—is that organized idea or working model of human nature.

And, once you have a working model of human nature, you can see quickly where everything belongs, and how and when and why it belongs there. With a working model of human nature, you know which data to pay attention to and what questions to ask those data in order to arrange human and natural information suitable for getting through the day, the week, the year and the lifetime.

2

For example, take this frequently asked question of "Where am I?" That being a point somewhere between where you have

161

come from and where you are going, it is necessary to locate these two places first in order to reply with information about where you are. And those two locations are quite easy to find if you have a working model of human nature that explains where everything is and how and why and when it fits there. To wit:

GENUS: *Alva Edisonthropus*
SPECIES: *Homo Tinkerectus*
VARIETY: *Skinnerens Newtoni Freudensis*

You can quickly find where you have come from by looking at this model of human nature with its cogs, wheels, drives and other mechanisms that run according to natural law. You are the issue of your parents' human and natural need, love and union. If they provide you with the proper environment, rearing, example and education, and if you obey and persevere, you can grow up to be President.

There is really nothing random about where you have come from. As a look at *Edisonthropus Tinkerectus* reveals, you are born of a functioning machine created and set in motion by a Great Mechanic. And you have the responsibility from birth to take your place in the machine and keep it functioning. If there is any accident of birth, it is only a mechanical failure of some sort—a faulty parent, an impoverished environment, a poor constitution. But these accidents and malfunctioning parts can be identified, corrected, compensated for or replaced. Look at Alexander Graham Bell, who overcame deafness. Look at Helen Keller, born both blind and deaf. Look at Abraham Lincoln, reared by a stepmother in a log cabin. As you can see clearly in this working model of human nature, there is a random origin only for the offspring of willfull people who refuse to obey the natural law and yield to sloth instead of persevering.

That is not the only explanation of where you have come

from, of course. Another working model of human nature locates these origins in another place. For example, take:

GENUS: *Tarzanthropus*
SPECIES: *Homo Inherens*
VARIETY: *Calvini Darwini Lorenzis*

You can find the starting point very easily in this model of human nature with its built-in components of personal feelings, individual memories, particular preferences and other fixed frequencies. You begin life as a little stranger who has come to live in your parents' home. And no matter what kind of rearing, environment, example or education are provided for you, your parents cannot help you to become President unless it is within you to be one. What you need is a varied, fertile and permissive climate in order to let your true personality unfold. Consequently it is not important that you become President—or anything else. It is necessary only to be true to thine own self; to realize thine own potentialities; to do thine own thing and thus achieve personal satisfaction and individual fulfillment.

Where you have come from may be an unknown and an unconscious place. But it is your very own place which has been carved out for you by a Great Creator. Something about you, your parents, their parents and on has been worthy of survival. So you have not come from a random place at all—and, in fact, it doesn't feel random. That is a basic test for validity provided by this working model of human nature. When you look at the *Tarzanthropus Inherens* model to find out where everything belongs, you can feel the resonance of meaning, unity and purpose when they strike on your genetic clock. You can feel vibrations of consistency. And, on the other hand, you can feel the clangor of discord when things are not consistent with your nature. Under the circumstances, the world you inherit at birth does not bring with it the responsibility to adjust to the machine and to keep it functioning. According to this organized idea of human nature, you inherit a world in which you must make your own way, find your own niche, cultivate your own garden. To violate those personal needs and persevere in disregard of them can bring on disastrous results.

That doesn't mean mistakes and accidents of birth are impossible. On the contrary, they happen all the time. But only in families with hang-ups—to people who cannot realize that a little stranger has come to live with them; to parents who do not allow for individual relevance and personal priorities; to adults who insist that children obey the universal principles of natural laws and obstinately refuse to understand that there are as many natures as there are people.

That is not the only other explanation of where you come from. There is at least a third working model of human nature. It puts the starting point in still another place. This is the model of:

GENUS: *Pierpons Morganthropus*
SPECIES: *Homo Exchangenesis*
VARIETY: *Adamusmithicus Woodrowilsoni*

You can readily see where you have come from by looking at this model with its IOUs, receipts for payment, certificates of origin, accreditation and possession—and all the other bits and pieces of paper for transacting life. You are a gift. Depending on the geography, you are a gift from God, a gift from the stork, a gift from mommy to daddy, a gift to the world, a gift of love, and so on and on.

In return for this gift, your parents owe you protection, care, love, and as many privileges and possibilities as they can afford, and so on. In return for these things, you owe your parents respect, honor, cooperation, loyalty, and so on and on through good report cards, gold stars and bronze plaques. If your parents meet their obligations and you repay them for their love and kindness, it doesn't matter whether you grow up to be President. The important thing is that you be successful at whatever you do—whether it is in earning degrees or stock options—and thus become a credit to your family, friends, teachers, community, nation and so on. And for their part of the bargain, they will strive to be a credit to you and to their families, teachers, friends, community and so on and on.

With this ongoing transaction and balancing of credits, there is nothing random about where you have come from. You are born with a membership in this or that nation, state, city, family. You have a birth certificate which establishes your credit rating among your kin, community and eventually the world. There is nothing chancy about it. A pauper cannot be conceived by millionaires. You are delivered with a participating interest in your family's portfolio of privileges, permissions and other credits. True, the value of the portfolio may change or you may abjure your claim to it. But that does not change the situation. As a look at the model *Morganthropus Exchangenesis* reveals about where everything fits, you have come from history—an orderly, knowable place. And as for the world you inherit, it is neither your responsibility to keep the cogs and wheels running nor your duty to yourself to find your own niche. As this organized idea of human nature shows, the world is your oyster; it is your obligation to make the most of it.

In this model there are certainly accidents of birth, too. But they usually happen only to families who do not see a baby as a valuable gift and so do not realize the debt they owe in return for the favor bestowed. These people do not build a portfolio of diplomas, licenses, certificates, receipts, honors and other securities. Consequently, they do not have a credit rating of worth. And as a result, the world does not know what exchange value to put on their babies—anymore than it knows what value to put on a dog without a pedigree or on a painting without a signature. That is bad enough. But in addition, without being born to a portfolio of any documents whatsoever, these babies are never properly paper-trained. And so they grow into messy children and eventually into non-negotiable people who, in their turn, do not see their babies as valuable gifts. And so on and on.

Well, those are the kinds of places you have come from—at least they are the places according to these three models of human nature. But that is not yet enough information to answer the question of "Where am I?" It still remains to find out where you are going in order to locate the place in between the two where you are now. And with a working model that shows where everything fits and how and when and why it fits there, it is quite easy to see where you are going.

If you look at *Edisonthropus Tinkerectus* with its drives, pulleys and gears doing the world's work, you can see that when life is done you are going to your rest. Naturally that does not mean a complete retirement because the devil finds work for idle hands. It just means that you have been advanced from daily laborer to consultant. You are frequently called on to counsel and advise those left behind, usually coming to them in the bedroom at night but also sometimes dropping into the kitchen or the back yard. This job not only keeps you around the house a lot, but in addition it requires that you speak, dress, behave and look as you did in life. Death may be a release from what the working model explains as misery, travail and suffering. But there is no liberation from your myopia, say, or your trick knee or your children. Beyond the grave you continue to wear eyeglasses or to limp. Beyond the grave you continue to wear a shirt and tie or flowered house dress. That is because you must stand ready at every moment to appear in recogniz-

166

able form and warn, comfort or hector your family when they invoke you to do so.

All in all, there is nothing chaotic about where you are going, as a look at *Edisonthropus Tinkerectus* clearly shows. Under the circumstances, it is very reasonable that a professor of chemistry at Cotton Mather College, who has won renown for unlocking a mechanism of the atom, should expect to see his mother in full form when he dies. The machine ticks along like clockwork—now and hereafter. It is a very optimistic machine in every way. With perseverance and better understanding of natural laws, even the mechanism of death may be unlocked, reassembled and reversed.

In similar manner, there is nothing chaotic about where you are going as you can see by looking at the other two popular models of human nature.

Take *Tarzanthropus Inherens* with its individually built-in components and fixed frequencies. As this working model organizes the data, everybody is unique. There are as many human natures as there are people, so there are no higher values and lower. There is only a spectrum of experience with people realizing their individual potentialities and doing their own things. There are no big wheels or little, no upward motion or backward, no gears meshing or clashing. There are only temporary geometric relationships of individuals with other individuals. You are part of an augmented chord here, part of an arpeggio there, a note in the melody in some other measure.

The arrangement changes irrevocably when you die. On this side of the grave your individual resonance lingers for a little while. In some measures it persists for a long time by its absence. On the other side of the grave you join a new choir of frequencies and figure in new geometric relationships with a host of angels. These frequencies are sometimes audible here, and the new geometry perceived—during some sunsets, for example, or in certain narcotic gloamings, when the world noise and mind noise are stilled for a moment.

As in any classical progression of music, which must finish on the home base of tonic note and chord, your career of individual experience and self-realization comes to a finale with a journey home. And that is hardly a chaotic destination. All in all, you see considerable harmony when you look at *Tarzan-thropus Inherens* to find out where everything fits, and what people are, where they're going, and how to get there. And in that regard, it is possible to locate you beyond the grave—or at least to call up your essential resonance—by using this working model of human nature. It requires first a triangulation of frequencies to find you, and second a particularly sensitive receiver to achieve communication. This fine band tuning is often accomplished in a quiet room with several wave-length generators holding hands so as to form a loop antenna. If reception is good, your individual resonance can be heard—frequently as percussion on the table top, but also sometimes as a brass, a woodwind or strings. On very rare occasions some of the lyrics come through, too. But they are almost always in an extremely foreign tongue, as you would expect when there is an individual human nature for each human being.

You can also see clearly where you are going if you look at the *Morganthropus Exchangenesis* model made of diplomas, promissory notes, licenses and other negotiable securities that inform a lifetime. As this working model organizes the data of human nature, you begin as a gift. Naturally you finish the same way. The gift bestowed at the outset must be returned. And for that transaction it is cleaned, polished, gift-wrapped so that people can pay their last respects before it goes back. But as for your portfolio of negotiable documents, you can't take it with you. As you can see within the model *Morganthropus Exchangenesis*, there is no final chord struck, no journey home, no last

168

resting place. There is no final death at all; there is only a death certificate negotiable in further transactions, such as lawsuits, inheritance taxation, patent and copyright assignments, estate auctions, insurance payments, lease and title transfer, contractual commitments, notes of condolence and so on and on.

All in all, there is nothing chaotic about where you are going. Beyond the grave, your corporeal entity is received back and some of it goes on in negotiations with St. Peter at the gates or with the devil regarding rewards and punishments. On this side of the grave, your corporate person persists, exercising its will and testament, negotiating with heirs and assigns regarding rewards, punishments, directives and controls. On either side, the datum that is you can be located by consulting with the working model of human nature, *Morganthropus Exchangenesis*.

Depending on the kinds of transactions you have made and thus the credit rating you have accumulated in this papered, corporate world, you can be found in political developments, for example, or in economic measures; or in scientific progress; or in the annals of crime; in the history of cat fancying; in a cornerstone; or in the wedding announcements of your great-grandchildren. And if your corporate person cannot engage in those kinds of posthumous transactions, then you can probably be found in perpetuity in the hall of records, the grade school transcripts, the credit association files, the census figures or the FBI microfilm archives. And if you cannot be found in those documented transactions, then you can always be found within the hearts of your family and loved ones where negotiations continue with you over unrequited affection, unfulfilled promises, unanswered questions, unrepaid kindnesses, unsettled scores and other unfinished business. In any event, you belong to the sequence of past transactions called history. And that is where you are to be found on this side of the grave.

On the other, naturally, you can be located in the same way:

either through written documents such as a tombstone or a paid memoriam advertisement in the newspaper; or else by flowers on the grave, a prayer or some other transaction conducted between the living and the non-living.

Those are the kinds of places you are going to, depending on the working model you look at to find out where everything fits and why and when and how it fits there. And between your destination and the place you started from is the place where you are.

3

Once upon a time there was a balloonist who hired himself out as an attraction to fairs and lodge picnics. One day while he was aloft, a strong wind came up suddenly and carried his balloon far across the countryside for hours and hours. Finally the wind died down. As dusk approached, the balloonist saw far below him a farmer plowing a cornfield.

Very carefully the balloonist let enough gas escape from the balloon until he was hovering above the farmer.

"Where am I?" the balloonist called out, unaware that the farmer used the *Edisonthropus Tinkerectus* model of human nature.

"You?" the farmer called back. "You're 43 feet above a point 85 degrees east and 41 degrees north on the third planet from the sun in the solar system. That's probably not where you're supposed to be at all. But wherever it is, you'll never find it in the dark. What you need is a hot meal, a hot bath and a good night's sleep so you can start out at 7:49 in the morning when the sun comes up. But you won't make it through to this evening if you keep leaning out of your gondola basket that way. A fall of 43 feet is pretty hard on a body."

Once upon a time there was a balloonist who hired himself out as an attraction to fairs and lodge picnics. One day while he was aloft, a strong wind came up and carried his balloon far across the countryside for hours and hours. Finally the wind died down. As dusk approached, the balloonist saw far below him a farmer plowing a cornfield. Very carefully he let enough gas escape from his balloon until he was hovering above the farmer.

"Where am I?" the balloonist called out, unaware that the famer explained human nature according to the *Tarzanthropus Inherens* working model.

"You?" the farmer called back. "Only you can answer that question. One man's balloon is another man's hang-up. All I can tell you is where I am at. I'm hungry and tired and mad as hell that I missed the county fair. But as for where you are— well, the most I can say is that you're up there. And from the way you're leaning out of that gondola basket, it looks to me like a bad trip."

Once upon a time there was a balloonist who got carried away by a strong wind. It was dusk when the wind died down, and he let enough gas escape from the balloon so that he was hovering over a farmer plowing a cornfield.

"Where am I?" the balloonist called out, unaware that the farmer used the *Morganthropus Exchangenesis* model of human nature.

"You?" the farmer called back. "You're over my cornfield in the town of Bryant, township of Bear Creek, Jay County, Indiana, United States of America. You don't belong here. You belong at the county fair. But I'll give you supper and a place to sleep tonight if you'll give my kids a ride in your balloon tomorrow. You can also use my phone to call your family so they won't worry about you. But you'll have to pay the toll charges.

171

If you're not insured, take care not to fall out of that gondola basket because I won't be responsible if you get hurt. . . ."

So, there are three ways to answer the question. There are three working models of human nature, each making valuable information out of observed data in order to tell you where you are.

That is the great advantage of a working model of human nature. It tells you where everything fits and belongs. And consequently it tells you when things are out of place and out of order, and how to set them to rights again. A working model of human nature not only tells you to ask "Where am I?" but it also tells you the *answer* to the question.

With a working model of human nature, you can make vast quantities of that kind of important information—asking and answering all those questions necessary to get through the day, the week, the year, the lifetime.

4

"WHAT TIME IS IT?"

Now, that is one of those questions. And it is very important to receive an informative answer because you cannot get through the day, the week, the year and the lifetime unless you know when those times are. In order to tell what time it is you have to know not only where everything belongs, but also when it belongs there. You have to know how things are organized before you can tell when it is time to reorganize them. So it requires a working model of human nature in order to ask and answer the question of "What time is it?"

If you look at *Edisonthropus Tinkerectus* with its gears and wheels running like clockwork, it is very easy to see the time. You can tell at once when it is time to rise and shine, when it is lunchtime, quitting time, dinnertime and bedtime. You can also tell when it is time to begin, time to celebrate and time to retire. To everything there is a season in this model, and a time to every purpose under the sun. So you can also tell when it is time to laugh, time to weep and high time you put away childish things and settled down.

If you look at the working model *Tarzanthropus Inherens* made of individually built-in memories and message units, you can see what time it is, too. It is time to mate. It is time to take a breather. It is time to find out who you are. It is time to join hands or time to split up. On the calendar it may be March, but it's three-quarter time on the drum you hear. It may or may not be lunchtime; but you know when it's time to get something to eat. It may or may not be time to retire; you're only as old as you feel.

When you look at the *Morganthropus Exchangenesis* model of human nature made of its leases, receipts, statements and other documents of transaction, you can certainly tell what the time is. Like any other commodity on the exchange, time is limited, time is money, time can be wasted, time can be well spent. You can be left with plenty of time, with time on your hands, with not a minute to lose. You can get rid of a couple of hours, lose a weekend, fritter away a month at the seashore and have leftover life to kill. But in the *Morganthropus Exchangenesis* model there is no universal clockwork ticking endlessly along, nor a built-in metronome beating out individual time. That could make it difficult to get the kind of information provided by the other two models, such as when it's time for breakfast or time to mate. But you can get this kind of information in the transaction market place. For example, if you're nice to people then they'll give you the right time of day. And if you

173

propose a marriage contract, then sooner or later you will find somebody with whom to make time and with whom to spend your breakfast hours. To make that kind of an investment you should start early—before you lose your prime. There's not much time available, so it's first come first served.

"WHAT DO YOU WANT TO BE WHEN YOU GROW UP?"

The question put that way is usually addressed to small children and seems to imply a wide open choice of being for growing up to. It is a question that also seems to imply human freedom, dignity and similar possibilities of a democracy. So, if you look at the question that way, it is a violation of human rights to tell a little boy that he cannot grow up to be a woman if he wants to. At least that is the theory.

But in actual practice, the question of what you want to be when you grow up belongs to the working model *Edisonthropus Tinkerectus* with its gears and mechanisms doing the world's work according to natural law. If you look at this model, you see that people grow up and do this or that job of work. Consequently, this scale model of human nature contains in its parts scale models of man's nature, woman's nature and children's nature, each performing its human function in the machine. And if they do not for some reason or other, then an adjustment of the parts is required. And as for freedom and dignity, they do not apply in a model where there is only the meshing of gears and interchangeable drives and pulleys.

That is not the case with the other two commonly employed working models of human nature. As you can see by inspecting *Tarzanthropus Inherens* with its individually built-in potentialities, you cannot grow up. You can only grow into. You can only actualize. You can only realize your potentialities. So it is impossible to ask people what they want to be when they grow

174

up. The only applicable question is what will you become, and that is impossible to answer until the journey is finished and you can look back. And inasmuch as there are as many human natures as there are people, it is difficult to divide them according to man's nature, women's nature and children's nature. The only real differences are among individuals and their particular resonances.

In the working model *Morganthropus Exchangenesis,* there is no growing up, either. There is only coming of age. You can transact some business as soon as you have a birth certificate and a fingerprint. But there are other documents you cannot give or receive until you are eighteen and twenty-one. So it is not necessary to grow up. It only requires that you hang around until you age—and eventually trade away. Whether you are a man or a woman from time to time in this due process of aging is unimportant, just so long as your credit rating is good and your power of attorney is strong. When you use the model *Morganthropus Exchangenesis* to find out where everything fits and how and when and why it fits there, you cannot ask people what they want to be when they grow up. All you can ask is where they want to be when they are twenty-five, thirty-five, fifty and so on and on. And it is impossible to answer with much sense or will unless you are holding winning cards, controlling stocks or similar currency. In this working model of human nature you cannot foresee how the cookie will crumble, how the ball will bounce or what other breaks and vicissitudes will befall future negotiations.

That is the trouble with the question of what you want to be when you grow up and its variations. They cannot be asked when you have a working model of human nature. Once you have an organized idea of where everything belongs—once you have a body of knowledge about what people are and where

175

they're going and how to get there—once you see how everything fits together, there is only one way to put the question in order to get an informative answer. To wit:

"WHAT SHOULD YOU DO?"

If you look at the model *Edisonthropus Tinkerectus* with its machinery running according to natural law, it is very clear what you should do. You should do your share. You should do your job. You should do it the right way, not the wrong way. And you should do it to the best of your ability. If you are in school, your job is to study hard and get your education before you begin your life. Then you should grow up, be productive and adjusted, and do what you can to make the world a better place to live in. It is your generation's duty to improve on what has gone before, to right wrongs, to build better mousetraps, to take the helm and keep the world on its course for the generation that follows yours. But you should use your common sense and not try to change things overnight. You should be prepared to lose some of your ideals along the way and have the world change you. Your reason will tell you that in the end you will have to fit in, so you should be ready to do so. That means you should not be an artist, writer or poet because they do not fit in. But whatever you do, you should do it well. And if at first you don't succeed then you should never say die but should try, try again. If you obey those natural laws and persevere, that will do for all practical purposes.

When you look at the model *Tarzanthropus Inherens* with its personal potentialities and other components built in to individual specifications, it is also clear what you should do. You should do your thing. You should express yourself. You should be yourself and strive for fulfillment. And if you don't have a thing to express or a self to fulfill, that is probably because it was

176

suppressed or mashed by your family, your teachers, your prerequisites and the other gears and pistons of the *Edisonthropus Tinkerectus* model of human nature. If that is the case, then you should find yourself in your work and in the geometry of interpersonal relationships. You should try this job and that. You should be into art, into writing, into emotional involvements, into social work, into city planning and the like until you vibrate to your true resonance. The job is not important. It is the career of the self that you should think about. There is no right way or wrong way. There is only a good way or a bad way for each individual. There is no universal clock ticking according to natural law and measuring your progress. And in that regard, you should work to free the world of the oppression that keeps individual potentialities from being realized. You should challenge reactionary forces whether they appear in the guise of liberal or of conservative programs. And you should use your gifts to defend and help those who cannot do so for themselves. But you should also use your intelligence to understand that such a battle can never be fought to unconditional victory. You should have the self-assurance and courage of your convictions to cultivate your own garden if that is the most you can do.

The *Morganthropus Exchangenesis* model of human nature, pasted together with documents of transactions such as declarations and enactments, also turns the data of possibilities into the information of what you should do. As you can see in this organized idea, there is no right way or wrong way. Nor is there a good way or bad way. Instead, there is a just and fair way, and an unjust, unfair way.

Naturally, you should be just and fair in your dealings with your fellow man. You should fulfill your obligations and honor your pledges. Moreover, you should obey and uphold the law, and fight to see that everybody gets a chance to succeed. But that does not mean you have to give away the groceries. You should be prudent, politic and judicious. You should succeed and prosper. You should never lie but nobody is asking you for the truth. You should win all the prizes. But you should also remember that it is much better to give than to receive. That is not so paradoxical as it may appear. Hardly anybody can remember the names of the people who received the Nobel or Pulitzer prizes two years ago, or even last year. But everybody remembers the names of Alfred Nobel and Joseph Pulitzer.

It is not important that you do your own thing or be yourself on the job. In fact, you should not if it stands in the way of successful transactions and negotiation. On the contrary, you should make a good appearance, put up a good front, put on a good show, put a good face on things and hold your cards close to your vest. In that way you accumulate valuable coupons redeemable for the power and time necessary to do your own thing and be yourself. No matter the name of the game, you should play it to win. You should play your role professionally. So that means learning a negotiable and marketable trade. It is certainly all right to be an artist or poet—as long as your art and poetry sell. Naturally, they have to sell for money. That is the current medium of exchange. But you should expect more. Human nature does not live by bread alone. In return for whatever you do, and for whatever role you play, the transaction should provide a psychological pay-off, too.

5

In other words:

Don't worry if your balloon seems to be lost in the chaos of random world data. You can easily see where you are: you are located in an organized idea or working model that explains where everything human and natural belongs and how and when and why it belongs there. That is to say, you are conforming to a simulation of human nature. Or, in the words of molecular biologist and Nobel Prize winner Jacques Monod:

What the brain does is "to give a representation of the material world adequate for the performance of the species; to furnish a framework permitting efficient classification of the otherwise unusable data of objective experience; and even in man, to simulate experience subjectively so as to anticipate its results and prepare action.

"It is the powerful development and intensive use of the simulative function," Monod says, "that, in my view, characterizes the unique properties of man's brain . . . in man, subjective simulation becomes the superior function par excellence, the creative function." To be absorbed in thought, he says, "is to be embarked upon an *imagined experience,* an experience simulated with the aid of forms, of forces, of interactions which together only barely compose an 'image' in the visual sense of the term." But thought, he says, is not a spontaneous occurrence. Like a lost balloon, "thought reposes upon an underlying process of subjective simulation." And if that is so, then "we must assume that the high development of this faculty in man is the outcome of an evolution during which natural selection tested the efficacy of the process, its survival value. . . ."

This "power of simulation lodged in our early ancestors' central nervous system," Monod says, "was propelled to the level reached with *Homo sapiens.* The subjective simulator could afford to make no mistakes when organizing a panther hunt with the weapons available to Australanthropus, Pithecanthropus or even *Homo sapiens* of Cro-Magnon times. . . . As the instrument of intuitive preconception continually enriched by lessons learned from its own subjective experiments, the simulator is the instrument of discovery and creation."

So, of all living things, man is a simulation-maker—a model-builder—par excellence. But that is only half of it. In addition, man is almost wholly a model-living organism. It is questionable as to whether he could survive without his organized ideas of where everything belongs and how and when and why it belongs there.

The adult, say Donald Hebb and W. R. Thompson, "may think that he is not disturbed by strange places, darkness or solitude, although young children are. As our lives are usually arranged, this belief is easy to maintain. It is more difficult if one has tried being separated from one's companions in the deep woods at night; reportedly, it is also difficult for those who have suffered solitary confinement.

"All of this, it seems, casts grave doubt on the idea that man has intrinsically a greater emotional stability than the chimpanzee or other animals. The real difference may be in the protective environment man has created for himself, which he so takes for granted that he becomes unable to see how his stability is achieved, and how his behavior would look to someone not used to it."

It appears, then, that having to build and live within a model of what is human and natural is a natural and human characteristic that serves both the intellect and the emotions. The hypothetical "civilized man"—the goal at which approved social education aims—say Hebb and Thompson, usually does not "act so as to produce acute, strong sexual arousal, jealousy, anger or fear. He does not display disgusting objects openly; he is equally careful not to get into situations in which his own emotions make a display of him . . .

"Man is a rational, unemotional animal so long as there is nothing to disturb his emotions. Also the causes of strong emotion are few, as we usually consider them; for all we take account of are the causes that *do* operate in a society the main function of which may be to control and limit strong emotion, and we are almost incapable of thinking of an environment that differs from the social and physical one in which we live and which we have so carefully tailored to our needs."

With a working model of human nature that explains not only where everything belongs but also how you should feel about each, a human and natural life becomes accessible. With the exception of infants and certain psychotics, says Robert Zajonc, "all men actually make quite accurate predictions about various aspects of their social environment in the course of their daily lives." But that cannot be done without "some sort of generalized principles about social life. There must exist, therefore, on a subjective and private level, among members of societies, 'theories' of social behavior, of social structure, of interpersonal relations, etc. . . ."

Put that way, of course, it all sounds rather tentative and iffy, what with "theories" of human nature in quotes and those theories further qualified as "some sort of generalized principles." But that cannot be helped in some sectors of the human nature industry where even a hint of respectability about the concept of human nature may be actionable. However, there is some evidence that the organized idea or working model of human nature is not a jerry-built affair at all but is quite firm about which kinds of data are abstractable from the world rubble and the ways in which those data are organizable.

No reputable anthropologist today, says Clifford Geertz, seriously questions the "doctrine of the psychic unity of mankind," the doctrine that asserts "there are no essential differences in the fundamental nature of the thought process among the various living races of man." And French anthropologist Claude Lévi-Strauss, surveying and comparing data-organization principles from locale to locale, says that it is a mistake to think that primitive peoples have a "prelogical" mentality while we "modern" men enjoy a "logical" mentality. Even in very young children, says Noam Chomsky, you can see evolved human model building.

It appears that a child only a few months old, Chomsky says, "interprets the world in terms of perceptual constancies, and shows surprise if stimuli do not manifest the expected behavior of 'enduring and recurring physical objects.'" That observation, he says, would tend to indicate that this scheme of conceptualizing and perceiving "is primitive rather than acquired in the course of language learning."

Moreover there can be no doubt, he says in agreement with Monod, "that animals are capable of classifying objects and relations according to abstract categories, specifically geometric categories such as 'triangle' and 'circle' . . . So far as we know, animals learn according to a genetically determined program. There is no reason to doubt that this is also true of 'the fundamental categories of human knowledge'. . . ." And in addition, recent experimental work "suggests that there is a primitive, neurologically given analytic system which may degenerate if not stimulated at an appropriate critical period, but which otherwise provides a specific interpretation of some experience, varying with the organism to some extent." These discoveries, Chomsky and Monod agree, give support in a new sense to an hypothesis that has been held in disrepute by many sectors of the human nature industry for almost a century, namely, the hypothesis that forms of knowledge are innate.

If that is so, then the conceptual framework is there before birth—the cognitive skeleton, the form that must be filled in with a body of knowledge or organized idea about where everything human and natural belongs and how and when and why it belongs there.

So, it is not an iffy or tentative matter when it comes to abstracting data from the world rubble and organizing those data

182

into firm information. "The world of social perception," says social psychologist Kenneth J. Gergen, "tends to be a stable one . . . As a person is exposed to facts about another, such facts are ordered and assimilated . . . The concept is thus used to encapsulate a series of observations, and the conceptualization of a body of observation forms the cornerstone for what we know as 'understanding' of the others. Once such judgments are formed, they tend to remain intact and unchanging." When persons receive "contradictory information about another, they often misperceive entire sets of facts in order to develop an internally consistent view of the person. In these ways, persons tend to be seen as stable and consistent . . . we come to perceive, expect and assume personal consistency on the part of others in our social environment . . ."

Naturally it doesn't happen as piecemeal as a hasty reading of that dispatch from the knowledge foundry might indicate. You are not simply *exposed* to *facts* and *sets of facts* about others which you then either *perceive* or *misperceive*. It requires a nature—or a good simulation or working model of a nature—to abstract data from the world rubble and turn them into facts and organized sets of facts. It takes a working model of human nature to organize yourself and present that self as a consistent set of facts for others to understand and judge. But in many sectors of the human nature industry, nobody mentions the product which performs those feats of organization. In many sectors of the industry the talk is only about the organized consequences of that product—the information which the working model arranges, such as Society, Politics, Economics, Environment and Perception. In those sectors, everybody is busy parsing the sentence, but nobody ever tells you what the subject of it is.

But you cannot understand any of those consequences unless you consult a working model of human nature that explains where they belong and how and when and why they belong there.

183

Without such a working model you cannot be consistent, or perceive others to be consistent, or get a steady job in the human nature industry counting, measuring and analyzing Consistency, Perception, Society, Environment and so on.

An organized idea or working model arranges human and natural information about everything: time, space, relatives, names. Just name it and you've placed it. And, furthermore, you've placed it as good information or bad, right or wrong, just or unfair. It can't be helped. An informative list of human and natural data has an organized order of value: a top and a bottom; a more human and a less human; a natural and a not-so-natural. There is no such thing as value-free information: not about time, or about space or about relatives or names or any other abstractable, organizable data.

"We talk of measuring time," says E. R. Leach, "as if time were a concrete thing waiting to be measured; but in fact we *create time* by creating intervals in social life." And one of the functions of festivals, he says, may be the ordering of time. "The interval between two successive festivals of the same type is a 'period,' usually a named period, e.g., 'week,' 'year.' Without the festivals, such periods would not exist, and all order would go out of social life." Such festivals, of course, are value-laden with shoulds and oughts of proper clothing, etiquette, revelry, formality, rest, etc.

Says Edward T. Hall, "Man's feeling about being properly oriented in space runs deep . . . The fact that so few business men have offices in their homes cannot be solely explained on the basis of convention and top management's uneasiness when executives are not visibly present. I have observed that many men have two or more distinct personalities, one for business and one for the home. The separation of office and home in these instances helps to keep the two often incompatible personalities from conflicting. . . ." In addition, Hall points out, Americans

184

who have become dependent on the uniform grid pattern of most of our cities are often frustrated by something different. "It is difficult for them to feel at home in European capitals that don't conform to this simple plan." Should an American get lost there, "almost without exception, the newcomer uses words and tones associated with a personal affront, as though the town held something against him." And vice versa. Hall reports on a German newspaper editor who had moved to the United States and "had his visitor's chair bolted to the floor 'at the proper distance' because he couldn't tolerate the American habit of adjusting the chair to the situation."

If it is difficult to organize value-free information about time and space, it is just as difficult to do so for names and for clothing.

Expectant parents spend a lot of thought on the selection of a name for the as yet unborn. In a widely reported instance, the daughter of Senator Hubert Humphrey named her first-born Victoria because the child was a mongoloid and Nancy did not want to give the infant a name she really liked. Victoria, she said, seemed "impersonal."

In the final phase of a study of first names, psychologist N. Schoenfeld asked subjects to match a list of eight masculine and eight feminine names with personality characteristics "belonging" to each. Only 7 of the 248 subjects complained that the task was difficult or meaningless. Among the remaining 241, there was agreement well above chance about the characteristics belonging to each name.

Clothes may not make the man; but their information is not value-free, either. Whether the material is organized as dungarees, dinner jackets or cassocks, it is an organization that bespeaks a great deal about what data the wearer pays attention to. That is easiest to see, of course, in the most stylized clothing. As one Hasidic Jew expressed it to researcher Solomon

Poll: "With my appearance I cannot attend a theater or movie or any other place where a religious Jew is not supposed to go. Thus, my beard and my sidelocks and my Hasidic clothing serve as a guard and shield from sin and obscenity." Not so outspoken but just as clear is the information in children's clothing. As Philippe Aries puts it: "We have come from the sixteenth century, when the child was dressed like an adult, to the specialized childhood costume with which we are familiar today. The idea of childhood profited the boys first of all, while the girls persisted much longer in the traditional way of life which confused them with the adults." This change was also slow to appear in the lower classes whose young went on wearing the same kinds of clothes as adults, keeping up "the old way of life which made no distinction between children and adults in dress or in work or in play."

Even in so objective-appearing data as birth and death the information is hardly value-free. The range extends from "natural" childbirth and death from "natural" causes to the other end of the hierarchy of values. Insemination, too, is organized with values: natural, accidental, artificial, etc. And within the organized information of artificial insemination, says H. J. Muller, it is common practice in hospitals to pick as the semen donor an intern of the same religion as the mother, "as if there were such things as Catholic or Baptist genes." Clearly, it is natural to die. But even a natural death from natural causes is far from value-free information. As Hebb and Thompson point out: "Be reverent to the dead, speak in whispers, and make no jokes at the funeral service, and, if you are male, remove your hat . . . disgust must be expressed, for example, at a report that relatives have kissed the dead man after preparation for burial." You can get your own evidence about the value information regarding death if you "will obtain a human head from the dissecting room and try to carry it home openly in the subway."

Looked at that way, repugnance, reverence and cannibalism are parts of the same organization of data. A working model or organized idea of human nature that explains where everything human and natural belong also makes information to explain what you should do about each datum. If you have information of any kind, then you have a value for it.

Eating, digestion and elimination may appear to be undisputedly human and natural data. But they cannot be accomplished without a complete organization of information and its accompanying values. You cannot set a table without deciding on the appropriate tableware or eat without choosing the right food. And you cannot do either without a working model of human nature which explains where everything human and natural belongs. That holds for food and plates as well as for chamber pots. If you begin with a notion of an ordered universe as the England of the Georges had, then you develop a mind-set marked, says Henry Glassie, "by a bilateral symmetry which can be seen in architecture, furniture decoration, gravestone designs and farm layouts . . ." With that organizing principle, says James Deetz, the members of that Georgian social group were rigorously decked out with artifacts in matched sets. "In place of the older medieval asymmetrical relationship between individuals and their material culture," he says, a new one may have been operative—"a one man—one chamber pot relationship."

Language being an organization of informative symbols, it too is far from value-free. Communications, say Leonard Schatzman and Anselm Strauss, "may be handled haphazardly, neatly, dramatically or sequentially; but if they are to be communicated at all, they must be ordered somehow . . . Common assumptions suggest that there may be important differences in the thought and communication of social classes. . . ." But regardless of who is doing the communicating, the conceptual organization of the message "embodies not just anybody's rules, but the

187

grammatical, logical and communicative cannons of groups . . .
Both reasoning and speech meet requirements of criticism, judgment, appreciation and control."

Even the seemingly objective organization of information called numbers is not value-free, but is also locatable in the working model of human nature—which made those data abstractable in the first place. For example, take the number three. That number, says Alan Dundes, is a "folk cognitive category which pervades . . . a good many of the supposedly objectively and empirically derived analytical categories." Dundes cites not only Gaul but the whole world's being divided into three parts: animal, vegetable and mineral; solid, liquid and gas; troposphere, stratosphere and ionosphere; outer, middle and inner ear; cerebrum, cerebellum and medulla; Stone, Bronze and Iron ages; Old Stone, Middle Stone and New Stone ages; Lower Old Stone, Middle Old Stone and Upper Old Stone ages; head, thorax and abdomen and larva, pupa and adult. "The question is: are insects truly morphologically tripartite," Dundes asks, "or do we simply see them as tripartite?" Is nature divided that way —or is it the nature of the working model of nature held by observers, scientific and otherwise, that locates materials in threes?

Now, that is not a general rule in scientific observation. But it indicates that scientists, like everybody else who gets through the day, the week, the year and the lifetime, are not value-free from the shoulds and oughts and other information made by a working model of human nature which explains where everything belongs, and how and when and why it belongs there.

"Some of those who believe that science is or should be ethically neutral," says G. G. Simpson, "have fallen squarely into the naturalistic fallacy by their very efforts to avoid it. Insisting that they only describe and not prescribe, they deny that any consideration of right or wrong applies to their subject matter. Yet, in the social sciences, above all, what is described often does have an ethical aspect. From that point of view the 'objective' scientist runs into some danger of condoning what is wrong or rejecting what is right. Or, at least, his attempted withholding of judgement may in itself amount to an ethical stand."

The working model of human nature certainly determines the proper, right, good way for medical scientists to look at data. "A medical technique," says a student at New York University Bellevue Medical School, "is not to look at patients the same way you look at fellow human beings. In toxicology, you look at the human the way a butcher looks at meat. In surgery, the body is draped. You see only an area. You can pretend that the head belongs to somebody else."

In the behavioral sciences, inconsistency or cognitive dissonance, says Robert Zajonc, "is regarded as a noxious state" even though nobody has yet defined consistency or cognition. But even so, says Kenneth Gergen, that places a certain moralistic cast on personal consistency. Unity "becomes a goal of psychotherapy." And demands for consistency in psychological clinics and research laboratories "may well engender behavior" that makes such assumptions come true. "Personal consistency in these settings may itself be fostered by the social situation in which the behavioral scientist plays a significant role."

In the biology laboratory, too, the facts are not bare of value.

"Life appeared on earth," says Jacques Monod. But "what, before the event, were the chances that this would occur?" The a priori probability, he says, was virtually zero. "The universe was not pregnant with life nor the biosphere with man." It all looks like the product of a unique event. "Our number came up in the Monte Carlo game . . .

"This idea," Monod says, "is distasteful to most scientists. Science can neither say nor do anything about a unique occurrence. It can only consider occurrences that form a class, whose a priori probability, however faint, is yet definite." But in addition to the scientific reason, there is another reason why biologists recoil at the idea of life and man having appeared by chance. "It runs counter to our very human tendency to believe that behind everything real in the world stands a necessity rooted in the very beginning of things . . ."

That is to say, science like everything else can be located in the working model or organized idea of what is human and natural. Or, put another way, raw data and bare facts are manufactured by the human nature industry, and are not so raw or bare as they appear to the not-so-naked eye.

Chapter Eight

About that bare fact coming toward you on the street—well, only a complete ignoramus would disregard it. Only somebody who had no organized body of knowledge about human nature could ignore it. Only needy people without a working model showing where everything human and natural fits could tell themselves that it meant nothing and was not worth paying attention to. But as there are very few people like that, it is not a bare fact at all. Quite the contrary. It is a Naked Woman on Fashionable Fifth Avenue in Fabled Gotham in November. And that is not a bare fact. That is an information. That is a meaningful tale—a whole true-to-life story complete with a message of significance about what is human and natural.

There are no bare facts when you have a body of knowledge or working model of human nature. A working model tells you who, what, when, where, how and why. And that, as every lower journalist and higher anthropologist knows, is the whole story—including what it all means.

Now, what is the significance of this Tale of the Naked Woman? What is human and natural? What is the meaning of it all?

Only a partial ignoramus would say it was a meaningful event that signified an impending rainstorm. Only somebody with a very limited body of knowledge about human nature would say that it was an omen of a long, cold winter ahead. Only people with an obsolete explanation of where everything belongs would tell themselves that it signified a longer story of good luck if you made a wish on it.

But if you look at a more modern, more complete model of human nature, you can readily see that a naked woman on a New York avenue in November is a story with other significance. Listed below is the range of meanings assigned to the tale as gathered in a hasty survey of some observers of the story—

Meanings provided by the model *Edisonthropus Tinkerectus* with its pulleys, gears and other mechanisms: "She must be sick," and "It must be some sort of an experiment. Who's running it?" and, of course, "She's absolutely shameless."

Meanings provided by the *Tarzanthropus Inherens* model with its built-in components: "She must be awfully cold," and "She must be nuts."

Meanings of this true-life story are also provided by the *Morganthropus Exchangenesis* model constructed of contracts, declarations, proclamations and all the other negotiable documents of transaction. As you can find out by looking at this working model of human nature: "She must be protesting something," and "It must be an advertisement for a new musical comedy," and "They probably have a camera hidden somewhere. She must be an actress. They must be making a movie."

Now, this story of The Naked Woman And What It Means has been recounted here because it illustrates several relevant matters. First, it illustrates the relevance of knowledge. When you have a body of knowledge or working model of human nature, you can see what is worth paying attention to and what is worth ignoring. Moreover, this body of knowledge tells you not only what things mean but also what those meanings mean. You can see whether something makes sense or nonsense. And either way, you can also see whether it is a worthwhile significance or an insignificant significance. For example, would you let your brother marry a woman who walks naked on Fifth

194

Avenue? Would you let your sister marry a man who ignores a naked woman on the street?

So, it takes a complete body of knowledge or working model of human nature to organize every bare fact into significant information, and every significant information into meaningful stories to tell yourself. People with an incomplete body of knowledge do not know what to tell themselves about many bare facts. They cannot tell what is significant, what is not, and what may be. People who do not know what to pay attention to and what to ignore are ignorant people, and their advice is not worth much. But people who keep their body of knowledge up to date know what to tell themselves. They can see what is significant and also what it signifies. And if they don't know what it signifies, then they know where to get that significant information. They know whose advice to ask, whose assistance to require, whose example to follow, and whether it is worth the cost to themselves and to others.

That is the second lesson this story of The Naked Woman teaches. When you know what something means, you know where it goes in the story.

For example, if you look at the model *Morganthropus Exchangenesis,* you can see what a naked woman on Fifth Avenue means. Most likely she is involved in some nether transaction that engrosses her completely. She has become a bargaining table or a battlefield, and across it opposing forces negotiate fiercely for ownership of her. She is possessed. That is what she signifies in the story. And with that meaning, she would naturally go to the high priest where the demons would be exorcised and conflict resolved.

According to the model *Tarzanthropus Inherens,* you can also tell what a naked woman on Fifth Avenue means, especially in November. Clearly she is not capable of taking care of herself. She is potentially dangerous both to herself and perhaps to others. That means she is mad, insane, a lunatic. And with that meaning in the true-life story, she naturally goes to the police station and eventually to a locked asylum.

According to the *Edisonthropus Tinkerectus* model of human nature, there is a different meaning of the story. In this version, you can tell there is a malfunction somewhere. You can tell that something is not working properly and must be fixed. The meaning is plain: she is sick. And if she is sick, then perhaps she can get better. If that is the message of significance in the Tale Of The Naked Woman And What It Means, then she goes to the doctor rather than to the high priest or to the police.

In any event, it is a very exciting story once you pay attention to it. It has possibilities of hospital scenes, jails and courtrooms, bells, books and candles. It contains secret forces and hidden doings. It involves matters of life and perhaps death. Above all, it concerns questions of personal destiny. And in addition, the outcome is uncertain until the very end when meaning is conferred on it by one working model of human nature or another. So, that is the second moral of this Tale Of The Naked Woman. Once you know what it means, you know to whom to tell the story, and how and why and when to tell it there.

There is at least one more moral to the story, and that is that every story has at least one moral. If it is a story at all, then a working model of human nature has made it so. Consequently, it has meaning. And if you know what it means, then you have learned a lesson from it. A story might teach a moral or lesson about how to spend your money, for example, or about how to educate your children. It might teach a lesson about what is appropriate office architecture, or how to enforce the law. It might teach a lesson in how to get sick and how to get well, or how to die and where to go afterward and whether or not to come back. A story could contain a moral about any aspect of human nature. But in any case, if it is a story then it has a moral at the end. That is another great convenience in having a good working model of human nature. It is always instructing you as to how and when and where and why to use it.

Set out below is a true-life story with exactly that kind of a moral. It is the story of The Naked Woman And What It Means, and has been condensed from the account in the newspaper which, naturally, did not run the photograph. And as you can see, the lesson at the end of the story tells you which working model of human nature to pay attention to if you want to make the most popular meaning of a naked woman in a public place.

> A 26-year-old woman, employed as a secretary on the 19th floor of 767 Fifth Avenue, disrobed completely in the elevator of that building at noon yesterday and walked out of doors into the 33-degree weather and an astonished lunch-hour crowd of pedestrians.
> She proceeded south on Fifth Avenue for five blocks to East 51st Street where she entered St. Patrick's Cathedral. There, clergymen summoned the police who took her to Bellevue Hospital where doctors placed her under observation.

Suffice it to say that true-life stories and their morals abound everywhere. You cannot walk down the street without being assaulted by little lessons from everyday life: a baby in diapers here; a businessman with briefcase there; a wino asleep in that doorway; a wedding procession; a funeral cortege. At every moment a working model of human nature is making meaning and significance. Everything is for-example and for-instance and an-indication-of.

There is no place to escape to, either. You cannot rush off

to the country and sit under an apple tree without being in jeopardy of a lesson falling on your head.

Now, just because every story has a moral, that does not mean it is known immediately. Sometimes many years pass between a true-life tale and the lesson it teaches. It is impossible to say how many apples fell between the time of the first one in the garden of Eden and the one in the garden of Isaac Newton. But by and by the lesson is made clear. That is when people say, "Naturally I should have known better," or "How silly of me not to have thought of that."

Sometimes the story is not a true-life story, but the moral of it is valid anyway. Many people planning vacations or marriages or careers will gather brochures, tracts and other advice and then make up the story in several different versions in order to see how it comes out. And in the end they may learn that it is better to go by car, go alone or go to school.

Very frequently, the moral arrives before the true-life story is known. Many people learn that their marriages have failed, and then begin to look for the true-life story that has led up to that lesson. Many people get heartburn, palpitations, insomnia, sweaty palms and other morals, and then look backward to find out what the story was.

In any case, once you have a working model of human nature, you can find the sequence of meaningful events leading up to the lesson you have learned. That is a great comfort and reassurance as anybody knows who has ever taken a train through a railroad yard. If you stand at the front of the train, you cannot tell which track leads where and means what amidst the maze of rails ahead. But if you stand on the rear observation platform, you can easily look back and find the track you have traveled through the maze. That is another benefit of a working model of human nature. It gives you a rear observation platform to stand on. It lets you face the chaos of the past in a meaningful way, and at the same time it puts the unknown and uncertain future reassuringly behind you.

But regardless of whether the story comes first or second, the moral comes sooner or later. Regardless of whether it is a true-life story or only a rehearsal, there is a moral to it. It is there whether you want it or not, forcing its attention on you, nudging you meaningfully, glaring at you significantly in all sorts of ways. You have only to look at a printed column of type with its neatly justified margins, and you know that it must mean something. You have only to see a number of pages bound together between covers, and you can feel that it has a lesson to teach. You have only to see an entrance, an exit, a room, a fence and a moral looks back. You have only to see a painted canvas in a frame, and you begin to look for what it means. That is the way with a working model of human nature. It provides you with frames of meaning—borders, margins, paragraphs, days, weeks, years, lifetimes and the like—limits of stories, signs of significance that indicate a meaning is there and a moral is to be looked for.

2

When you have a working model of human nature that can set out frames of meaning and tell stories with morals, you can tell not only where it begins and ends—whatever it is—but also whether it is better to want it or begin it in the first place.

That is the chief advantage of these frames of meaning— these real-life stories with lessons or morals at the end. They explain not only *what* is worth paying attention to but also *how much* it is worth. They provide not only significance but also value. Consequently, you can tell when it is worthwhile to feel sad, bereft, defensive, defeated, and when to stop, and when it is worth starting to feel glad, appreciative, expansive, exultant. With a working model of human nature that sets out frames of meaning, you can tell not only what is a dream but also what is a dream worth worrying about. And once your feelings are organized by the model, you can begin to take appropriate action, depending, of course, on what the model explains as suitable steps. So it all works out very beneficially for getting through the day, the week, the year and lifetime. Once you have a frame of meaning, you can see not only what to do, and when and where to do so, but you can also see what makes the doing worthwhile. In short, with a good working model of human nature, you can answer the very necessary question of worth:

"DO YOU LOVE ME?"

It is a simple matter to find out your worth by looking at the model *Edisonthropus Tinkerectus*. According to this working model of human nature, the question of "Do you love me?" can be answered easily with a sincere and fervent "Yes because—"

Yes, you are worthy of love because you behave the way a child should behave: you are toilet trained; you wash your hands, face and behind your ears; you do your best in school. Yes, because you behave as a young person should behave: you are hard working, persevering, eager to learn how to take your place in society. Yes, you are worthy of love because you are an upright, right-thinking citizen: you are very manly or womanly; you are a good provider or good homemaker; you do good works; you do everything well. We were made for each other. You can see that because we work so well together.

If you look at the model *Tarzanthropus Inherens*, you cannot assay a person's worth by standards of work and activity. With this working model of human nature, made of individually built-in personal components, there is no standard scale or yardstick for measuring value. You are not worthwhile because of what you do. You are worthwhile because you exist. No further proof of value is necessary, so you don't have to prove yourself with clean diapers, stick-to-itiveness or any other high-quality performance. That makes it very easy to answer the question of "Do you love me?" The reply is always an unhesitating and cosmic "Yes! You are worthwhile because you are you."

Almost everybody is worthwhile according to this *Tarzanthropus Inherens* model of human nature inasmuch as there is no standard for individual wave lengths and personal geometries. And so, love is universal. Love is constant. Love does not change. Only the immediate object of it changes from time to time. But that is not a question of "Do you love me?" That is a question of frequencies, harmonics and congruence. And the answers to that question are generally put: "You turn me on;" or "We communicate;" or "I get good vibrations;" and, of course, "Sorry, but I'm already involved in a relationship."

When you look at the *Morganthropus Exchangenesis* model of human nature, the matter of what you are worth on the open market can easily be determined right down to the last mil. But the question of "Do you love me?" is somewhat harder to answer for two obvious reasons. First, love is a commodity in very short supply. That is what makes loved ones so precious, treasured and awfully dear. So that puts a very high price on love. It's not a thing you can give away easily, if at all. But exactly what the value and price are cannot be readily established because love is not usually traded on the open market. That is the second difficulty in answering the question of "Do you love me?" Most often love is just a game that two are playing. And the transactions, as everybody knows, include making passes, playing hard to get, bestowing favors, scoring, exchanging gifts and vows—in short, his move and her move. But there is no fair trade value and price in the negotiations of love. As everybody knows, all's fair in love and war.

What with the endless negotiations that make up the model *Morganthropus Exchangenesis,* you cannot really answer the question of "Do you love me?" with any sort of cosmic or fervent "Yes because." According to the way this model puts human nature together, the reply is always open for renegotiation, and generally comes out as "Yes, if—."

Yes, you are worthy of love if you're nice to me; if you fulfill your obligations and keep your promises; if you supply my wants; if you play the role of lovable child; if you get good marks in school; if you get a good job; if you win renown; if you are a faithful and constant lover. Yes, you are worthy of love if you are successful; if you give me a ring; if you swear that you belong only to me.

Once you have that information about the significance and value of data, you can tell when to feel loved and/or loving, and whether to be happy, worried and/or disappointed about it.

Furthermore, once you know why you should do it, whatever it is, you can easily find out the appropriate steps to take. That merely requires another look at the working model of human nature, this time to see not only why and when and where things belong, but also how they fit together. Here is an example arising out of this matter of "Do you love me?"—a common instance of:

"HOW SHOULD YOU DO IT?"

If you look at the model *Edisonthropus Tinkerectus* with its drives, gears chugging along according to natural law, you can see at once how you should do it. First, you should read a good, complete shop manual on the mechanics of sex. Everybody has needs, so you should know how to stimulate them and respond. But this is very delicate machinery and requires a careful setting in order to run well. The best setting is usually a private meal of heady foods and aphrodisiac potions, accompanied by venery music and served under inadequate lighting. Other settings for the proper functioning of the machinery include: the beach after a night swim in the nude; a soft, furry hearthrug before a glowing log fire; a haymow after a picnic lunch; a hotel room after an office party; a motel room during a convention.

As you can see in this *Edisonthropus Tinkerectus* model of human nature, an engine is at work with its pistons and valves at the ready. So the ignition can be turned on by either a male or a female—just so long as there is only one of each engaged and properly identified as such, with the male at the throttle and the female at the brake. A woman's place may not be in the home, but it certainly isn't in a man's pants.

In the event that the machinery fails to operate satisfactorily, you should naturally refer back to the shop manual first to determine whether the trouble lies in the setting, the fuel, the lubrication or the ignition. If no improvement comes with the adjustment of these parts, then a replacement is indicated—an easy matter when you have interchangeable parts and partners.

If you look at the *Tarzanthropus Inherens* model of human nature with its individually built-in wave lengths, you can also see how you should do it. You should rely on chemistry and vibrations. You should wait for love at first sight and let that take its course. There is no shop manual to consult or ignition and setting to adjust because there is no mechanical principle at work. Everybody may have needs, but they vary from one essential person to another. All you can do is to be your essential, fundamental self and wait for geometry to take over.

There are no essential places to do that waiting. Or, rather, almost any place is an essential one: outside of a modern dance class, say, or in a queue at a Humphrey Bogart film showing. The essential thing is that you dress and behave essentially so that you look like the fundamental person you are. And sooner or later another, proper frequency will reach you. After that, it is merely a matter of establishing clear reception and transmission. That, of course, is accomplished by going to fundamental places together such as slums—rural or urban—and Europe; eating fundamental foods such as bread, cheese and wine; talking in fundamental language; and doing fundamental things together such as social work and sexual intercourse.

If it doesn't work out—well, there's been no harm done. On the contrary, you've grown through the experience and discovered some new essential truths about yourself. In that event, you should take steps to change the geometry. The first step is usually a move from a straight line between two points to a triangle.

When you look at the *Morganthropus Exchangenesis* model of human nature made of declarations, promissory notes and all the other documents of transaction, you can see what you should do. You should make yourself pleasing and acceptable. You should be courteous, kind, attentive, loyal and true. You should anticipate needs of the other, thus instilling a sense of gratitude, dependence and obligation. You should say it with flowers, with candy, with expensive dinners. You should say it with birthday and holiday gifts, with theater tickets. And eventually it will pay off with pleasant dividends.

If it doesn't, then you should say it in writing, if you're willing to pay that price. It all depends on how much of yourself you have invested in the enterprise. In the event that it is a bad deal, there are other options available. In the *Morganthropus Exchangenesis* model of human nature there are always other options available. For one, you can buy your way out of the contract and negotiate a new arrangement elsewhere. For another, you can merge with a conglomerate. That is known in the trade as wife swapping—a transaction wherein you make your marriage a going concern and then take it public.

3

In other words:

A working model of human nature gives you the whole story. It tells you the who, what, when, where, why and how to pay attention to. And it gives you a moral at the end about what it all means. Or, as the Duchess said to Lewis Carroll's Alice in Wonderland:

"I can't tell you just now what the moral of that is, but I shall remember it in a bit."

"Perhaps it hasn't one," Alice ventured to remark.

"Tut, tut, child!" said the Duchess. "Everything's got a moral, if only you can find it. . . ."

Naturally you can find it. If you couldn't find it, you couldn't make up your mind about anything and consequently could never get through the day, the week, the year and the lifetime. A working model of human nature has to explain not only where everything belongs but also why it belongs there. Otherwise it's not a working model of human nature. "In order to make up our minds," as Clifford Geertz says, "we must know how we feel about things; and to know how we feel about things we need the public images of sentiment which only ritual, myth and art can provide." That is to say, we have to agree generally on the story so as to agree generally on the moral at the end of it—which is a consequence of having agreed generally on the working model of human nature and its explanation of where everything belongs and how and when and why it belongs there.

"Normal science," says Thomas Kuhn, "can proceed without rules only so long as the relevant scientific community accepts without question the particular problem-solutions already achieved." If the models are felt to be insecure—if there is disagreement about them—then concern about rules arises. The period before a new model is agreed upon by the relevant scientific community is "marked by frequent and deep debates over legitimate methods, problems and standards of solution, though these serve rather to define schools than to produce agreement."

If Kuhn's story *The Structure of Scientific Revolutions* is true for all working models including scientific models, then the moral of that story may be that this is a pre-model period in human nature. It certainly seems to have all the earmarks: questions about solutions achieved; deep debates over legitimate methods, problems and standards of solution; enough insecurity about the model of human nature to make visible a human nature industry and the models it produces, distributes and advertises. There is great concern about accepted rules and axioms, and they are now being scrutinized as assumptions. To wit:

"Whatever their other differences," says Alvin Gouldner in *The Coming Crisis of Western Sociology,* "all sociologists seek to study something in the social world that they take to be real; and, whatever their philosophy of science, they seek to explain it in terms of something that they *feel* to be real. Like other men, sociologists impute reality to certain things in their social world. That is to say they believe, sometimes with focal and sometimes only with subsidiary awareness, that certain things are truly attributable to the social world. In important part, their conception of what is 'real' derives from the dominant assumptions they have learned in their culture."

If it is a pre-model period, then it is no wonder that the human nature industry does not want to mention the name of the product. To do so would be meaningless. But if it is a pre-model period in human nature, then that means a new model is coming. And so it is reasonable for Margaret Mead to suggest that: "We are on the verge of a tremendous change in the nature of man, a change as far reaching as the great changes of the past, when man's precursors learned to use tools, to speak, to plant seeds, to build cities and to write. Perhaps even a greater change."

That may be true. But it requires a working model of human nature to suggest that meaning. Without a working model of human nature that explains where everything belongs and how and when and why it belongs there you cannot locate this as a pre-model period, or a post-model period. Without an organized idea that gives you the whole story including a moral at the end about what it all means, you cannot say that something is meaningless, or that it is a dominant assumption of the culture, or that it means a great change is coming, or that it means something is wrong and should be fixed. To wit:

"That Americans have been willing to study the rat and the pigeon as paradigms [models] of man confirms the fact that we have learned to consider ourselves as little more than pigeons or rats," says Jules Henry, questioning solutions achieved, methods, problems, rules and standards as seem to be consistent with activity in a pre-model period. But he can offer that critique only with a working model of human nature that gives him the whole story including a moral about what it means. "Our humility is to be admired perhaps, but the resulting contribution to a science of man is questionable."

Tut, tut, as the Duchess said. It requires a particular working model of human nature before you can postulate a *science of man* and debate its methods, problems, rules and models. You need a working model of human nature that gives you the whole story before you can see that story's heroes, villains and fools and evaluate their *admirable humility* or *questionable con-*

207

tributions. You have to get the whole story including the moral at the end about what it means—what *fact* it *confirms* about being human and natural—before you can see the message of significance in rats and pigeons, and *learn* from that lesson to consider yourself as little more, the same or little less than those animals.

Making meanings about what is human and natural from rats, pigeons and other animals is not a new story. As the Duchess says, everything's got a moral. And as Ronald Fisher says, "Ancient man argued from animals to men and back again with sophistication and success." Such lessons about human and non-human anatomy were "indispensable to man's survival . . . and constituted a substantial part of the biologically founded culture with which humans conducted their own evolution from the earliest times." That is to say, if you don't get the whole story including the moral about what it all means, then you can't learn how to treat illness, how to prevent injury, how to assign blame, what to regret or when to anticipate change and/or recurrence. It is hard to say whether cats and dogs see morals in the birth of their kittens and puppies. But certainly ancient man learned the lesson of what happens to people as a result of close inbreeding. In order to learn that, you have to draw a moral from a story that is nine months old at the very least, but more likely you may not be able to see the significance of the story until two or three years have passed.

*   *

As Alexander Marshack puts it:

"Even the simplest names, the nouns or words such as 'man,' 'woman,' 'old man,' 'infant,' 'boy with changing voice,' 'girl first menstruating,' 'mountain wearing green' or 'mountain wearing white,' all imply stories. Such stories would, of course, differ somewhat in each culture, with each person and with the age of the person, but as a reader you nevertheless sense at once the 'stories' implied and contained in such words."

Naturally, Marshack does not mention the nature, or the working model of it, which gives you those meaningful stories with their who, what, when, where, why and how. Instead, as is the case in many sectors of the human nature industry, he talks about the nature of the consequences—the nature of the story.

The term "story," he explains, "refers to the nature of the communication of meaning, and, even more . . . it is the communication of an event or process that *is* happening, *has* happened, or *will* happen. There is a beginning, something happens, and there is a change or result, an understood solution. . . . It is in the nature of the 'story equation' that it must always be told in terms of someone or something," whether it is told in words, mime, dance, ritual or in the symbolism of dream or trance.

But clearly the who of the story is locatable in the working model of human nature; otherwise there would be no *someone or something* to tell the story about. It requires a working model that explains where everything belongs in order to locate the *beginning* of the story, to note a *change* and see that something *has happened* or *will happen,* and to recognize an *understood solution.* It certainly requires a working model of human nature in order to talk of a *story equation.* Without a working model that explains where everything belongs and how and when and why it belongs there, you cannot tell the difference between a waking-state story and a story told in a *dream or a trance.*

In its broadest sense, every story you get is a lesson about the model itself. That is to say, if you get the story at all, then you are getting a story about human nature—about what is human and natural. In other words, the moral organizes the story.

For example, new stories usually put the moral first, leading off with a meaningful event or statement of significance by a meaningful person. Fiction stories, on the other hand, usually put the moral at the end, finally making clear the meaning of the information set out at the beginning and the middle. Anthropology, of course, begins with the moral—people—and works back from that meaning in an attempt to organize the story of when and why and how and where people got that meaning. But in any case, the moral or lesson about what it all means organizes the story. If there is no moral or lesson, then there is no story.

If a moral emerges, then a story emerges. If a moral changes, then the story changes. For example, many people suddenly discover that an insignificant cliché or maxim has become a message of significance and meaning. And by the light of that newly illuminated lesson, they are able to look back and tell themselves a reorganized story of where they have been and what they have been doing all these years. An illustrative instance is the recent lesson learned by Alexander Marshack and the story he was then able to reorganize.

Beginning with a moral about what is human and natural— a plan to put a man on the moon—Marshack set out to organize the story of how *Homo sapiens* had reached that point. And while gathering the information, he discovered that *Homo sapiens* was just that—Man the knower: the scientist, the organizer of knowledge and, specifically, the knower of a body of knowledge about time. The human brain, Marshack realized, was an organizing "time-factoring" organ. By the light of that moral, he was able to look back at what had been called decorative markings on Ice Age bones and reorganize that story. Those marked bones, he says, could well be calendar notations made by man's ancient precursors who were organizing time by attending to the regularity of the moon's phases.

And the moral of that story is that a working model or body of knowledge which can give you a meaningful story is a very handy thing to have on hand. "No matter where this early man who was capable of recognizing a pattern in the sky migrated," Marshack says, "some aspect of this recognition would go with him. Climate, animals and landscape might change as he wandered, but the sky went with him, and to that extent he was psychologically and culturally 'at home' anywhere on earth."

And the moral of all that, in turn, is a story about what human nature is: it is human to look for a message in marked Ice Age bones; it is natural to look for meaning in the phases of the moon; it is human nature to want to put a man on the moon. In short, it is human nature to be curious about the meaning of everything, and that includes being curious about the meaning of human nature. In its broadest sense, the lesson being taught in every story is that a model of human nature is at work all the time and everywhere, moralizing about itself—teaching lessons about where everything human and natural belongs, pointing out the meaningful data to pay attention to and framing the significant questions to ask those data in order to arrange them into human and natural information.

In its narrowest sense, a story may be an anecdote, a lullaby, an encounter between two people, a surgical operation, even a dictionary definition. But if it is a story at all, then it has been organized by a moral about what it all means. And in that sense, the moral is always the same: a working model or body of knowledge is at work organizing meaningful stories of the HUMAN and the NATURAL for the wakeful, the dreaming, the entranced, the young, the old and even the anesthetized.

"In every culture," says Margaret Mead, "no matter how simple, no matter how complex, no matter how impoverished or decayed, how exuberant and efflorescent, the children receive a total impression. The deepest ignorance and the state of the most esoteric knowledge is conveyed to them, inarticulately, by the way they are held and sung to, fed and punished, permitted to wander or kept close to home . . ."

"Songs," say Alan Lomax and Herbert Yahraes, "are meta-communications about norms. Their function is to reflect and reinforce norms and to pass this information across time. It is normal everywhere for the grandmothers to sing to the children. What are they telling them? We think they are telling them about the very roots of their being. They are giving them a message that very early becomes part of them . . . that you belong here: this is your place . . . Song constantly orients the child to his society; it tunes a person in on the tradition and values of his group." That is to say, song gives you the meaningful story about where everything human and natural belongs.

Under anesthesia, reports the British medical journal *Lancet,* patients in the operating room may "hear sounds which are personally meaningful." Many patients awaken angry and resentful on account of having heard the surgeon invite guests to observe the operation, or ask the resident to finish it, or in other ways refer to the supposedly unconscious patient as an insignificant object in an unimportant story. One patient reported by *Lancet* underwent one operation to free his blocked nasal passages and nine more to cure the severe headaches he began to suffer whenever he breathed through his nose. Finally, he began treatment with a hypnotherapist. Under hypnosis, the patient was able to recall having heard while anesthetized in the first operation the surgeon comment to an assistant, "Whenever air is inhaled, he'll have sharp pains and a severe headache." But investigation by the hypnotherapist revealed that the patient had got the moral of the story wrong and had consequently misorganized the story. As it turned out, he had missed the first words of the surgeon's remark, namely: *"For a few days,* whenever air is inhaled . . ."

The Chinese and Japanese word for man is *jen.* And like any definition of something human and natural, it is the moral of a story. The Chinese conception of man, says Francis L. K. Hsu, "is based on *the individual's transactions with his fellow human beings.*" So, when the Chinese say that so-and-so is not a *jen*, "they do not mean that this person is not a human animal. Instead they mean that his behavior in relation to other human beings is not acceptable." Other morals, of course, organize other stories of human behavior. For example, the phrase *not-a-jen* may tell the story of "a man who abandons his parents," while *bad-jen* be a story about "one who cheats his friends." In addition, other stories can be organized and told: *the endeavor of being jen,* and *one who is learning to be jen.*

In Yiddish, the word for man is *mensch.* And like any definition of something human and natural, it is the moral of an organized story of human nature. The meaning of *mensch,* according to Leo Rosten, is "rectitude, dignity, a sense of what is right, responsible, decorous."

There appears to be no escape from it. If it is a story at all, then it has been organized by a moral about what it means. And what it generally means is that a working model of human nature is at work.

As Lister Sinclair points out, the English, Italian and Greek mother will usually tell her child, "John, be good," which implies an organized story of bad, naughty or wicked behavior; the French mother corrects by saying, "Jean, *sois sage*"—be wise —implying a meaningful story of foolish, imprudent, injudicious and similar inappropriate behavior; the Scandinavian mother tells her child to be "friendly" or "kind," and the German mother corrects with "Hans, *sei artig*"—be in line.

Sooner or later it must dawn on those children that somewhere there is a line to stay in, a kindness to find, a sagacity to grow into, a goodness that exists: in short, a particular organization of the world. These mothers are not merely playing with

213

words. They are teaching lessons about a working model of human nature.

Meanings, says Edward Sapir, are "not so much discovered in experience as imposed upon it because of the tyrannical hold that linguistic form has upon our orientation in the world." In other words, the organization of symbols called language bespeaks an organized idea. That is to say, language is a mirror of the mind. "This is true," says Noam Chomsky, insofar as "properties of language are 'species specific' . . ." And it appears that one of the specific characteristics of the species is a language of organized symbols for what is human and natural. It appears that a working model of human nature is at work all the time, organizing figures of speech, illustrative anecdotes and meaningful stories about itself.

Without a working model that made its meaning clear, you would not know whether to permit a child to wander, keep it close to home, keep it in line; you would not know what kinds of lullabies to write and sing; you would not know which operation to perform, whether to invite spectators, whom to blame in the event of failure, where to turn for recourse. And, moreover, without a working model that explained itself, you could not recognize wandering children, singing grandmothers or resentful patients as meaningful events in larger significant stories. But it is possible to see, recognize and observe all of these data because a working model *is* a meaning, a moral, a message of significance. And that is true for a working model of human nature as well as for a working model of science. Physics *is* meaning. So is biology. So is anthropology or journalism or medicine.

A model teaches its lesson in the stories you are able to tell to yourself and to others. That is how people learn lessons: by example, application, anecdote, illustration.

"Scientists, it should already be clear," says Thomas Kuhn,

"never learn concepts, laws and theories in the abstract and by themselves. . . ." If, for example, a student of Newtonian dynamics ever discovers the meaning of such terms as "force," "mass," "space" and "time," Kuhn says, he learns those meanings not so much from the definitions in his textbook as from the applications of those concepts to problems and their solutions.

The term "human nature," of course, is seldom defined in any textbook because textbooks are usually organized by official spokesmen of an industry that doesn't name its product. So, although you cannot look up the meaning of human nature in most textbooks these days, you can readily see that they are applications or examples of a working model of human nature. A textbook, like any story, is an illustrative anecdote exemplifying the working model of human nature and teaching its lesson.

Once you learn that lesson and get that meaningful story, you can tell what is significant, where it belongs, and how and when and why it belongs there. You can then proceed to abstract your own data, make your own arrangements, organize your own story of the universe. In addition, once you learn the lesson which the working model teaches about itself, you can become a judge of human nature. You can pay attention to the kinds of stories other people tell themselves and each other, noting the kinds of data they pay attention to as meaningful and the significant questions they ask those data in order to arrange them into such informative stories as the day, the week, the year and the lifetime. And if, in addition, you can see the stories other people tell themselves as being significant incidents in a still larger and more meaningful story, then you can very likely get a top job in the human nature industry—being a publisher, for example, or funding big research projects or even making public pronouncements on such critical human issues as reality and marriage. To wit:

"The plausibility and stability of the world as socially defined," say sociologists Peter Berger and Hansfried Kellner, "is dependent upon the strength and continuity of significant relationships in which conversation about the world can be continually carried on. . . . The reality of the world is sustained through conversation with significant others. This reality, of course, includes not only the imagery by which fellow men are viewed, but also includes the way in which one views oneself."

Well, that is clearly a story about the kinds of data people pay attention to and the kinds of questions they ask those data in order to arrange them into meaningful information. So it is a story about a working model of human nature at work—bestowing *significance* on others; organizing significant *relationships;* giving people not only *plausible* and *stable* stories to tell each other about the world, but also giving people the *imagery* and point of *view* for telling those stories. But which working model of human nature is this story about?

Why, it is about *Morganthropus Exchangenesis,* the model of human nature made of birth certificates, marriage licenses and the other negotiable documents which people put in their portfolios and pass along from generation to generation.

Society, Berger and Kellner explain, has a set of meanings ready for the individual born into it: "great universes of meaning that history offers up for our inspection." People select from those meanings and confer reality on them in the "many little workshops in which living individuals keep hammering away at the construction and maintenance of these universes." One such workshop is the institution of marriage where reality is made and maintained by the husband and wife. For example, the male partner's friends from before the marriage "rarely survive the marriage or, if they do, are drastically redefined after it. This is typically the result of neither a deliberate decision by the husband nor deliberate sabotage by the wife. What happens, very simply, is a slow process in which the husband's

216

image of his friend is transformed as he keeps talking about this friend with his wife. Even if no actual talking goes on, the mere presence of the wife forces him to see his friend differently. . . . Marriage thus posits a new reality. . . ."

This new reality of marriage, say Berger and Kellner, is "legitimated" by other societal agencies such as psychology and religion, which have "established their own rites of passage, validating myths and rituals, and individualized repair services for crisis situations. Whether one legitimates one's maritally constructed reality in terms of 'mental health' or of the 'sacrament of marriage' is today largely left to free consumer preference. . . ."

In other words, heavens are made in marriages.

But that is a different story from the one told by the *Edison-thropus Tinkerectus* model of human nature made of gears, drives and other mechanisms ticking along according to natural law. As this working model told Sir Arthur Conan Doyle, who told it to Sherlock Holmes, who in turn told it to Dr. Watson: "I think she is one of the most charming young ladies I ever met, and might have been most useful in such work as we have been doing." But, said Holmes, "I should never marry myself, lest I bias my judgement. . . ."

And that, in turn, is a different story of what marriage does to reality from the story organized by the model *Tarzanthropus Inherens* with its individually built-in resonances. There is no meaning to be chosen from the selection presented by history. There is no reality to be constructed in the husband-and-wife workshop. Instead, there is only a geometric configuration of two individuals, a harmony—or dissonance—of two individual notes. As William James said in a letter to his father:

> *We have been so long accustomed to the hypothesis*
> *of your being taken away from us, especially during*

the past ten months, that the thought that this may be your last illness conveys no very sudden shock. You are old enough, you've given your message to the world in many ways and will not be forgotten; you are here left alone, and on the other side, let us hope and pray, dear, dear old Mother is waiting for you to join her. If you go, it will not be an inharmonious thing . . . it comes strangely over me in bidding you good-by how life is but a day and expresses mainly but a single note. It is so much like the act of bidding an ordinary good night. Good night, my sacred old Father! If I don't see you again—Farewell! a blessed farewell! Your

William

Chapter Nine

And the moral of all that is: that is how a working model of human nature works. It gives you the whole story—who, what, when, where, how and why—complete with a moral about what is human and natural. And it does so for everybody everywhere, including lower journalists and higher anthropologists.

It is very reassuring to get stories of that sort to tell. They organize the chaotic rubble of world data into a landscape of meaningful information. They weed out what is not worth paying attention to and they make a place for everything else. Moreover, they are very captivating stories to tell. Once you are into such a story, it does for you what it does for everything and everybody else. It pulls you out of the random rubble of unlimited possibilities and combinations and it puts you into the human condition—organized and informed—able to tell the time, the place, the method, the reason and whether to go home afterward, or to sleep, to dinner, to the beach or back to the office. Furthermore, it is very exciting to be able to tell yourself stories of that nature. When you can tell where you belong, and how and when and why you belong there, you can also tell when you are not where you should be. Consequently, you can tell when to feel guilty, shameful, disappointed or envious. When you can tell yourself that kind of story, you are also able to tell when others are not where they should be. And so you can tell yourself when to feel shocked, indignant, resentful, angry or jealous. And on the other hand, you can tell when everything and everybody are where they belong. That makes it easy to tell yourself when to feel relieved of anxiety and satisfied.

All in all, you can tell at every turn how things are developing in the story: whether they are getting better or worse; whether there is tension, conflict or crisis; and when there is resolution and harmony. And that is because you are able to tell yourself at the outset how people are supposed to get along and how the story is supposed to work out. So, if people don't get along and things don't work out, then you can tell yourself why they don't and what to do about it. Naturally, that depends on which working model of human nature gives you the story in the first place.

If you look at the *Edisonthropus Tinkerectus* model with its meshing gears, you can see immediately how people get along. They get along by means of accordance among the working parts. That is known as a functioning society, with everybody having a job to do. Policemen have theirs. Wives and mothers have theirs. Teachers have the job of teaching; students have the job of learning; the President has the job of running the machinery of government. It is a natural accordance that people should do their jobs as well as possible if things are to work out in cooperation, harmony and accord. God helps those who help themselves—those who are self-reliant; those who exercise their will power; those who do good work and good works.

By the same measure, when people fail to get along and things do not work out, it is most likely because somebody fell down on the job. You can readily tell why such people conform to the natural accordance among the working parts of society. It is because they are inefficient, unhealthy or otherwise faulty in some drive or gear. They may be lacking in will power, self-reliance or other mental or physical stamina. Or they may be poorly brought up without the advantages—ignorant of the natural accordance. Whatever the reason, you can tell that what they are doing is wrong, is sick, and simply isn't done. Moreover, with the *Edisonthropus Tinkerectus* model of human nature with its reversible mechanisms and interchangeable parts, you can tell what must be done to repair the damage. First, these faulty people must be removed and replaced. And then, if they are young enough to salvage, they must be sent somewhere for an overhaul. Depending on the fault, they are to be dispatched for rehabilitation, adjustment, retraining or correction. In addition, preventive steps must be taken to teach others the accordance so they will not fall down on the job. That means further research into the individual cogs, wheels and other, smaller working parts in order to find out what makes them misfire and malfunction. You have to know what faulty mechanism makes people violate the natural law and defy the accord. Only then can you tell yourself how to treat asthma, sloth and crime effectively.

Naturally, these faulty parts of society are in the minority. For the rest, the social accord works quite well. And that is because it is so uncomplicated. Almost anybody can learn to be a good soldier, teacher or haberdasher. And they, in turn, can become President and run the machinery of government. In fact, the social accordance among people is so simple that even little children can tell how it works and what to tell themselves. As Ralph Waldo Emerson summed up the way the working parts of this model of human nature work together:

> *So nigh is grandeur to our dust,*
> *So near is God to man,*
> *When Duty whispers low,* Thou must,
> *The youth replies,* I can.

If you look at the model *Tarzanthropus Inherens* you can also tell yourself at the outset of the story how people get along and how things should work out. In this working model of human nature there are no meshed gears and other interchangeable mechanisms running in accordance with each other. Instead, there are individual message centers, unique frequencies and wave lengths and other solid state components built-in to personal specifications. Consequently, people get along by clear communication—expressing their individual needs in order to satisfy them, and receiving similar messages from everybody else. It requires a considerable sensitivity to be able to transmit needs and receive them at the same time. And that is known as understanding: interpersonal understanding, intergroup understanding, interfaith understanding, international understanding; in short, human understanding.

Now, it is not difficult to achieve such understanding. In the first place, everybody's components are made of the same basic materials: primordial slime, prehistoric vapor, unconscious soot, crystals and other precipitates, all trapped in an electromagnetic field. So that makes common ground for human understanding to begin with. And in the second place, all people have their individually built-in capabilities and potentialities differing uniquely from person to person. So there is no reason to fight over rights to the common ground. It can be shared by everybody for the benefit of all. For example, there is no need for a teacher to stake claim to the front of the classroom and direct the student personnel. This is not the model *Edisonthropus Tinkerectus* with people in accord about their particular jobs. On the contrary, according to the model *Tarzanthropus Inherens*, it is not human nature to have a job. Rather, you realize your own potentialities: you do your own thing as you understand it. Teaching is not a job, nor is learning a job. The two are merely specific parts of the general human need to relate: to communicate and understand. And looked at that way, the students have as much to offer in the relationship as the teacher. Naturally, it works the same way everywhere with everybody. Complete transmission and reception require a free and equal relationship among the individual components of the family, the group, the nation, humanity. Once that kind of geometry is established, clear communication is possible. Self-understanding and mutual understanding follow, and with them come harmony.

Similarly and congruently, when people fail to get along in harmony, it is usually because somebody did not communicate. You can readily tell what interferes with the natural need to understand. It is most likely a problem in geometry. It may be a built-in error in or among the individually built-in components—a poor memory, a confused set of emotions, etc. Or the problem may be found in the external geometry, among the constellation of relationships in the family, classroom, peer group, etc. Or else the difficulty may be that some other model of human nature is impinging. The prerequisites of *Edisonthropus Tinkerectus* or the accreditations of *Morganthropus Exchangenesis* may be causing static in the harmony of natural and individual frequencies of *Tarzanthropus Inherens*. So, you can tell yourself that things will not work out well because somebody in the relationship is distorted, alienated, unilateral, temperamental or poor stuff and rotten through and through. And by looking at this *Tarzanthropus Inherens* model of human nature with its inalienable human rights and other built-in components, you can tell how to redress a grievance against a component individual in the geometry who communicates poorly. The solution, like the problem, is to be found in geometry. If the error is built-in—a faulty conscience or communications system, say—the entire solid-state unit, including the good parts, must be removed from the relationship and shelved or disposed of because there is no way to replace individually built-in components. But as there are few errors in nature, the static and interference in the harmony are more likely to be caused by the shape of the constellation in the family, school, neighborhood, community, etc. These geometric forms must be examined and rearranged so as to restore communication and understanding;

and alien models of human nature must be weeded out and disposed of. Harmony will prevail only when society has been reconstructed along lines that more closely approximate human dimensions. Criminality, for example, will cease when the relationships among people have been clarified and the parameters of living have been broadened. People must be free to realize their own, individual potentialities. This need for self-understanding is so human that it can be felt by children. Out of the mouths of babes, so to speak. Or, to rephrase Emerson's stanza for application in the *Tarzanthropus Inherens* model of human nature:

> *So nigh is grandeur to our dust,*
> *So near is God to man,*
> *When Duty whispers low,* Thou must,
> *The youth replies,* I don't
> feel like it; it's not consistent
> with my nature; and besides, who
> says it's my duty?

If you look at the model *Morganthropus Exchangenesis* you are also able to tell yourself at the outset of the story how people get along and how things are supposed to work out. They do so without a geometry of built-in components or a natural law governing working parts. As you can see, this model of human nature is a paper-thin collage of deeds, leases, diplomas, titles and other negotiable documents of ownership and participation. People get along by the rules of the game. So that requires something more specific than an accordance or an understanding. In this model, things work out by means of a social contract. Everybody has a share of the responsibility, and with it everybody gets a share of the credit and the benefits.

In the endless transactions of the social contract, accredited individuals fulfill the obligations of policemen, exercise the options of children, undertake the commitment of medical doctors, swear to uphold the office of President, and so on and on. In negotiating by the rules of the game, women play the roles of wife and mother; men take their parts as husband and father; people of all ages do their bit as citizens; and so on and on.

By the same measure, when people fail to get along and things do not work out, it is most likely because somebody broke the contract. You can readily tell why such people do not meet their obligations or play their parts. It is because the rewards or the penalties have not been high enough. Whichever the reason, it is impossible to say that what they are doing is wrong or bad. History is filled with revised documents which made outlaws into patriots, princes and patrons of humanity. When people break the social contract and get out of their obligations, the most you can tell yourself is that "It's not fair!" and "How dare they!" And by looking at the *Morganthropus Exchangenesis* model made of clauses, amendments and the like, you can tell what measures are needed to restore harmony and accord. First, the defaulters in the transaction must pay their debt to society. Next, the pot must be sweetened and the stakes increased. Government will improve if you attract better accredited officials with higher pay. Crime will abate when it becomes more dangerous for criminals than for victims. As a third measure, the name of the game can be changed. Colleges will improve when there are more celebrities on the faculty; when people who understand negotiable documents are in the administration; and when the classroom is redefined as what it really is—a market place of ideas and information run by a good salesman and packager for the benefit of the tuition-paying customers.

Now, this is not to say that the social contract always works perfectly inasmuch as it is under revision and in negotiation somewhere or other all the time. But generally things work out with it. You can usually tell where you belong and to whom, and whether you can afford to do it, whatever it is—because everything has a price, and you don't get something for nothing. And that is how people get along according to this model of human nature: by making promises and keeping them; by doing favors and having them repaid; by negotiating their ways through the day, the week, the year and the lifetime. Even small children know what allegiances to pledge, what obligations they owe, whose flock they belong to, and vice versa what is owed to them. To recast Emerson's lines for use in the *Morganthropus Exchangenesis* model of human nature:

> *So nigh is grandeur to our dust,*
>   *So near is God to man,*
> *When Duty whispers low,* Thou must,
>   *The youth replies,* Okay, if
>   it doesn't violate the Ten
>   Commandments or the Bill of
>   Rights. But you'll have to
>   specify how, when and where—
>   and of course put it in writing.

2

So that is how a working model of human nature works. It provides you with a frame of meaning and puts you in the picture. And once you are there, you can see where you stand on such diverse issues as life and death. You can find your point of view about taxes and clothing. You can fix your position with regard to the schoolhouse, the alehouse, the whorehouse, the courthouse and the electric chair. In other words, a working model of human nature makes things visible, and you visible as well.

That is to say, it gives you the whole story about what to pay attention to and where it belongs. Once you are into the story, you can tell what is order and what is chaos. In addition, you can tell yourself whether it is good order or bad. And moreover, you can tell whether it is worthwhile to do anything about it one way or the other. When you have a working model of human nature, there are all sorts of things you can tell yourself. That is how a working model works. It tells you what is tellable and what is not—in other words, what is speakable, what is unspeakable and what is not speakable at all.

Now, if something is not speakable at all, that is because it has no place in any working model of human nature. And if it cannot be located in any model, you cannot tell where it belongs, nor how, nor why, nor when it belongs there. If something is not speakable at all, it is not thinkable at all, either. So there is nothing you can tell yourself about it at all.

On the other hand, if something is unspeakable, it most certainly can be located in a working model of human nature. You can tell exactly where it belongs, and how and when and why it belongs there. And if it belongs in one model in unspeakable condition, then quite possibly it can be located in another model as well—where it may turn out to be completely speakable. For example, if you look at the model *Tarzanthropus Inherens* with its unique potentialities, you can see that it is unspeakable to buy and sell people as though they were produce. But by locating this matter in another model, you can tell yourself that it is simply a variety of game transaction (*Morganthropus Exchangenesis Baseballibus*), and you can speakably negotiate the sale and purchase of players at the going market price. For another example, if you look at the model *Morganthropus Exchangenesis* made of negotiable obligations which begin with a gift and end with the gift returned, you can see that it is unspeakable to traffic in dead people and mutilate and dismember them. But by locating this matter in another model, you can tell yourself that these are not dead people but rather medical problems to be solved—a variety of bio-mechanical engineering (*Edisonthropus Tinkerectus Postmortems*)—and then you can do your job very speakably every day as a medical examiner in the city morgue.

These are not examples of merely playing with words. On the contrary, there is nothing mere about it. This is very important stuff with very serious results at the end. When you play with words, you are quite likely to be moving from one model of human nature to another and changing the whole story, including the moral about what is human and natural. It is one thing to tell yourself that you have to treat an illness called crime. But when you tell yourself that you must exact a debt owed to society, different events are liable to occur; and still others may arise when you say that criminality is built into individual components or is a function of interpersonal geometry. That is to say, payment of lip service can range in cost. Results may vary widely depending on whether you tell yourself that something is wrong, or is rotten, or is unfair. In the same way, euphemisms are not necessarily euphemistic; they do not inevitably say the same thing but in a nicer way. Grave proceedings can follow if you say that people have passed away when you actually mean they are living in Argentina.

In other words, other words may not clarify things but instead may only put them into another, more generally speakable model of human nature in order to achieve other ends. As this book illustrates so clearly, the self-asserted communications of the *Tarzanthropus Inherens* model are followed at the end of each chapter in other, more popularly speakable words—the accredited, documented words of the *Morganthropus Exchangenesis* model and the counted, measured, laboratory-tested words of the *Edisonthropus Tinkerectus* model—in order to make the story more tellable by giving it a more acceptably engineered plot and a more widely salable form. In other words, these working models or bodies of knowledge about human nature organize chaotic data into speakable information. And they do the same for you, whether it is for the purpose of selling, of buying, of educating, or of surviving a lifetime, a death, a disappointment or a Sunday afternoon. What you tell yourself may be a matter of playing with words. But that is a matter of playing with working models or organized ideas of human nature, and consequently playing with consequences.

Well, what do you tell yourself speakably?

In other words (*Morganthropus Exchangenesis*), what words do you play with?

That is to say (*Edisonthropus Tinkerectus*), what are the facts?

In other words (*Tarzanthropus Inherens*), what's the true story?

Inasmuch as a working model of human nature explains where everything belongs, and how and when and why it belongs there, the questions answered by one model can usually be answered by the others—but, of course, in other words. So, to begin with *Morganthropus Exchangenesis'* question:

WHAT WORDS DO YOU PLAY WITH?

There are many more words to play with when you use the working model *Edisonthropus Tinkerectus* instead of the others. That is because this machine is a very popular model of human nature nowadays. These are words you can count on, words that measure out a day, a week, a year, a lifetime. Some of the words to play with in this model are: public opinion, productive, input, pressure, stimulus, per capita, average family, logistical, isolated, mental health.

In addition to countable, measurable words to play with, this model also provides a long list of operative, functional words such as: subliminal, ecological, operative, functional, frustration, educable, workable, brain washing, gimmick, cope, hang-up, therapy. Then, too, there are many other words for the machine and its working parts, to wit: terminal ailment, terminal degree, subjective, experimental, peer group, Oedipus complex, class struggle, transplant, mercy killing, conscience formation, mind-expanding, working models. With words like these to play with, you can in the last analysis get it out of your system—whatever it is, work it through, straighten out your life.

There are not as many words to play with in the working model *Tarzanthropus Inherens* as in the other two. That is partly because this is a solid-state model with few working parts to designate. That makes it hard to establish yardsticks and scales for counting and measuring. Another reason for the paucity of words to play with is that this model is made of raw materials such as primordial slime, unconscious soot and other prehistoric precipitates and personal potentialities. So it is difficult to isolate items and experiment with them in repeatable, scientific fashion. And if items are not repeatable, then they are not very tellable. As a result, the words to play with in the model *Tarzanthropus Inherens* are not very scientific: thing, basic, essential, inherent, relate, impinge, communicate, commune, ethnic, charisma, human animal, lust, aggression, hostility, territoriality, prophecy, eye-opener, wired-in, nitty-gritty, loser, introvert, visceral, innocent, sexy, frigid, identity crisis, masculine, feminine, latent homosexual, preschizophrenic, sensitized, idle curiosity, human nature.

The working model of human nature *Morganthropus Exchangenesis* has still another list of words to play with. This model is made of such negotiable documents as are used in transacting the business of living and dying. So the words to play with are of a similar nature, having a great resemblance to the business game vocabulary: score, rules, gain, loss, profitable experience, saving energy, paying compliments, and so on and on.

In addition, there are many other words available inasmuch as this model is very popular: popular, viable, revered, compromise, public servant, relevant, in, revisionist, coveted, reputation, an in, image, contacts, face lift, case history, precedent, etiquette, promise and commitment, hot and cool media, myth and fable, compassion and revenge, liberal, conservative, moderate and reactionary, letter and spirit of the law, and so on and on. With such words to play with, you can bank on *Morganthropus Exchangenesis* to put you in a good bargaining position. By profiting from experience, you can tell yourself what policy to adopt, how to draw the claws of criticism, and whether you can afford to do it with the personal and human resources at your command.

These lists of words are not a summary of a controlled experiment (*Edisonthropus Tinkerectus*) or a consensus of usage (*Morganthropus Exchangenesis*) in any way. They are set down only as an illustration, to show that playing with words may be a matter of playing with models and thus with consequences. Putting things another way can place them in another organized idea of human nature with other events arising.

That tabulation could go on and on, as it does every minute with people telling themselves and each other: "What you're really saying is;" and "What I'm trying to explain is;" and "To look at it another way." And as a result of this translation from word to word and from working model to working model of human nature, people find themselves in one consequence or another—liking this friend more than that one; choosing this job, career or profession or that; in love or out of it; hired, promoted or fired; getting elected, defeated, appointed, disappointed, arrested, released and so forth. And all of those consequences can arise because the words you play with talk about the data you pay attention to. In other words (*Edisonthropus Tinkerectus*), what is tellable breaks down to a question of:

WHAT ARE THE FACTS?

Inasmuch as facts are made by organized ideas, it requires only a look at these ideas or working models of human nature to tell where the facts of life belong and which human data to pay attention to.

If you look at the model *Edisonthropus Tinkerectus*, you can tell what the facts are. They are information about how the working parts of the human machine work. As a consequence, the data to be isolated, counted and measured include such mechanisms as brain waves, hormones, digestion and nutrition, urbanization and bureaucratization, sleep, dreams, sexual and reproductive mechanics, child-rearing practices and other operating gears, drives and pulleys. Once you can tell how the working parts work regularly, you can tell what facts are irregular. And in consequence, you can isolate, count and measure such eccentric and anomalous functions as obsessions and compulsions, ghosts, deviants (including criminals, homosexuals and geniuses). So the range of facts in the working model of human nature *Edisonthropus Tinkerectus* runs all the way from viruses and intelligence quotients at one end to business cycles, computer systems and coprolites at the other.

In contrast, the model *Tarzanthropus Inherens* sets out a different order of data to pay attention to. To begin with, there are the facts of the solid-state components that have been built-in to each person, so to speak. That means you have to contemplate data about individual resonances: deathbed words; diaries

232

and letters; ethnic history; your own navel, metabolism, dreams, hates and other feelings; and the emotional and intellectual differences between twins.

And inasmuch as there are as many different human natures as there are people, there are the facts of how they get along with each other. That means paying attention to data about cognitive mapping and communication: extra-sensory perception, precognition, DNA-RNA, mediumship, trance states and promiscuity, to cite a few examples. Furthermore, the individually built-in components are basically made of primordial stuff, so it is necessary to collect the data of evolution such as: old bones from the Olduvai, manifestations of the unconscious and race memory, child development, linguistics, apes, angels and Trobriand Islanders.

Finally, if you look at the model *Morganthropus Exchangenesis,* you can also tell yourself which data of human nature to pay attention to. This is the information about obligation, negotiation and transaction. For example: kinship systems in Chicago and Chicopee, Chihuahua and China; old clay pots from Sumer; jewelry and provisions from tombs; fads and taboos; class and power structures; myths and legends; prayers, paintings and revolutions; birth, courtship, marriage and death rituals; laws and in-laws; the feudal system; coins; life cycles and so on and on.

3

Now, that catalogue of facts is not complete (*Edisonthropus Tinkerectus*) or definitive (*Morganthropus Exchangenesis*) by a long shot. But the essential picture (*Tarzanthropus Inherens*) is there. You can see at a glance what the valid data are. And that is because a working model of human nature tells you the sorts of facts that validate it. In other words (*Tarzanthropus Inherens*), what is tellable boils down to a question of:

WHAT'S THE TRUE STORY?

If you look at the model *Edisonthropus Tinkerectus,* you can tell how to weave the facts into a coherent whole. The true story is that man is the hyphen between the stimulus-response. And as soon as you know how the working parts of that hyphen work, you can tell yourself how to live a better-ordered, more-integrated, more-satisfactory life. Once you see how the drives drive and the pulleys pull human nature, you can tell yourself how to spend your money, how to educate your children, how to get along in your family, whom to elect and in general how to react to the world.

Naturally, that requires an investigation into the natural laws —a thorough study of the working parts, and of the smaller parts that make them, and of the parts that make those smaller parts, and so forth down to the smallest working parts and their pieces. That is very hard work, of course. It requires great objectivity and precise measurement of tiny details, so you must wear comfortable shoes and assume nothing. But in the end you have gained information about what makes people tick. You can tell what makes men men; what makes women women; how people learn; how the ship of state sails; what kids are like; and, in short, what makes the world go around.

A great deal of piecework has already been done in the investigation into the *Edisonthropus Tinkerectus* model of human nature. Consequently, there is a thick thesaurus of words to play with, a great storehouse of facts available, a vast story to tell yourself. For example, there are charts and graphs to show what babies should have learned at this age or that. There are tables and indices of how a child should be performing with this IQ or that. There are profiles and statistics, based on carefully controlled laboratory experiments, on how a satisfactory sex act is performed, complete with diagrams of the working parts and their internal mechanisms and the smaller working parts of those. There are books by experienced researchers about the mechanics of maleness and femaleness and how and when and why they do not function properly. And because such mechanisms can be taken apart and examined and adjusted, there are books about how to be satisfactorily married.

Those subjects are too big for the magazines to handle, so they break such matters down to smaller working parts. The newsstands are filled with recipes by expert and master mechanics who explain such specialized parts of the operation as how to make love premaritally, maritally or extramaritally; how to isolate and cope with problems about money, in-laws, vacations; ten questions (or multiples of ten) to ask yourself in order to find out if you are stable; how to feed a baby; how to talk to a boy child or a girl child; how to live with an older person; and so forth among the cogs and wheels and their parts that make up a day, a week, a year and a lifetime.

That is only the beginning of the true story according to the model *Edisonthropus Tinkerectus* with its gears within gears meshing in conformity to natural law. Hardly a month goes by without another installment, report, breakthrough or pilot study about the machinery parts. Even a moderately alert television viewer or newspaper reader can tell how to improve the education process, the urbanization process, the presidential function—and what may be in the works for slowing down the aging process, the bureaucratization process, heart and mental disease. Almost anybody who looks at the personal advice columns can tell what machinery to set in motion in order to get over such obstacles as bereavement, children, loneliness, Christmas, perspiration, unrequited love, unsatisfactory schoolwork and the muss, fuss and tedious effort of preparing food and eating it. Even many young people know that is the true story. They can tell what educational levels to pass through in order to find out how the machinery works, and what experience is necessary to master the particular piece of a mechanism that interests them.

And as that is the story, it is like any other story—it has a moral. To wit: if you learn how the working parts work, you can make the necessary adjustments in yourself to become more human and thus make the world a better place to live in.

If you look at the *Tarzanthropus Inherens* model of human nature, you can also tell how to arrange the words and weave the facts into a coherent whole. This model has built-in components evolved of primordial stuff and tailored to individual specifications. So the true story is that man is the missing link between the ape and the human. That makes man an animal and you an individual of the species.

As soon as you know the specific characteristics of the animal and the particular characteristics of yourself, you can tell yourself how to live in closer touch with your feelings, less alienated and more content. Once you find your individual resonance in the chorus of mankind, you can tell yourself how to spend your money, how to educate your children, how to communicate with your family, whom to elect to office, and in general what life style to choose in order to supply essential creature comforts and to satisfy individual needs.

Naturally you have to conduct that quest in two directions. You have to look outward to find the built-in, wired-in species—specific capabilities, instincts and other characteristics of the animal. And you have to look inward, trying on this life style and that, in order to find your own potentialities, feelings and other individual characteristics as they unfold and actualize.

That is not only hard work; it is also a lifetime career to get the true story. The part about the characteristics of the animal may be available in the field and on the bookshelf; but the other part of the story about your own capabilities and instincts continues to unfold until you die. And that makes it quite difficult to tell the story in discreet chapters. There are no mechanisms to isolate and examine, so you cannot simply learn how to begin your education, finish your education and begin your life. Nor can you learn how people tick because people do not tick. This one may tick; that one may tock; another may tick-*tock;* you may *tock*-tick. So you cannot get the story on how to be content in marriage, or how to be a man, or how to be stable. And certainly you cannot feed the baby every four or six hours because his individual biorhythm may not be hungry on mechanical, clockwork schedule. And as for such events as loneliness, bereavement, unrequited love and unsatisfactory schoolwork—there is no mechanism or machinery to adjust or replace. There are only built-in inner resources, irrevocably changed geometric relationships and a failure to communicate.

Under the circumstances, there are few shop manuals or books, articles, documentaries, advice columns and similar reports by master mechanics that can give you the true story about your individually built-in potentialities and feelings. According to the *Tarzanthropus Inherens* model of human nature, there are as many natures as there are people. As a result there are no scales, tables, per-capita numbers or other how-to instructions. About the best you can look to on this half of the quest are other individuals and their resonances: biographies, poetry, anecdotes about unforgettable characters, etc. For the rest, you have to commune with yourself, meditate, get in touch with your essence, and then tell the story to yourself and to anybody else who will listen in order to find out if the echo vibrates properly.

It is a lot easier to get the story about the other half of the quest—the capabilities, instincts and other characteristics of the animal. The bookshelves, newsstands and air waves are full of true stories about how to be a chimpanzee, a jackdaw, a salmon, a baboon, a pigeon, a graylag goose, a timber wolf and other animals. And man being an animal, that part of the story may be found somewhere among the pair-bonding, nest-building, territorial, aggressive and other built-in, wired-in stuff that have evolved to make everybody's components in general.

The other part of the story—about your individually tailored components—is not so readily researched. But it is a much more popular story. Compared with your own feelings, capabilities and unfolding destiny, those of the salmon and graylag goose are rather dull. Nature walks may have their place in the *Tarzanthropus Inherens* model of human nature. But they do not approach the excitement and dangerous thrill of a trip into your own unconscious. It has become one of the most-visited tourist attractions in the Western world, gaining new devotees and addicts all the time. Even many young people, who cannot tell a chimpanzee from a baboon, know how to get there by themselves and, finding the story so engrossing, sometimes do not come back.

In any event, that is the story. And like any story, it has a moral, namely: when you know what you are essentially, then you can re-create the world and make it more human.

If you look at the pasted-up *Morganthropus Exchangenesis* model of human nature, you can also answer the question of what the true story is. The true story is that man does not have a nature—at least not the kind of nature that has clockwork mechanisms to adjust or inherent characteristics to reveal. Instead, man has only that portfolio of negotiable documents he is born to, adds to or deletes from as he lives, and bequeaths when he dies as a portfolio to the newborn, and so on and on. The true story is a script that has been written and rewritten in the past, is being written and rewritten now, and will continue to be so in the future. And that makes everybody both a player and playwright at the same time.

As soon as you learn the script, or at least your part in it, you can tell yourself how to live a successful life. That includes how to spend your money prudently; how to educate your children profitably; how to negotiate wisely with your family; which party to elect to office; and in general what obligations you should incur and what roles you should choose to play.

Naturally, you cannot get that story by looking inward—neither into the paper and ink of the script, nor into yourself. The atomic structure of the role is irrelevant, and beneath the role is nobody but another role. Deep inside an Albert Schweitzer, where it really counts, is a birth certificate that says Albert Schweitzer. And beneath that document are others: his father's birth certificate; his grandfather's; his great-grandfather's; and an enactment signed and sealed by a long-since dissolved Napoleonic government. So the true story is that you have to look backward in order to profit from the mistakes of the past, and forward in order to prepare and rehearse the parts you choose to play. And because it is largely scripted, the story is available to be read, heard and seen everywhere.

You cannot turn around without getting the story on how to play your part. The bookshelves are filled with stories about how to be a teen-ager; how to be a lover or mistress; how to be a husband or wife; how to be a father or mother. The streets are lined with places that tell you how to be graceful, charming, the belle of the ball, suitably dressed, a wonderful cook, a better provider. The newspapers are crammed with stories of documentation, certification, ownership and lease-hold—who was born, who was married, who died, who was graduated (with or without honors), who signed what treaty, who sought asylum in which embassy, who was traded for whom, who was kidnaped for how much worth of negotiable paper, and so on and on. In addition to stories like those, television is filled night and day with backward looks at how the script got to where it is. You can tune in at almost any moment and get an adequate recapitulation on the story thus far in foreign policy, labor negotiations, the political campaign, the presidency, the baseball season and Western civilization. And moreover, just to make sure that the story is being told well, magazines frequently offer tests you can take regarding your achievement in role-playing and image-building: What does your living room say about you? What is the girl in this picture telling you? So you think you speak English properly? Would anybody buy a used car from you? Do your kids think of you as Daddy? and so on and on.

Well, that is the story, or at least part of it, according to the *Morganthropus Exchangenesis* model of human nature. The final true story is impossible to tell because the script is always under revision and the portfolio is constantly in review. There is no inherent animal characteristic to guarantee roles against reversal. There is no natural law to insure credits, accreditations and other negotiable documents against devaluation. The image of man changes from place to place and time to time. In this part of the planet, it no longer includes child labor, public executions, slavery, inequality at the polls and so on. It is a different image of man from the past's, and reflects more or less clearly all sexes, all colors, all incomes, those who are in jail and out, in hospitals and out, in kennels and out, and so on and on. The image of man in this part of the planet does not yet include chimpanzees and computers. But that part of the *Morganthropus Exchangenesis* story is subject to change, too, inasmuch as negotiations with both seem to be developing.

In any event, that is a story according to *Morganthropus Exchangenesis*. And because it is a story, it has a moral: forget

240

about changing human nature. You can make people more human by changing their images of themselves. But it takes a two-thirds vote to do it.

4

In other words, *other words* have consequences. That is to say, even so disreputable a phrase as human nature conjures up true-life events in the way you educate your children, go to the polls, spend your money, and in general get through the day, week, year and lifetime. In other words, the story works out largely according to which working model of human nature you look at. To consider a few endings side by side by side:

CHILD REARING

According to the model *Edisonthropus Tinkerectus,* the true story is that it takes everybody's effort in this world to keep the machine functioning smoothly. Consequently, you feed the children on schedule, toilet-train them on schedule, dress them the way children should be dressed, mark them in achievement and deportment, and try to show them in similar ways that everybody has a place and a responsibility—if only for bowels, towels, napkin rings and silence in the presence of adults. So the true story is that healthy babies are happy babies. And the best mothers are adjusted, tranquil, or at least tranquilized, mothers.

According to the *Tarzanthropus Inherens* model, the true story is that there are as many natures as there are people and each unfolds at its own speed. Consequently, it doesn't matter whether you dress the children according to standards of age or sex because such standards are unimportant. It is individual growth and self-realization that make the difference. For the same reason, you feed children only when they demand food; toilet-train them when they seem to be ready for it; mark them for leadership, cooperation and creativity; and try to show them in similar ways that the world can be their oyster. It depends on the personal action they take. So the true story is that healthy babies may or may not be happy babies; it depends on their natures. And similarly, not all mothers are cut out for motherhood; it depends on their natures.

According to the model *Morganthropus Exchangenesis,* the true story is that everything is negotiable—including death and taxes. Consequently, it doesn't matter whether you feed the children on schedule or on demand. The important thing is that child rearing pay off and be fun. So, you give love when the children perform successfully on the toilet or bottle, and withhold love when they fail. And sooner or later they will learn to play their roles so that they get their just desserts and everybody gets happiness. Furthermore, you see to it that they get good marks in appearance and courtesy; make sure that they go to parties dressed in gift wrapping; and try to show them in similar ways that rewards can come whether or not they are useful, excellent or special. So the true story, according to the model *Morganthropus Exchangenesis,* is that happy, lovable babies act happy and lovable. And if they don't project that image, then they can't expect to get much love and be happy.

EDUCATION

According to the *Edisonthropus Tinkerectus* model of human nature, you must adjust the parts or replace them with better ones. Consequently, you hire qualified, experienced teachers; install up-to-date audio-visual equipment; put in optimum lighting, seating and desk space; make sure that lessons are bite-sized for the average student; and in general build better schools so that subject matter can be mastered more readily.

According to the model *Tarzanthropus Inherens,* the true story is social engineering. If the components aren't in harmony, you have to redesign the geometric relationships among them. Consequently, you hire talented, understanding teachers; set up a guidance and counseling office for individual attention; put in independent study projects; reduce interpersonal tension by doing away with grades; set up a school-busing program; and in general ease the way for total communication.

According to the model *Morganthropus Exchangenesis* made of report cards, diplomas, degrees, licenses and other documents of transaction, the true story is negotiation and accreditation. If education isn't paying off, you must review the portfolio. Consequently, you must see to it that the school building is attractive and lures students; you must see to it that all students earn good grades—or better yet, let them grade themselves; you must hire popular or widely published or well-celebrated teachers in order to invite the right students—the kind who are good for contacts in later life. You must offer negotiable securities in your catalogue of courses. School-building and school-busing may be all right. But they aren't the cartes blanches of eased requirements and open enrollment.

POLITICAL LEADERSHIP

According to the *Edisonthropus Tinkerectus* model, the true story is that the political machine is necessary but iniquitous. Power tends to corrupt. Consequently, the best presidency may be a six-year term with no re-election possible—leaving the office-holder free of the lures and entanglements of party, patronage and political pressure.

According to the model *Tarzanthropus Inherens,* the true

story of political leadership is charisma—the inherent talent of giving voice to the harmonious will of all without muffling the individual's resonance. Consequently, if a presidential office-holder has the charismatic capability, it may be in the best interests of all to re-elect the incumbent term after term until the general harmony changes and a new charismatic voice is needed.

According to the model *Morganthropus Exchangenesis* made of favors, platform planks, campaign promises, contributions and the other documents of negotiation, the true story is that you don't get something for nothing—especially in politics. Consequently, the best check on presidential power may well be the political IOUs, obligations and allegiances the officeholder owes to the party. That could mean a four-year presidential term, or even shorter, with at least one option to be renominated. And with it, of course, comes an added check: the threat of defeat at the polls for both the incumbent and the party in the next election.

Now, that is not to say you always know what to tell yourself. Sometimes the true story is not clearly speakable or readily available. That sort of difficulty can crop up for a number of reasons. For example, your body of knowledge about human nature may be too narrow to reveal where some things fit and how and when and why they fit there. That condition is known as blocked, limited, stunted, underdeveloped, obsessed, poorly reared, ill-prepared for life, overprotected and the like, depending on which working model of human nature you look at. For another example, sometimes the true story is elusive because you do not have the words to play with and the facts to pay attention to, and thus cannot weave them into a coherent narrative. That is a condition known as ignorance, stupidity, poor education and the like, depending on the model of human na-

244

ture you look at. Or, for still another example, sometimes the landscape seems to change so drastically and quickly that you cannot organize it and yourself in it without redesigning the working model. That condition is known as a miracle, a catastrophe, a nervous breakdown, a crisis, an altered state of consciousness, a revolutionary development and the like, depending on the model you look at.

There are many other instances when the true story is not readily or completely tellable. But whichever the case, sometimes the sky appears to be falling down and you cannot organize the hurtling data into a coherently speakable whole. In that emergency, you usually have to bring the pieces to other people and ask them for the true story they tell themselves about it —where it begins, its settings and locations, and the rest of the narrative according to the working model of human nature, including a moral about which data to pay most attention to. And the same is the case regarding these other people whom you ask. In the event that they cannot tell themselves the true story when the sky appears to be falling down, they usually refer themselves to still other people, bringing the shards of data and asking what story these other people tell themselves about it: where it begins, its setting and location, a moral about which pieces to pay most attention to, and the rest of the true story according to the working model of human nature.

Which people do you begin to ask for the true stories they tell themselves? Where are they located? And which people do they begin to ask?

That part of the story depends, of course, on which working model you consult to begin with. If it told you that the sky was falling out of proper location, then it can probably provide the beginning of the story as well—including somebody or other to tell it. So, looked at that way, the story organizes the tellers: the way a news event organizes the sources; the way a court trial organizes the participants; the way ailments organize doctors; the way tribal rites separate the men from the anthropologists. In other words (*Tarzanthropus Inherens*), birds of a feather flock together. That is to say (*Morganthropus Exchangenesis*), company is known by the man it keeps; and vice (*Edisonthropus Tinkerectus*) versa.

Take a hypothetical true story illustrating the way the story organizes the tellers. Say you are a higher journalist and notice one day that the human nature sky appears to be falling down. As you can quickly see, the story involves such items as the creation of the world and the location of human nature in it. And that makes it quite easy to figure out whom to ask for the true story. It simply depends on which working model of human nature you look at.

If you look at the model *Edisonthropus Tinkerectus,* you can see that the world was created a long time ago by a Master Engineer who set its machinery in motion and keeps it running like clockwork. Consequently, this working model of human nature is a simulation of something located "out there" where the other natural laws are kept. So, when the human nature sky appears to be falling, you ask the king what he tells himself only if he rules by divine right. Otherwise, you ask for the true story from such people as: medical doctors, pharmaceutical detail men, psychiatrists and others who are engaged in adjusting the mechanisms that make the human machine; military specialists, advertising agents, political speech-writers and others who are engaged in engineering consent; clergymen who know the ways of God; cultural anthropologists; spiritualists; and others who deal daily with natural laws and understand them—school-building experts, cab drivers, old wives and Iowa farmers.

If you look at the model *Tarzanthropus Inherens,* you can see that the world was created on July 27, 1900, or on June 8,

1952—or on the birthday of whomever you ask for the true story according to this model. Moreover, the world was created by a Master Artist out of common, garden variety clay but fashioned individually for each person who ever lived or will live. Consequently, this working model of human nature is a simulation of something "inside," built into each person, where it exists in potential ready to leap into actuality as needed. So, when the human nature sky appears to be falling and you have to ask other people for the true story they tell themselves about it, you begin with: ethologists, geneticists, microbiologists and others who know about common clay; clergymen who know about the Divine Spark that makes man potentially special; neurophysiologists; physical anthropologists; psycholinguistics experts; astrologers, palmists and others who deal daily with what is wired-in to mankind and built-in to each person's individual specifications—adolescents, mediums, bartenders and their steady customers, drug pushers and theirs, judges, mothers, Vermont farmers, etc.

If you look at the model *Morganthropus Exchangenesis,* you can see that the world has not yet been created. Or, rather, it was created today and will be re-created again tomorrow and the next day and so on and on. But just how the world will be created tomorrow is anybody's guess because it depends on the roll of the dice, the bounce of the ball and the other kinds of negotiations people have with each other. Consequently, this working model of human nature is a simulation of something "in-between" everybody where the transactions go on and on. So, when you have to ask other people for the true story they tell themselves about human nature, you begin with: archaeologists, musicologists, art curators and other historians who keep track of the way the world was created yesterday and the day before; politicians, salesmen, tycoons, and others who know where everything is for the moment; clergymen who know about

247

the transaction of prayer; social anthropologists; morticians; faith healers; sociologists and others who deal daily with the world's negotiations and understand them. That list also includes newspaper editors, lawyers, prostitutes, therapy-group leaders, swingers, witches, motivation researchers, architects, Indiana farmers, etc.

Well, there is a true story about human nature—namely that people go around talking to themselves all the time, telling themselves true stories about where everything belongs, and how and when and why it got there and belongs there.

Chapter Ten

In other words:

People everywhere get a complete set of human nature when they are very young or before, and they are in accord, or understand, or contract to keep it in good order forever and ever.

As anthropologist A. I. Hallowell says, the "functioning of any human society is inconceivable without self-awareness, reinforced and constituted by traditional beliefs about the nature of the self. This hypothesis receives support from the universal fact that, as compared with the societies of animals lower in the scale of organic evolution, any human society is not only a social order but a moral order as well. A moral order being one that is characterized by the fact that not only norms of conduct exist but organized or unorganized social sanctions to reinforce them, an inevitable conclusion must be drawn: the members of such an order are expected to assume moral responsibility for their conduct. Such an assumption, in turn, implies self-awareness of one's own conduct, self-appraisal of one's conduct with reference to socially recognized standards of value, some volitional control of one's own behavior, a possible choice of alternative lines of conduct, etc."

So, people not only get a complete set of human nature at birth or before, but they also have been in accordance, understanding or contracting to keep that set in good order for quite a long while now.

Whether one model is older than the others in the set depends, of course, on which model you look at in order to find out where everything belongs. But certainly the model *Morganthropus Exchangenesis* is very old, with its vows, permissions, favors and other negotiable scrip. As French structuralist Claude Lévi-Strauss points out about primitive societies, exchange is not a matter of economic transactions so much as it is a negotiation in reciprocal gifts. That exchange, he says, is "an event which has a significance that is at once social and religious, magic and economic, utilitarian and sentimental, jural and moral." That working model of human nature is readily apparent in North American society today, even in its particular, primitive gift-giving aspect. "The exchange of gifts at Christmas, for a month each year, practised by all social classes with a sort of sacred ardour," Lévi-Strauss says, "is nothing other than a gigantic *potlatch,* implicating millions of individuals, and at the end of which many family budgets are faced with lasting disequilibrium."

The model *Morganthropus Exchangenesis* is also very old, as Lewis Mumford describes it: "Man does not simply live his life from day to day, in a sober, matter-of-fact way: he dramatizes and enacts it. For every phase of his development, he creates a plot and a dialogue, a sequence of actions, an appropriate costume, and a special stage . . . By losing himself in role after role, drama after drama, man explores passages that the fixed parts assigned by nature would never have opened up . . . His being is always involved in becoming, and that becoming involves a self-transformation." By this process of working over his original nature, Mumford says, man brought forth a second self: "a new image of himself . . . a more truly human self." In time, all of his artful masquerades "touched every part of his society and his environment, not least his inner self."

There is certainly nothing recent about the solid-state *Tarzanthropus Inherens* model.

"The psychologist," says the opening sentence of *Ethical Standards of Psychologists,* "is committed to a belief in the

250

dignity and worth of the individual human being." But psychologist Isador Chein doubts that such a belief is "implicit in the images of Man presented in our textbooks or represented in the pages of our scientific journals." The belief in the dignity and worth of the individual, he says, derives from extrascientific indoctrination, one such extrascientific source being the Bible wherein God said: "We will make man, in our image and of our likeness . . ."

A Talmudic commentary on the biblical narrative of the Creation, Chein says, "remarks on a unique aspect of the creation of Man. Unlike all others, Man was created in the singular. From the contrast, the rabbis deduce that each man must justify himself in his own life . . . the Creator of the universe stamped millions of pieces of clay in His own image and no two human beings are alike."

In the ancient Greek civilization, this *Tarzanthropus Inherens* model of human nature can clearly be seen at work. As psychologist Bernard Rosenthal points out, "an integral fact of humanism was the optimal development of one's potentialities . . . while happiness resulted from the aspiration to and practice of excellence," which provided a "full-bodied fulfillment" of each man's "impulses, talents and penchants."

But when each man's potentialities are individual and no two human beings are alike, it is difficult to think of "humanity" as a function of natural law—as a term for all people—the way you can think of "space" and "time" as universal phenomena obeying some higher principle. The *Tarzanthropus Inherens* model of human nature makes it much easier to define the "human" as yourself and perhaps your group, too, and locate "others" and "outsiders" elsewhere in the model. As Lewis Mumford puts it, "the 'human' has never so far been the generically human: the image man coins in one culture does not yet pass as human legal tender, without a heavy discount in other cultures."

Each group tends to conceive its own type, "with its own characteristic expressions and projections, as the truly human one."

Under the circumstances, you might think that the model *Edisonthropus Tinkerectus* is a more recent addition to the set of human nature—drives, cogs, wheels and other mechanisms being largely the inventions of the seventeenth and eighteenth centuries. And, in fact, many sectors of today's human nature industry see it that way.

In the early Renaissance, says historian of science E. A. Burtt, "the people had *thought* themselves living in a world rich with color and sound, redolent with fragrance, filled with gladness, love and beauty, speaking everywhere of purposive harmony and creative ideals . . ." But during the seventeenth century, says Hallowell, the idea of the world as animate "gave way to the idea of the world as *mechanism*—a world machine, no longer animate but mechanically responsive to the laws of nature."

The discoveries of Isaac Newton, says Burtt, were "squarely behind that view of the cosmos which saw in man a puny irrelevant spectator . . . of the vast mathematical system whose regular motions according to mechanical principles constituted the world of nature . . ." Not only did Newton contribute to this new model, many spokesmen for the industry say, but also John Calvin lent his authority to it. As sociologist Robert Merton says, if the Calvinist God was "irrational in the sense that He cannot be directly grasped by the cultivated intellect, He can yet be glorified by a clear-sighted, meticulous study of His natural works."

By the eighteenth century, the *Edisonthropus Tinkerectus* model appears to the industry to have been almost completely operational as an organized idea of human nature. "All phenomena were to be subsumed within the giant mechanism," says historian of science Floyd Matson. "What could not be stretched or shrunk to fit its procrustean framework was simply no 'phenomena' at all . . . a fallacy of vision which the scientific lens would soon correct, and which meanwhile might better be disregarded. In short, all that mattered was matter." The result in the nineteenth century, Matson says, was a systematic reduction of all subjects and fields of knowledge to the dimensions and categories of natural science. "Philosophy tended to become 'natural philosophy,' biology virtually a branch of mechanics, and psychology the anatomy of the human machine." In fact, historian of science Michael Foucault goes so far as to say that until two centuries ago "man did not exist." The human sciences, he says, could not appear until "man constituted himself in Western culture as both that which must be conceived and that which is to be known." That man "should have become the object of science—that cannot be considered or treated as a phenomenon of opinion: it is an event in the order of knowledge."

That is to say, the past two or three centuries have brought about a change in human nature with the addition of a new body of knowledge or working model of it: *Edisonthropus Tinkerectus*. At least that is how much of the industry sees it. According to that model, as Baron d'Holbach saw it in 1770, "Man is the work of nature; he exists within nature and is subject to nature's laws. . . . There is neither accident nor change in nature; in nature there is no effect without sufficient cause. . . . Man is therefore not free for a single instant of his life." According to that model, as Oliver Wendell Holmes saw it a century later, "We must study the lines of direction of all the forces that traverse our human nature. We must study man as we have studied stars and rocks." According to that working model of human nature, as William James saw it a generation later, the *Edisonthropus* "God whom science recognizes must be a God of universal laws exclusively, a God who does a wholesale, not a retail business. He cannot accommodate his processes to the convenience of individuals." And according to that model of human nature, as the central character in B. F. Skinner's novel *Walden Two* sees it now, "I deny that freedom exists at all. I must deny it—or my program would be absurd. You can't have a science about a subject matter which hops capriciously about."

What the human nature industry does not mention usually, however, are all the evidences that the model *Edisonthropus Tinkerectus* was operational right along with the other two models in the dim, dead days beyond recall. This organized idea of human nature with its regularities, generalizations, causes and effects was certainly referred to by people who in the Ice Age marked time by the moon's phases; people who in the time of Peking man knew that saplings did not feed a fire; people who thousands of years ago noted the effects of close inbreeding and successfully hunted big game by observing, for example, that an antelope—like other ungulates—always runs in an arc.

That sort of thing is not generally mentioned by most spokesmen for the human nature industry today. In fact, the other two models are seldom referred to at all, except perhaps as former and now-obsolete stages of development which are supposed to have culminated in the modern marvel—the invention and perfection of the *Edisonthropus Tinkerectus* model and the selection and breeding of the high-quality mechanics who keep it in good working order.

As everybody knows, official spokesmen for rich and powerful industries often ignore their competition and close their eyes to the models being turned out across the street. It's human nature.

So, for quite some time people have been given a complete set of human nature, and have been in accord or understanding or contracting to keep those models in good order. Why they do so, of course, is because it is their nature to abstract human and natural **DATA** from the world rubble and organize them into human and natural INFORMATION. That is to say, people cannot live in chaos. The newborn infant does not taste reality "raw," as cognitive psychologist Ulric Neisser puts it. The very "structure of our sense organs is assimilative . . . information is heavily condensed by processes that are ready to operate at birth. Even the youngest baby can make at least some 'abstractions' about color, brightness, crude form and rough dimensional position." As the infant develops, he must abstract and organize more and more human and natural data. Anthropologist Mary Ellen Goodman says that "The child must absorb the culture of his group if he is to survive and to become socially adult. He does so because it is the nature of man to learn from others of his kind."

In other words, it is human and natural to organize an idea or working model of what is human and natural; and it is human and natural to live within that idea. Man is "an incomplete, an unfinished animal," says Clifford Geertz. What sets man off most graphically from non-men are the "particular sorts of things he *has* to learn before he is able to function at all." Without an organized idea of where everything human and natural belongs, people "would be unworkable monstrosities with very few useful instincts, fewer recognizable sentiments, and no intellect: mental basket cases . . . We live in an 'information gap.' Between what our body tells us and what we have to know in order to function, there is a vacuum we must fill ourselves. . . ."

And vice versa: ourselves are vacuums we must fill. "The human individual," says Hallowell, "must be provided with certain basic orientations in order to act intelligibly in the world he apprehends. Such orientations are basic . . . and peculiar to a human. . . . They all appear to revolve around man's capacity for self-awareness."

Looked at that way, **YOU** are a datum abstracted from the world rubble by your nature. **YOU** are an item on the landscape which must be organized into the picture—placed within the frame of meaning. Like any other abstracted datum, **YOU** must be arranged into human and natural information. You must be able to locate YOURSELF in the complete set of human nature which explains where everything belongs and how and when and why it belongs there. Consequently, you have to pull yourself together, find yourself, be yourself. So it is no grammatical accident that you are designated by a plural: "You are." It requires an organized idea or working model of human nature to arrange the plural you into a seemingly singular self that can express itself, say what it thinks, speak its mind, reveal itself, keep to itself and tell itself stories about where everything belongs and what it means.

"Behavior," says psychologist Theodore Sarbin, "is organized around cognitive structures, the result of responses of the organism to stimulus objects and residual stimuli. The self is one such cognitive structure or inference. Like all cognitive structures, it is organized around substructures . . . called empirical selves."

There are at least three such empirical selves which humans abstract from the world rubble and organize into their human and natural selves. Every human language, as Franz Boas pointed out, refers to at least an *I,* a *thou* and a *he;* "the underlying idea of these pronouns is the clear distinction between the self as speaker, the person or object spoken to, and that spoken of . . ." Those three observed data are organized into information known as the self.

"We appear as selves in our conduct insofar as we ourselves take the attitude that others take toward us," says George Herbert Mead. We "assume the attitude of assent of all members in the community. We take the role of what might be called 'the generalized other.' And in doing this we appear as social objects, as selves . . ." What we thus develop and arrange, says Charles H. Cooley, is a "social self" or "the reflected or looking-glass self." As Cooley sees that organization, it is pulled together from three principal elements: the imagination of your appearance to the other person; the imagination of his judgment of that appearance; and some sort of self-feeling such as pride or mortification.

Now, that is a great deal of data to abstract and organize into human and natural information. There is the way the *I* looks to the *thou;* there is the way the *thou* looks to the *he;* there is the way both the *thou* and the *he* look to the *I;* and consequently there is the way the *I* and the *me* look to each other. It requires considerable effort and a firm idea of where everything belongs in order to keep those data in their proper time, place and order so as to know who you are and to be able to express yourself. The job of organizing a self is not as easy as falling off a log.

For one thing, those three elements of yourself—the *I,* the *thou* and the *he*—are themselves information organized of all sorts of data, including wood, tin and sometimes even grass.

"It is quite clear," says Thomas Rhys Williams, "that many of an infant's earliest and continuing life experiences are set in the context of a particular type of shelter and its details. These experiences appear to contribute substantially to the structuring of perceptions of the self of the individual and to the ways individuals come to view objects, space and time . . ." Among the Dusan people of North Borneo, for example, there is disgust, fear and aggression regarding a few people who have built houses of wooden sides and tin roofs rather than the traditional Dusan dwelling. One old woman, spitting on the ground and pointing to one wood-and-tin house, said to Williams: "You

257

know that one draws the attention of every evil spirit in this place; is it any wonder so many babies have died here this year with that man and his house in the middle of us."

The elements of your self can also be organized of other materials. For at least a thousand years, says Margaret Mead, the Chinese "have used seals denoting the power of office, and seals containing the characters for names cut upon stone, wood, bone, ivory, crystal, china, glass, brass and other substances have been—and still are—used to establish the identity of particular individuals, artists and businessmen. . . . Objects provide a method of storing information—a system comparable to, but quite different from, storage by words."

Moreover, there is a past and a present in the elements which are organized into your self. As psychologists Ulric Neisser and Jean Piaget agree, "the very act of processing information causes a change in the system which carries out the process. . . . A piece of music that is heard for the fifth time does not sound as it did at first. . . . It is important to note that *both* the listener and the music he hears are altered."

Says sociologist Edward Tiryakian, "I am today what I am in part because of my historical past, and in part because of what I anticipate to be my historical future. I am also historical in a collective or social sense, that is, I am open to take as mine the history of my people, and this leads me to realize that I am not contained in my finite and solid appearance but that my being goes out spatially and temporally. . . . Moreover, the historical consciousness of the self is also a historical *conscience;* human historicity is not just cognitively perceived but also morally interpreted and evaluated. Self-awareness, in its fullest sense, then, is not just cognitive awareness of one's finiteness but also awareness of one's historical transcendence, which includes solidarity with one's fellows."

And, in addition, the elements of your self—the *I,* the *thou* and the *he*—are also organized of data which have been imagined only. "The king can be told so often that he is a lion that he comes to believe it," says James Fernandez. "He roars at his subjects and stealthily stalks those he thinks are enemies to his interest . . ." At a deep level of fantasy, Fernandez says, men "may hold to predications which cause them irresistibly to organize their world, insofar as they can, so as to facilitate or make inevitable certain scenarios. . . . Whether fantasies are lived out or not, they may still be defined as scenarios arising from metaphoric predication on pronouns."

That pronoun *you* is not easy to organize into human and natural information. "The difficulty of developing self-identity in childhood," says psychologist Gordon Allport, "is shown by the ease with which a child depersonalizes himself in play and in speech." Until the age of four or five, Allport believes, personal identity as perceived by the child is unstable. Beginning at about this age, a perceived self or personal identity "becomes the surest test a human being has of his own existence."

And even after your self is organized, the organization has to be reaffirmed constantly. You have to keep telling yourself and other selves where the past ends and the present begins, and where you end and the rest of the world begins. Anthropologist Rosalie Wax, reporting on field work in a foreign culture, says, "I often felt like a mental defective, and for about six weeks I felt as if I were losing my mind." Says another anthropologist who did field work in a mental hospital: "My initial period at the hospital was one of disorientation, shock and disequilibration. It lasted for about three or four weeks and it was highlighted by my need and attempt to find firm ground upon which to stand and to reconstitute an integrated 'self' with which to operate."

But for all that it is a difficult, tedious, tentative and hazardous business to organize **YOURSELF** into human and natural information, there is no way out of informing YOURSELF that way. If you are aware of yourself in the rubble—if you are an observable datum to yourself—then you are locatable in the working model of human nature which explains where everything belongs, and how and when and why it belongs there. And quite plainly the model has given you the story of yourself and what it means. Otherwise you would not be able to see the wood, tin, time, ivory, lion, thou and other elements which have been organized to make the plural you a singular self. Without a working model of human nature, you could not see yourself as *disoriented, depersonalized, unstable* or their contraries.

What kind of a self you organize, of course, depends on which model you consult. Each organized idea of human nature arranges its own particular kind of self from the elements: a self that tells itself particular kinds of stories about where everything belongs; a self that is seen in a particular kind of way by other selves; a self that sees other selves in a particular kind of way. Each working model of human nature organizes a human and natural self whose consequences in action differ from the consequences of selves organized by the other models.

If you look at the working model *Edisonthropus Tinkerectus* with its interchangeable cogs, replaceable gears and other mechanisms ticking along according to the clockwork of natural law, you can see that your self is quite plastic to begin with and is arranged by the application of external influences. As Don Wolfe puts it regarding the self ordered by this model, "Man's character is mechanistically determined by the forces, constructive or destructive, brought to bear upon his youth."

This kind of self comes to see itself as a replaceable cog in the great natural law machine that is the world. This kind of self has great confidence in counting and measuring the world as a method of understanding its natural laws and behaving

260

in accordance with them. Here is a judge awarding an adopted child to its "real" mother because that is where children belong. Here is John Goddard, aged forty-seven, having achieved 103 goals of the 127 he wrote down for his self to accomplish when he was fifteen. Here is the National Institute of Mental Health financing a study to determine whether homosexuality is caused by an endocrine error in body chemistry—a mistake of nature in violation of its own laws.

The *Edisonthropus Tinkerectus* model of human nature teaches its own particular lesson to the selves it organizes. As Don Wolfe states that moral: "There, but for the grace of God (my parents, my community, my playmates, none of which I chose) go I." And with such a moral, you can readily organize the story to tell your self.

"What is man?" asked Abraham Lincoln in a letter to his law partner. "He is a mere child moved and governed by this vast world machine, forever working in grooves, and moving in deep-cut channels; and now what is man? He is a simple tool, a cog, a part and parcel of this vast iron machine that strikes and cuts, grinds and mashes."

Naturally your self can see the consequences of such a story. "The bubbles on the foam which coats a stormy sea are floating episodes, made and unmade by the forces of the wind and water," says William James of this model of human nature. "Our private selves are like those bubbles—epiphenomena . . . their destinies weigh nothing and determine nothing in the world's irremediable currents of events."

That is a very compelling lesson and story, of course, because a model of human nature organizes everything so well. Consequently, it is easy to forget that *Edisonthropus Tinkerectus* is only one model in the complete set—especially as that model is so widely advertised and distributed by the industry.

While all psychoses, says Bruno Bettelheim, "are due to

conflict within the person, his specific delusions will reflect the hopes and anxieties of the society he lives in." In the Middle Ages, "even Lucifer was viewed as a person, though a distorted one. What is entirely new in the machine age is that often neither saviour nor destroyer is cast in man's image any more. The typical modern delusion is of being run by an influencing machine."

Bettelheim cites the case of Joey, a boy who thought he was a machine—"a child devoid of all that we see as essentially human and childish, as if he did not move arms or legs but had extensors that were shifted by gears. *Often it took a conscious act of will to make ourselves perceive him as a child.*" He plugged imaginary power lines into imaginary outlets to run his digestive apparatus. Around him he placed imaginary transistors. "Machines are better than people," he told Bettelheim. "Machines can stop. People go farther than they should. . . ."

Machines don't feel. Machines can be adjusted and parts replaced.

If you look at the model *Tarzanthropus Inherens,* you can see the particular kind of self that is organized for you. This model of human nature is made of primordial slime, unconscious soot and so forth formed into personal wave lengths, potentialities, resonances and other solid-state components built-in to individual specifications. So your self is not an arrangement of plastic and interchangeable parts, an adjustable mechanism that can be regulated to run according to natural law. It is with a self arranged by the model *Tarzanthropus Inherens* that you can say with William James:

"The world of sensations and of scientific laws and objects may be all. But . . . I hear that inward monitor . . . whispering the word 'bosh!'"

This kind of self has greater confidence in its feelings and in the unfolding of its personal destiny than in the countable,

262

measurable behavior of other selves. As Samuel Taylor Coleridge put it for the self of this model: "We murder to dissect."

Here is a dues-paying member of the American Parapsychology Association walking out of a meeting in great disgust. "The whole trouble with these people in these meetings is that none of them has ever had an extrasensory or clairvoyant experience. They don't realize that it can come to you only once or twice in your lifetime and never be repeated again. Look at them in there: analyzing a haunted house by means of statistics about knockings put through a computer."

Here are heart-transplant patients, as reported by Paul Ramsey, believing they have undergone a basic change in themselves: one man worried that he was becoming feminine on account of receiving a woman's heart; one forty-five-year-old man thinking he was twenty, the donor's age. Here is the American Declaration of Independence based on selves that have been created equal and endowed by their Creator with certain inalienable rights. Here is one journalistic report after another about the individual, circumscribed "World of" or "The Little World of" this person or that. Here are the anthropologists reappraising the human data, past and present, organized on the basis of sex rather than personal resonance—with Sherwood Washburn pointing out the tendency to consider all fossils as male; and Sol Tax calling for a word to replace "man" which will denote both males and females.

Whether such terms as "Neanderthal Person" and "Genkind" are put into general use will depend on whether the *Tarzanthropus Inherens* model of human nature is more widely advertised and distributed by the industry.

In any event, that model teaches its own particular lesson to the self it organizes. As William James puts the moral taught by this idea of human nature: "Our responsible concern is with our private destiny, after all." And with such a moral, you can readily organize the stories you tell your self. To wit:

"One of the strangest features in the thought of the present time," says G. N. M. Tyrrell, "is the widespread acceptance of that conjunction of irreconcilables: the belief that humanity matters as a collective, while the individual is intrinsically devoid of importance and merely exists as a unit to serve the community; as if the community had some invisible and supernatural existence of its own apart from the lives of the individuals who constitute it. . . . We forget how slender are the links which bind human individuals into these collective wholes, and in what abysmal depths of isolation the springs of thought and action are hidden."

As William James continues the story: "Individuality is founded in feeling; and in the recesses of feeling, the darker, blinder strata of character, are the only places in the world in which we catch real fact in the making and directly perceive how events happen . . ."

Naturally your self can see the consequences of a story like that if *Tarzanthropus Inherens* is the only model allowed to organize your self.

"During the past one hundred years," say Ray Helfer and Henry Kempe, "the rights of children have gradually been recognized. The duties of small children, on the other hand, are less easily defined. . . ."

The middle class, says historian William Irwin Thompson, "is filling up with the occult prophecies of [Edgar] Cayce. . . . Bookstores frequented by far-out students and hippies have special sections filled . . . other old, occult classics that have taken on a new life in Aquarian Age culture."

About the Declaration of Independence, Abraham Lincoln said, "I think the authors of that notable instrument intended to *all* men, but they did not intend to declare all men equal *in all*

264

respects. They did not mean to say that all were equal in colour, size, intellect, moral developments, or social capacity."

When you look at the paper-thin model *Morganthropus Exchangenesis* you can see that your self is neither a clockwork mechanism running according to natural law nor a solid-state generator of individual resonances which whisper, "Bosh!" According to this model's arrangements, your self can best be described by Erving Goffman:

"What the individual is for himself is not something that he invented. It is what his significant others have come to see he should be, what they have come to treat him as being, and what, in consequence, he must treat himself as being if he is to deal with their dealings with him." Among those others who see this self, there are "those who are concerned to find in him someone unalarming whom they can disattend in order to be free to get on with other matters. So what the individual in part must come to be *for himself* is someone whose appearances are ones his others can see as normal. His show of being safely disattendable is deeply him; he has no self that is deeper although he has some that are as deep."

This kind of self, obviously, is not concerned with discovering natural laws to obey or personal resonances to vibrate to. This kind of self has much more confidence in the local rules, regulations and cues necessary for playing its many roles as dictated by the script—fulfilling obligations, making reciprocal gestures, coming in and going out on the proper lines. As Mark Twain put it for the self organized by the model *Morganthropus Exchangenesis:* "From the cradle to the grave, during all his waking hours, the human being is under training . . . He is a chameleon; by the law of his nature he takes the color of his place of resort."

Here are people saying, "Much obliged" or "I am in your debt," or all those other phrases of double-entry social book-keeping—"This day has been a real gift," and "You owe it to yourself" or, more colloquially, "You ought to." Here are children attaining self-consciousness and learning to be themselves by "endless imitation" as William Wordsworth called it. In the more modern language of Margaret Mead, "The child is continually acting as a parent, a teacher, a preacher, a grocery-man, a policeman, a pirate or an Indian." Here is a Michigan druggist who misfilled a prescription, giving a woman tranquilizer pills instead of contraceptive pills. For that error, he is now playing the role of father to the woman's unwanted child. By court order the druggist must pay the costs of rearing the baby, the expenses of the pregnancy and the amount of the wages lost by the mother who had to give up her job. And here is a group of Australian aborigines finding that the women in their dwindling population were unmarriagable—having been designated as "sisters" and therefore incestuous marriage partners and so taboo. But the aborigines have solved the problem by reclassifying the women. The data are no longer called "sisters" and consequently can become Married information.

As you would expect, a self created and re-created by a change in the script and the roles it calls for can often appear to itself as little more than a rewritten part put together in an out-of-town tryout. So, one moral taught by the *Morganthropus Exchangenesis* model to the self it organizes can be, in Mark Twain's words: "If God created man, He was disappointed in the monkey."

More popularly, however, the moral that organizes this self is, in Goffman's words: "Rules of conduct are fundamental to definitions of a self, and . . . just as fundamental to corporate social life." And with that kind of moral to organize your stories, you can readily see the consequences in action for a self that has been defined by rules of conduct. For examples:

Subjects in psychology laboratory experiments, says Ulric

Neisser, are quick to pick up "subtle cues from the experimenter's behavior to guide their responses." That can result in reports of spectacular scientific discoveries—especially if the subject of the experiment is a clever horse or sensitive college student who has been picking those subtle cues from the experimenter who knows the right answers to the experiment's questions. "There are many such cues in every study," Neisser says, "even a totally automated one . . ."

A self that has been defined by the rules of the game can also be seen acting its parts on the real-life stage outside of the laboratory stage.

"The physician," says Thomas Szasz, "has it in his power to decide whether or not the patient is playing the medical game, that is, the real-life drama of being ill according to the rules. If he plays fairly he is rewarded ('treated'); if he is caught cheating, he is punished (sent away, scolded, subjected to unnecessary or sadistic measures, etc.). . . . Such rules, however, are not God-given, nor do they occur 'naturally.' Since all systems of classifications are made by people, it is necessary to be aware of who has made the rules and for what purpose." During the past sixty or seventy years, Szasz says, "a vast number of occurrences were reclassified as 'illnesses.' We have thus come to regard phobias, delinquencies, divorce, homicide, addiction and so on almost without limit as psychiatric illnesses. This is a colossal and costly mistake."

From time to time, too, people invent autobiographies, thus making fictitious documents of past transactions for themselves in order to play more lucrative roles in business and industry, receive awards and medals, make more believable images of themselves as leaders and spokesmen, and in general accumulate more valuable negotiable securities in the present and future.

But that is not so surprising. The *Morganthropus Exchangenesis* model of human nature is, after all, only a paste-up of man-made rules and regulations and the other documents pertaining thereto. So forgeries and spurious accreditations are expectable if this is the only model of human nature you consult to find out what is human and natural. And under the circumstances, it is only natural to find that the rules and regulations have been changed from time to time, and with them the self they organize has been changed accordingly.

"Professors are increasingly looking the other way when cheating occurs," reports *The Wall Street Journal*. These teachers argue that cheating is a product of the educational system—which can also be looked at as an organization of rules, regulations, accreditations and other documents of negotiation. "I'd lose all the rapport I've built up with my classes," a Midwest professor told the newspaper. "Anyone, teacher or student, who turns in a cheater is branded forever as a rat." Other widely distributed documents of negotiation, the report indicates, are examinations signed by the student but written by a paid professional exam taker, and term papers signed by the student but bought for negotiable cash from a term paper-writing agency.

Clearly it is very difficult to organize your self by using one model of human nature exclusively for the job.

Beneath the roles written by the model *Morganthropus Exchangenesis* there is no self. There are only other roles, some played better than others. And there is no way to add them all up to a self because the organizing rules and regulations, like any negotiable documents, are subject to change without notice.

It is also hard to organize your self with the exclusive use of the model *Tarzanthropus Inherens*. True, your potentialities, wave lengths and natural frequency are built-in to your personal specifications. But what they are cannot be seen until your life is over and you have finally realized your self, sounded your note, given your message—and then it is too late to organize, recognize and be "yourself."

Just as clearly, you cannot organize your self by using only the *Edisonthropus Tinkerectus* model of human nature. There is no self to organize. There is only a stimulus and response mechanism that you can call your self, and its parts are interchangeable, replaceable or adjustable. It is very difficult to say that a clock has a self. If it tells its own time then it needs repair. Even a self-winding watch is being its proper self only when it tells the time of another clock or, better still, the time of the stars.

In other words, if you organize your self by consulting only one model, you will be hard put to establish your identity. It takes a complete set of human nature to pull your self together and tell your self the complete story about such things as how old you are (*Edisonthropus Tinkerectus*); how old you feel (*Tarzanthropus Inherens*); and whether you're at the proper age to have an identity crisis (*Morganthropus Exchangenesis*).

Chapter Last

So, that's one thing human nature seems to be—an organized idea or working model or body of knowledge that tells you what things to pay attention to, where they begin and end, and how they work out in between. And with that informative story, people talk themselves through the day, the week, year and lifetime, telling themselves and each other where everything belongs, and how and when and why it belongs there. The story organizes the tellers. It simply depends on which working model of human nature they consult as to what the true story is.

But is it the real story?

What you tell yourself may get you through the day, week, year and lifetime. But that's no guarantee of its being the genuine story of real human nature. It might be only an ad hoc organization called to order for this particular day, week, year or lifetime; and the report it makes may narrate reality, and then again may not. The true story you tell yourself might be only a provisional simulation that will have to suffice until somebody can come back with the really true story and the truly real blueprint.

That is the trouble with working models. They are only simulations at best, only provisional organizations. You can stand away from them and watch them work. You can reach in and tinker with them, or climb inside and inspect the premises, or snip off one piece and paste another over the hole—depending, of course, on the kind of model it is and the kind of data it assembles into information. So, when it comes to a working model of human nature, it is awfully hard to say that your nature is real if you can climb out of it, look back in to evaluate its premises, tinker with them, refurnish them, calk the seams, and then climb back into the reorganization. Besides, you cannot tell yourself that your nature is real when there are three different working models of it to look at and climb back into.

Naturally, the same is the case with the you and yourself who are involved when you tell yourself stories in order to get through the day, week, year and lifetime. It is quite difficult to say which of you is telling, which of you is listening and asking for more details, and which other of you is monitoring those two and butting in from time to time with such asides and footnotes as: I was amazed to see myself doing that; I couldn't help myself; I wasn't myself; I can't explain myself; I'd like to get back to being my old self; but I want to be myself first. That is the perplexity when you have to tell yourself stories about where everything belongs. You have to be beside yourself to do it. But just how many of you are in the line is impossible to find out. It's one thing to go around telling yourself, "To thine own self be true" and "Don't exceed yourself." But it's something else to tell yourself which of yourselves to be true to, which is the real you not to transcend.

So, with at least three simulations of human nature to choose among and at least three of you to tell yourself about them, there is no guarantee that the true story is the real story. For example, a lot of people who have spent many of their days, weeks and years in school often explain to themselves that they are preparing for real life. But once they get there, they find themselves saying that it is not to be believed. For another example, a lot of people who have got through many days, weeks and years in prisons and military institutions frequently talk about the real world outside. But if they go there, they are quite likely to say that is like a nightmare or like a dream. Similarly, a lot of people who live what they call an everyday life every day, week and year often go to very opulent or very rustic places for their vacations. And once they get there, they hear themselves saying that this is really living. On the other hand, a lot of people who take vacations from their usual ways of organizing the data of human nature often come home telling themselves that they are returning to reality. At home, they see and talk with people. On vacation, they saw and spoke with Latins, Anglo-Saxons, Cape Codders or other natives, and observed their customs and folkways.

There also appears to be considerable disagreement about the real words that tell the real story. For example, nobody doubts the truth of such nouns as feces, nasal mucus or coitus. But whether those nouns are less real when you tell them in the Latin and more real when you tell them in fifth-century Low German is a matter of great dispute. There are many other examples of this difficulty in the language; real words for telling the real story are very hard to find. And as a result, people have to work quite hard to explain not only that an event was real, but also just how real it was. Generally speaking nowadays, there seem to be twelve levels of realness in common local usage. At least those are the markings on an unofficial plumb line dropped into hundreds of true stories many people have told to themselves and to a higher journalist and a lower anthropologist.

The following list of these twelve levels of realness begins with the average, ordinary real which is usually expressed, "It was just like in real life." This list descends to the depth of the most completely, wholly, perfectly real—usually expressed, "It was completely unreal."

1. IT WAS LIKE IN REAL LIFE.
2. IT WAS NOT TO BE BELIEVED.
3. IT WAS ANOTHER WORLD.
4. IT WAS FANTASTIC.

5. IT WAS LIKE A DREAM.
6. IT WAS ABSOLUTELY ABSURD.
7. IT WAS LIKE IN THE MOVIES.
8. IT WAS RIDICULOUS.
9. IT WAS INCREDIBLE.
10. IT WAS NOT REAL.
11. IT WAS UNREAL.
12. IT WAS COMPLETELY UNREAL.

A more scientific sounding of the language of realness might dredge up a more precise enumeration. But it would add up to the same sum, namely: there is widespread suspicion that the true story is not the real story. Quite the contrary, there is widespread belief that none of it is real—not the working model of human nature; not the data it abstracts; not the teller who has been informed or organized.

The popular theory seems to be that ideas of human nature are all right to talk about, but that somewhere apart from them nestles the real McCoy—in some real place outside of the ad hoc, provisional simulation, and unconnected from it, sits the real human nature waiting to be discovered. According to this common theory, it requires only the proper method of investigation to get away from the organized ideas or working models and on to the genuine human article.

You can see this theory at work in all sorts of ways. Lower journalists are always being warned by their editors to get all the facts and to get them accurately. And the way to do so, as every newsman knows, is to wear comfortable shoes and assume nothing. In the same way, higher anthropologists are forever coming back dusty and exhausted from expeditions into the steaming mores, worried that they have not worked hard enough at asking the real questions. The way to do so, as anthropologists know, is to pry off your preconceptions about where every-

274

thing belongs and look objectively at the who, what, when, where, why and how. Many more examples of this sort abound, supporting the widespread yearning to find the real human nature in some real place apart from the working model. A moment after somebody has advertised himself as a realist, there are six investigators trying to find out what he's really like. Just try to explain working models of human nature, and you find a number of people nodding kindly in agreement and saying, "Yes, yes, of course: bodies of knowledge, organized ideas. But what about the real human nature? What about that?"

Well, there is very little you can do for people like that—except perhaps to ask them: Where are they? What time is it? How do they cooperate and divide the work load? and all of the other questions that a working model of human nature answers. True, those may not be the ultimately real questions. But everybody everywhere asks them in order to live, so they are certainly true questions of human nature. And that is all a working model of human nature has to answer for. Besides, nobody has said that these models of human nature are real. The only claim made for them is that they may be actual and true. The only claim made for any organized ideas of human nature is that everybody everywhere needs them in order to tell what is human, what is natural, what is worth knowing, what is worth having and how to get it, and all the other information necessary for getting through the day, week, year and lifetime.

But many people cannot listen to that story. Or if they listen, they cannot believe it to be a true story about human nature. Or if they believe it, they cannot remember it for more than a moment. And at the very next moment they are asking about their real self or selves, and looking for the real place of the real human nature which sits beneath the model, behind the organized idea, aside from the true story.

Naturally, they are concerned about getting this real place located. That is human nature—to organize the data of human nature into a body of knowledge or working model. That is what a working model or organized idea of human nature does: it gives you the story about where everything belongs, and how and when and why it belongs there. Consequently, it depends on which true story, organized idea or working model of human nature you consult as to the location of the real human nature and the real you—beneath the model, behind the idea, or aside from the story.

If you look at the model *Edisonthropus Tinkerectus* with its gears, drives and other mechanisms running according to natural law, you can see that the real place of real human nature is aside from the story you tell yourself in order to get through the day, week, year and lifetime. The conscious mind, filled with such notions as freedom and dignity, is a marginal by-product of evolution. That kind of machinery is jerry built, local and biased although it appears to be enduring, universal and true. These cogs and wheels can be replaced with others such as duty and obedience without impairing the smooth functioning of the real machinery. The real place of the real human nature is in the autonomic mechanisms—breathing, digestion, habituation, conditioning, etc.—which run according to natural laws of survival. What you think of as the true you with its hopes, fears, joys and ideas of human nature is only a mirage, or at best an epiphenomenon.

In any case, that true you is beside the point. The real you is a creature of habit, a creation of conditioning, a blind response to the stimuli of existence such as hunger, cold, loneliness and the other natural forces. Real human nature is cell nature and the nature of the cell's working parts. If you want to find real human nature, according to the model *Edisonthropus Tinkerectus,* then forget about what people tell themselves and each other. Instead, observe what people do everyday. Count and measure their behavior under this set of conditions and that: in test kindergartens, in test marriage beds, in test kitchens, in sense-deprivation rooms, etc. Just be careful not to pollute the test samples with your own ideas of human nature, even if you're observing the mechanisms of rat behavior. It's the mechanism that counts in getting you through the day, week, year and lifetime. That everyday machinery is the real human nature. The rest is largely random, and very distracting, mind noise.

If you look at the *Tarzanthropus Inherens* model made of primordial stuff tailored to individual specifications in the built-in components, you can see that the real place of the real human nature is beneath the working model—amid the brambles, snakes and jagged bedrocks of basic survival. The components that are built-in to individual specifications may make for as many ideas of human nature as there are people. But the primordial stuff of those components exists because it was able to slither, lash out, claw and bite in order to stay alive and procreate. So, beneath all its bodies of knowledge, the human mind is always *in extremis*.

The true you may sound as an individual resonance. But implicit in that tone are at least three component pitches. They are sometimes called by Latin names and sometimes by Greek. But whatever the language, the real you is a minimum of three separate voices: the individual, personal *I;* the generalized *Everybody* who is or ever was; and the questing, primordial *That*. And all of them are talking among themselves about survival. At least one third of real human nature, and maybe a lot more, is animal nature, mammal nature, primate nature. If you want to find real human nature, according to the model *Tarzanthropus Inherens,* then forget about what people do in everyday life or under controlled conditions. Instead, observe people at death's door, in catastrophe, in war, in desperation. Observe people having to make their own shelter and clothing, having to grow

277

their own food—and the more rocky their soil, the better. Don't bother to observe intellectuals or urban dwellers. Real human nature is rural and manual. Real human nature is what people do in crisis and emergency at the hazardous, subsistence edge of existence. That's the stuff that gets you through the day, week, year and lifetime. The rest is superfluous, and very distracting, world noise.

When you look at the working model *Morganthropus Exchangenesis* made of declarations, promissory notes and the other negotiable documents with which people transact the day, week, year and lifetime, you can see that the real place of real human nature is behind the organized idea of human nature. Clearly there is nothing intrinsically real in printed tickets, canceled checks, embossed passports and the rest of the man-made portfolio of negotiable paper. It is only by contract that such scrip has a true face value. And as for the bearer, he has only a true face value, too, with his contractual family obligations, education diplomas, clean record and so on and on.

The true you may appear to be kind, courteous, loyal, trustworthy, honest and poor. But behind that image is the real you, playing your roles well as neighbor, child, sibling, parent, taxpayer and higher journalist or lower anthropologist—but not doing so well in playing your part as wage earner. If you want to find the real place of the real human nature according to the model *Morganthropus Exchangenesis,* then forget about the nature of the primate *in extremis* and the nature of the cell and its working parts. Instead, you have to look behind such ideas as love, charity, freedom and dignity and all the other images which people project. If you want to find real human nature, you must look at the roles people play on the stage of life. You must inquire as to how those roles came to be written in the script; how they are played in other places and at other times;

how the roles are learned; and how they are passed on from actor to actor or newly created when the script changes.

In any event, there is no need to look for the mechanisms of natural law or the emergency regulations of survival. On the contrary, real human nature is the name of the game that has evolved to the present moment. Real human nature is what existence says it is locally and immediately. Behind the sound and fury, there are only stage directions and cues for a script that will be rewritten for every performance. Behind the roles there are only other roles, played well or poorly. And behind those roles there is nothing except dust.

2

At least that is the general theory. But in actual practice, it is awfully hard to find the GENUINE human nature in that REAL place beneath the working model, behind the organized idea, aside from the story you tell yourself in order to get through the day, week, year and lifetime. In actual practice, only a few people are able to live for very long in such a REAL place. And those who are found there, unencumbered by any working models, true stories or organized ideas of human nature, are frequently said to be animals or vegetables. If somebody returns intact from that GENUINE existence, he is often said to have made a superhuman effort or a miraculous recovery.

In actual practice, people who have no organized idea of human nature are usually said to be out of touch with reality. They are usually locked away. Moreover, people whose organized ideas of human nature fall into disrepair and disarray are commonly said to be suffering from a nervous breakdown, an emotional illness, an identity crisis or some other incapacitating disorientation. People with these kinds of pathological conditions are commonly reported to be in real pain until they can rebuild their worlds. In addition, people whose organized ideas or working models of human nature are attacked and shaken are often said to become anxious, nervous, rigid and otherwise fearful. Depending on which model is in threat of demolition, such people may drop out, turn off or call for a return to law and order.

In actual practice, people who advertise themselves as realists almost always turn out to have very definite ideas about where everything belongs, and how and when and why it belongs there. As for the question of what people are really like, that is usually another way of asking what working models of human nature they consult: what data they pay attention to, and how they organize it into information. And as for realists who consult only one working model of human nature, claiming that everything can be located exclusively in the cogs and wheels, or in the built-in components, or in the portfolio of negotiable paper—such people with only one organized idea of human nature are often said to be inhuman, not humane, unnatural, weird, warped, monomaniacs or totalitarians.

All in all it is not easy to get at the data beneath the model, behind the organized idea, aside from the true story you tell yourself about human nature. The informative facts in those places, like the informative facts in any place, do not speak for themselves. You have to collect the data first, call them to order and ask them questions before they will give you any information.

But just what questions to ask, and just who may ask them—that depends, naturally, on which working model of human nature you are looking at. As everybody knows, the best researchers are well trained and experienced (*Edisonthropus Tinkerectus*); or they are highly talented and capable (*Tarzanthropus Inherens*); or they are very professional, qualified and accredited (*Morganthropus Exchangenesis*). In other words, people who are usually allowed to inquire publicly into the real facts generally prepare for the quest by amassing a body of knowledge. And with it, such people can tell the difference between really good questions and questions that are wrong, unproductive, irrelevant, superficial, frivolous. But people who do not have the talent or capability to learn the really good questions to ask—those people often get poor report cards, limited accreditation and guarded recommendations. That is to say, people who have not been well trained in the way the working model works seldom get the opportunity to be experts. They have not mastered the body of knowledge or organized idea and so cannot inquire publicly into the real facts. And as for people who wear comfortable shoes and assume nothing, they are usually killed very young while trying to cross the street. Such people have no idea whatsoever about where anything belongs, or how and when and why it belongs there. That makes it very difficult to stay alive, let alone to locate the real facts. People who assume nothing have no working model of human nature to begin with and thus no way to assemble even the true story with its moral about what to pay attention to.

Under the circumstances, it appears that just about everybody is an employee in the human nature industry. Just about everybody abstracts human and natural data from the world rubble and processes those data into HUMAN and NATURAL information. And those few people who cannot or will not—they are ordered and placed so as not to jeopardize the industry.

From time to time, of course, there are changes in the good questions to ask data and in the right answers. That usually happens when the index at the end of the true story is revised and the data of human nature are reclassified. For example, **DREAMS** may be moved from the list entitled PROPHECY to the list entitled PATHOLOGY. Or **ANIMALS** may be moved from AESOP to ETHOLOGY. In that event, different kinds of questions are asked by differently trained people with different talents and accreditations. But that is still no guarantee that the later true story is more real than the earlier one. The most you can say about it is that the investigation of the matter has been assigned to another working model of human nature. Dreams have been moved from the transactions of God with man (*Morganthropus Exchangenesis*) to the workings of the cogs and wheels of the unconscious (*Edisonthropus Tinkerectus*). The behavior of animals has been taken away from such natural laws as Prudence and Folly (*Edisonthropus Tinkerectus*) and removed to the province of the built-in and wired-in (*Tarzanthropus Inherens*).

It is also hard to say that one organized idea or working model of human nature is more real than any of the others. For example, it might be a great comfort to know that the questions asked in the laboratory according to the model *Edisonthropus Tinkerectus* are the real questions. And with enough money and equipment, and plenty of well-trained, experienced researchers to ask these real questions of the data, eventually but surely the real answers will be forthcoming—such as the mechanisms which misfire to cause drug addiction, brutality, rapaciousness and even death.

But as it turns out, the questions asked in the laboratory are not always exclusive to the model *Edisonthropus Tinkerectus*. Quite often the questions asked and the experiments designed involve other items—including the future careers of the askers, the reputations of their seniors and administrators, the image of the laboratory, the funds available for such inquiry and other questions belonging properly to the *Morganthropus Exchangenesis* model of human nature. And those careers, reputations, images and negotiable bank checks may very likely be committed in this ten-year period to research in neurophysiology, genetics, the behavior of great apes and other questions belonging properly to the *Tarzanthropus Inherens* model of human nature. Under the circumstances, you cannot really call one organized idea more real than the other two. And the same perplexity crops up outside of the laboratory as well.

More than one college faculty has re-evaluated and tentatively redesigned the undergraduate curriculum because the administration sees a way of luring financial support to the campus. More than one funding agency has redesigned its program regarding elementary school education, revising its grant giving because of the invention of novel audiovisual machinery, and revising the program again because of recent findings in the wired-up brains of white mice and cats. Newsstands and bookracks are filled with such explanatory reading matter as: *How to Know Yourself*, *How to Know God*, *How to Be a Successful Lover* and *How to Make Money on the Stock Market*. These tracts set out the mechanisms of self-fulfillment, role-playing and negotiation by applying the methods of the model *Edison-thropus Tinkerectus* to the other two working models of human nature—the one made of unadjustable, irreplaceable, built-in components; the other made of pasted-up clauses and amendments; and neither amenable to the pliers and wrenches of the first.

Similarly, the organized idea of *Tarzanthropus Inherens* has actual consequences in the organized idea *Morganthropus Exchangenesis*. Judges frequently decide against responsible foster parents who fulfill their obligations, and award custody of children to their careless, cruel, irresponsible—but genetic—parents. And vice versa, the model *Morganthropus Exchangenesis* often has consequences in *Tarzanthropus Inherens* model of human nature. Rich men often marry good-looking women. Their daughters tend to be better looking if the men amassed their negotiable documents before marriage.

What with these overlappings and interweavings among the models, there is no way to say for sure which working model is the most real. Nor is there any guarantee that a working model of human nature conforms to reality or manufactures it. Consequently, it is very hard to get at the real story of human nature. But you really don't need it when you have the true story of actual working models of human nature to look at.

3

It appears that the idea of human nature is real. And the more care and attention you give it, the better it will work. The more often you climb out of the working models, look back inside to inspect the premises, paste up the holes, adjust the gears and calk the seams, the more real it will become. But if you disregard the idea and let it fall into disrepair and disarray, two terrible consequences can follow.

First, the idea may fall apart. And without a working model of human nature at work, there is only chaos.

The second consequence is equally terrible and much more probable. If you disregard the organized idea or body of knowledge—if you let the working model answer your questions about human nature before you have asked them—then the model will very likely get out of hand and go into business for itself. Where it will go, of course, depends on which model of human nature is going.

The model *Edisonthropus Tinkerectus,* with its clockwork drives and mechanisms, will run away and carry people with it, turning them into unfeeling, automatic monsters. Every experience will be counted and measured. And those that do not measure up will be discounted. People will be sent here or there to be adjusted, using drugs and other mechanical devices in order to achieve a feeling of personal, individual experience. If this working model of human nature gets out of hand, the proper study of mankind will be the molecule, the atom, the nucleus and so forth into the smaller and smaller working parts that make up each per capita figure.

The model *Tarzanthropus Inherens,* with its wired-in components built-in to individual specifications, will run away, carrying people with it and turn them into brutes who follow their feelings of the moment. People will be on the street at every hour, searching for their personal identities and asserting their individual resonances. Naturally that will make the streets noisy and dangerous. Human nature will be what the loudest, most coercive voice says it is. Communication will become communiqué in the name of instant self-expression. Inalienable rights and personal self will fall into constant jeopardy under the pummeling of instant satisfaction of immediate individual needs. Instant diets, instant euphoria, instant learning, instant access, instant money, instant gratification will be the organizing idea. And as a result, charisma will become tyranny in the name of safety for humanity. If this working model of human nature gets out of hand, there would be no proper study of mankind.

The model *Morganthropus Exchangenesis,* a collage of contracts and other negotiable documents of transaction, running wild will turn people into marketable merchandise. Everybody will have his price. Accreditations, like state secrets, will be bought and sold. Personal images will be designed, painted, framed and auctioned off to the highest bidder, with the rosier the identity the more costly. History, like fiction, will be written and rewritten to attract the consumers. Term papers will be for sale. So will teachers, wives, generals, doctors, lawyers, judges and all the other roles which are occupied temporarily by people. College presidents, like stock market presidents and other kinds of presidents, will be chosen for their credibility and marketability. Whom you know and what you have will be more worthwhile than what you know and what you are. The people who are allowed to ask about human nature, like the people who are allowed to tell about it, will have to be properly authorized and ticketed. But because images and roles, like documents of accreditation, are only paper thin, nobody will dare ask or tell for fear of jeopardizing the entire portfolio. The body of knowledge will be guarded closely along with other secret documents. Like espionage, life will be a game played for very high stakes. If this working model of human nature gets out of hand, the proper study of mankind will be the ways and means of rewriting the script in order to produce a more acceptable performance.

Those gloomy hypotheses are not true, of course. At least they are not wholly true as of this writing. They have been exaggerated only in order to show clearly that an unexamined hypothesis can take on a real life of its own. They are theoretical examples illustrating how easy it is to forget about human nature and instead take the theory for granted simply because it appears to be so well organized.

But then, that's human nature for you—very orderly and very oblivious. Everybody everywhere is filled to the brim with knowledgeable information about the right time, the best place, the proper way to get there and what to do afterward. Oh yes, when it comes to human nature, people have all sorts and classes and kinds of answers. Where they falter is in remembering the question. And that is how human nature falls into disrepair and disarray: by taking the reply before making the inquiry. That is how the idea of human nature goes into business for itself, turning people into unfeeling monsters, unthinking brutes, marketable produce: by mistaking the Word of the Year for the topic of the sentence; by memorizing the answers to the question of human nature and neglecting to ask that humanizing question itself.

286

Actually, people are not so oblivious as all that. Almost everybody everywhere remembers to ask the question. It's just that most people don't realize they are asking it when they inquire as to what? who? when? where? how? and why? Those are plainly the queries about the location of everything inside the organized idea or body of knowledge. Obviously, those queries add up to the question of human nature. But naturally, the question is almost never put that way—human nature being so disreputable a term, and the organized idea of it being so completely engrossing as to be invisible. Instead, the question generally comes out as:

"WHAT'S NEW?"

Well, what is new?
"So-and-so is dead."
No! Really?
"And so-and-so is engaged."
Who would believe it!
"Hadn't seen so-and-so in twenty years or more. Looks so old."
Shocking!
"And so-and-so is pregnant."
Wonderful! Congratulations!
"And so-and-so made high honors, made a trip to the moon, made a cure for the common cold, made a war, made a treaty."
Incredible!
"And so-and-so got a raise, got a home run, got a divorce, got assaulted, got elected."
Absurd!
"And so-and-so had a sale, had an ulcer, had a brilliant hunch, had a collation at a late hour."
Fantastic!

Looked at one way, there is very little new. People have been getting born, getting old, and dying for quite a long while. And, in between, people have been fighting, bartering, mating, making discoveries and voyages, playing and working. Looked at that way, *"What's new?"* is a rote question organized beforehand by the answers. Looked at that way, people keep telling themselves and each other the same surprising, amazing, shocking stories over and over again. Even surprise, amazement and shock appear to be institutionalized and can easily be located in the working model of human nature under the heading *"What should I do?"* Looked at that way, human nature is very obliging. People will usually come down with the condition as diagnosed —depending, of course, on which model they consult.

But looked at another way, *"What's new?"* is a question of human nature, and makes the organized idea or working model of it visible to anybody who cares to look at it another way.

What's new is that the world data are being classified and reclassified at every moment. And from time to time, classifications open up new levels of abstraction making new data abstractable from the world rubble. Either way, human nature is under review all the time.

Moment by moment, arrangements and rearrangements are being made for who, what, when, where, how and why. An old so-and-so is being disorganized; a new one is being organized. So-and-so has moved the moon to within walking distance. So-and-so is no longer a daughter-in-law, but has been reordered and is now the mother of a grandchild. So-and-so has renamed the capital of China, from Taipei to Peking. So-and-so has reordered the standings of this ball team and that. So-and-so has shifted the place of the common cold in the subdivisions of pathology. So-and-so knew it was appropriate to be outraged and has changed his place of domicile. So-and-so has got out of the social contract, accordance or understanding and is constructing another. So-and-so has had a flash of insight, illuminating an organization of data she had not noticed before.

Just what that organization is depends, of course, on which organized idea or working model she was looking at. Just what all of those arrangements and rearrangements of data are depend on which model of human nature is being consulted to explain where every datum belongs.

Looked at that way, the question of *"What's new?"* pulls you out of the working model and allows you to peer back inside and make the necessary adjustments, listen to the individual resonances, erase the misspellings and paste over the mistakes. But that does not make a model of human nature less true, simply because it is visible—simply because you can stand outside of it and inspect and evaluate its premises. Naturally you can do that sort of thing when you and your models of human nature are all data inside a larger model of human nature which describes humans as essentially model-builders.

When you hold an organized idea of humans as organizers, then you can inquire into their organizations. When your basic model of human nature explains humans as having to build models of their own nature, then you can report on the human nature industry and the models it manufactures, distributes, advertises and consumes.

And simply because your basic model of human nature is also visible, that does not make *it* any less true, either. That merely raises the human and humanizing question of whether your basic model is a datum inside another organized idea.

In other words:

Chapter I—REFERENCES

Pages   References

21   Anthony F. C. Wallace, "Anthropological Contributions to the
         Theory of Personality," in Edward Norbeck, Douglass Price-
         Williams and William M. McCord (eds.), *The Study of Personality: an Interdisciplinary Appraisal*, New York: Holt,
         Rinehart & Winston, 1968, p. 42.
22   René Dubos, *So Human an Animal*, New York: Charles
         Scribner's Sons, 1968, p. 5.
22   Marston Bates, *Gluttons and Libertines: Human Problems of
         Being Natural*, New York: Random House, 1967, p. 226.
22   Nixon Commission on Population Growth: the New York *Times*,
         March 12, 1972.
22   British scientists on population growth: the New York *Times*,
         January 14, 1972.
22   Interview with Roger Sperry by Cannel, New York City, 1971.
23   Lecture by Arthur Ferrari delivered at Connecticut College,
         1971.
23   Harry Gershman, the New York *Times*, February 25, 1972.
23   Arnaldo Apolito, the New York *Times*, February 25, 1972.
23–24   Lieutenant Calley: the New York *Times*, March 30, 1971.
24   Blackbirds and starlings: the New York *Times*, February 21,
         1971.
24   Jules Henry, *Culture Against Man*, New York: Random House,
         1963, p. 426.
24   American Psychiatric Association: the New York *Post*, November 17, 1969.
25   Raymond S. Duff and August B. Hollingshead, *Sickness and
         Society*, New York: Harper & Row, 1968.
25   Sherwood L. Washburn and Irven DeVore, "Social Behavior
         of Baboons and Early Man," in Sherwood L. Washburn (ed.),
         Social Life of Early Man, Chicago: Aldine, 1961, pp. 91–
         105.

25   Billy Graham, *Time*, July 11, 1969.

26   William Masters and Virginia Johnson, the New York *Times*, June 27, 1971.

26   Emile Durkheim, *The Rules of Sociological Method*, 8th ed., transl. by Sarah A. Solovan and John H. Mueller, and edited by George E. G. Catlin, Glencoe, Ill.: The Free Press, 1958, pp. 65–66.

26   Crime rate: Alvin Rudoff, "The Soaring Crime Rate: an Etiological View," *The Journal of Criminal Law, Criminology & Police Science*, 62: 543–47, 1971.

26   Lionel Tiger and Robin Fox, *The Imperial Animal*, New York: Holt, Rinehart & Winston, 1971, p. 2.

27   Myles Lask, the New York *Post*, February 9, 1972.

27   President Richard M. Nixon, *Time*, January 3, 1972.

27   Organized swingers: the New York *Times*, May 10, 1971.

28   Ruby Jo Kennedy, in lectures at Connecticut College, 1956.

Chapter II–REFERENCES

Pages   References

47   Dorothy Lee, "Are Basic Needs Ultimate?," in Lee, *Freedom and Culture*, New York: Prentice Hall Spectrum Book, 1959, p. 75.
47   Napoleon Chagnon, *Yanomamö: the Fierce People*, New York: Holt, Rinehart & Winston, 1968.
47   Ruth Benedict, *Patterns of Culture*, New York: New American Library Mentor Books, 1934.
48   E. Adamson Hoebel, *The Law of Primitive Man: a Study in Comparative Legal Dynamics*, Cambridge, Mass.: Harvard University Press, 1954, p. 88.
48   Ralph L. Holloway, Jr., "Human Aggression: the Need for a Species-Specific Framework," in Morton Fried, Marvin Harris, and Robert Murphy (eds.), *War: The Anthropology of Armed Conflict and Aggression*, Garden City, N.Y.: The Natural History Press, 1968, p. 30 ff.
48   Sherwood L. Washburn and Irven DeVore, "Social Behavior of Baboons and Early Man," in Sherwood L. Washburn (ed.), *Social Life of Early Man*, Chicago: Aldine, 1961, pp. 91–105.
49   R. Allen Gardner and Beatrice T. Gardner, "Teaching Sign Language to a Chimpanzee," *Science*, 165: 664–72, 1969.
49   John C. Lilly, *Man and Dolphin*, New York: Pyramid Books, 1962.
50   Dr. Louis Leakey, cited in Jane van Lawick-Goodall, *In the Shadow of Man*, Boston: Houghton Mifflin, 1971, p. 37.
50   Interview with Rabbi Martin Freedman, by Cannel, Paterson, N.J., 1971.
50   Lee, op. cit., p. 71.
51   Interview with Harry Demapoulous, by Cannel, New York City, 1970.
51   Sherwood L. Washburn and C. S. Lancaster, "The Evolution of Hunting," in Richard B. Lee and Irven DeVore (eds.), *Man the Hunter*, Chicago: Aldine, 1968, pp. 293–303.
51   Hoebel, op. cit., pp. 80–81.

51   E. W. Nelson, quoted in Hoebel, loc. cit.

51–52   Carl O. Sauer, "The Agency of Man on the Earth," in William
        L. Thomas, Jr., (ed.), *Man's Role in Changing the Face of
        the Earth*, Chicago: The University of Chicago Press, 1956,
        pp. 49–69.

52   Washburn and DeVore in Washburn (ed.), op. cit., p. 99.

52   Charles and Rebecca Palson, "Swinging in Wedlock," *Society*,
        February, 1972.

52   Ray E. Helfer and C. Henry Kempe, *The Battered Child*, Chi-
        cago: The University of Chicago Press, 1968.

53   Edward A. Shils and Morris Janowitz, "Cohesion and Disin-
        tegration in the Wehrmacht in World War II," *Public Opinion
        Quarterly*, 12, 1948.

53   Dorothy Lee, op. cit., p. 72.

54   M.I.T. Computer Study: the New York *Times*, February 27,
        1972.

54   Lawrence Wright, *Clean and Decent: The Fascinating History
        of the Bathroom & the Water Closet*, New York: Viking, 1960,
        p. 82; Alexander Kira, *The Bathroom: Criteria for Design*,
        New York: Bantam Books, 1966.

Chapter III—REFERENCES

Pages   *References*

57   John Greenleaf Whittier in Burton Egbert Stevenson (ed.), *The Home Book of Verse: American and English 1580–1920*, 6th ed., New York: Henry Holt, 1918, p. 261.

61   Fertilized egg in laboratory: the New York *Times*, April 14, 1971.

71   Twenty-two kinds of wink: Ray L. Birdwhistell, "Kinesics and Communication," in Edmund Carpenter and Marshall McLuhan (eds.), *Explorations in Communication*, Boston: Beacon Press, 1960, pp. 54–64.

75   Alfred L. Kroeber, *Anthropology*, New York: Harcourt, 1948.

75   Orrin E. Klapp, *Collective Search for Identity*, New York: Holt, Rinehart & Winston, 1969, p. 3.

76   Interview with Abraham Edel, by Cannel, at the College of the City of New York, 1970.

76   Interview with John R. Everett, by Cannel, at the New School for Social Research, 1970.

76   Interview with F. Champion Ward, by Cannel, at the Ford Foundation, New York City, 1970.

76   Interview with René Dubos, by Cannel, at Rockefeller University, 1970.

77   Bertrand Russell quoted in Herbert J. Muller, *Science and Criticism: the Humanistic Tradition in Contemporary Thought*, New Haven, Conn.: Yale University Press, 1943, p. 66.

77   James Whitcomb Riley did not write this poem. He wrote "When the Frost Is on the Punkin'".

78   Robert Glasgow, "The Urban Crisis," *Psychology Today*, 2: 18 ff., August 1968.

79   Hans Bethe quoted in Herbert J. Muller, *Freedom in the Modern World*, New York: Harper & Row, 1966, p. 132.

79   Computer-selected spouses: the New York *Times*, December 25, 1970.

80   Adult Development Program: *Behavior Today,* April 26, 1971.

80   William H. Whyte, Jr., *The Organization Man,* New York: Simon & Schuster, 1956.

80   Henry Fielding, *The History of Tom Jones, a Foundling,* New York: Dutton Everyman's Library, p. 3.

81   Matthew Arnold, "Dover Beach," in C. B. Tinker and H. F. Lowry (eds.), *The Poetical Works of Matthew Arnold,* London: Oxford University Press, 1950, pp. 210–12.

81   George Bernard Shaw, *Man and Superman,* New York: Brentano's, 1916.

82   Edna St. Vincent Millay, in Whit Burnett (ed.), *This Is My Best,* Garden City, N.Y.: Halcyon House, 1944.

82   Solomon Asch, *Social Psychology,* New York: Prentice-Hall, 1953.

83   Paul Radin quoted in Asch, ibid.

83   John R. Everett, "Sex and Politics," a lecture delivered at the New School for Social Research, July 15, 1969.

83   Man, a course of study: "Teaching Man for Children," *Time,* January 19, 1970, p. 56.

84   Desmond Morris, "The Disguises of Intimacy," *McCall's,* 99: 90 ff., March 1972.

84   Ann Faraday, "How to Make Your Dreams Work for You," *House & Garden,* 141: 84 ff., March 1972.

84   Arlene Silberman, "How Report Cards Can Harm Children and Mislead Parents," *Ladies' Home Journal,* 99: 32 ff., March 1972.

84   Ross Macdonald, *The Instant Enemy,* New York: Knopf, 1968, pp. 122, 227.

85   Julius Richmond, the New York *Times,* March 15, 1970.

85   Curing homosexuality by electric shocks: *Behavior Today,* October 26, 1970.

85   Alcoholic patients: *Behavior Today,* October 26, 1970.

85   Kenneth Oakley, "A Definition of Man," *Science News,* 20, New York: Penguin Books, 1951.

85   Rollo May, *Love and Will,* New York: W. W. Norton, 1969.

Chapter V–REFERENCES

Pages   *References*

111   Edmund Sinnott, *Cell and Psyche,* New York: Harper Torch-books, 1961, p. 21.

111   Herbert J. Muller, *Science and Criticism: the Humanistic Tradition in Contemporary Thought,* New Haven, Conn.: Yale University Press, 1943, p. 107, quoted in Sinnott, ibid.

112   Peter H. Ravin, Brent Berlin, and Dennis Breedlove, "The Origins of Taxonomy," *Science,* 174: 1210–13, 1971.

113   David McNeill, *The Acquisition of Language: the Study of Developmental Linguistics,* New York: Harper & Row, 1971, p. 55.

114   Clifford Geertz, "The Growth of Culture and the Evolution of Mind," in Jordan M. Scher (ed.), *Theories of Mind,* New York: Free Press of Glencoe, 1962, pp. 713–40.

114   Sherwood L. Washburn quoted in Geertz, ibid.

115   Richard B. Lee and Irven DeVore (eds.), *Man the Hunter,* Chicago: Aldine, 1968, p. 3.

115   Margaret Mead, *Continuities in Cultural Evolution,* New Haven, Conn.: Yale University Press, 1964, p. 38.

116–17   J. B. Birdsell, *Human Evolution,* Chicago: Rand McNally, 1972, pp. 94–95.

117   William S. Laughlin, "Hunting: an Integrating Biobehavior System and Its Evolutionary Importance," in Lee and DeVore (eds.), op. cit., pp. 304–20.

118   Laughlin, ibid., p. 313.

119   Bernard G. Campbell, *Human Evolution: an Introduction to Man's Adaptations,* Chicago: Aldine, 1968, pp. 202–4.

119   Robbins Burling, *Man's Many Voices: Language in its Cultural Context,* New York: Holt, Rinehart & Winston, 1970, p. 200.

119   Jane Goodall, "Chimpanzees of the Gombe Stream Reserve," in Irven DeVore (ed.), *Primate Behavior,* New York: Holt, Rinehart & Winston, 1965, pp. 425–73.

119   Anne Roe, "Psychological Definitions of Man," in Sherwood L. Washburn (ed.), *Classification and Human Evolution*, Chicago: Aldine, p. 324.

119   Campbell, op. cit., p. 78.

120   Campbell, loc. cit.

121   William James, *The Principles of Psychology*, New York: Dover, 1950, pp. 461–68.

121   James, ibid.

122   R. L. Gregory, *Eye and Brain: the Psychology of Seeing*, New York: McGraw-Hill World University Library, 1966, p. 8.

123   Interview with Frederick Marx, by Cannel, Rego Park, N.Y., 1972.

123   Interview with Campbell Wyly, by Cannel, New York City, 1970.

124   Gregory, loc. cit.

125   James, loc. cit.

125   Campbell, op. cit., p. 294.

125   Eric H. Lenneberg, "A Biological Perspective of Language," in Lenneberg (ed.), *New Directions in the Study of Language*, Cambridge, Mass.: The Massachusetts Institute of Technology Press, 1966, pp. 65–88.

126   Susan Ervin, "Imitation in Children's Language," in Lenneberg (ed.), op. cit., pp. 163–89.

126   David McNeill, *The Acquisition of Language: the Study of Developmental Psycholinguistics*, New York: Harper & Row, 1970, p. 55.

126   Burling, op. cit., p. 140.

126   William S. Laughlin, "Acquisition of Anatomical Knowledge by Ancient Man," in Sherwood L. Washburn (ed.), *Social Life of Early Man*, Chicago: Aldine, 1961, pp. 150–75.

128   Campbell, op. cit., pp. 202–4.

128   Adolph H. Schultz, "Some Factors Influencing the Social Life of Primates in General and of Early Man in Particular," in Sherwood L. Washburn (ed.), *Social Life of Early Man*, Chicago: Aldine, 1961, pp. 58–90.

128   Margaret Mead, "A Working Paper for Man and Nature," *Natural History*, Vol. LXXVIII, No. 4, April 1969.

129   Ulric Neisser, *Cognitive Psychology*, New York: Appleton-Century-Croft, 1967, p. 287.

129   Goodall, loc. cit.

130   Campbell, op. cit., pp. 294–95.

130   V. Gordon Childe, *Man Makes Himself*, New York: New American Library Mentor Book, 1951.

131   David A. Hamburg, "The Relevance of Recent Evolutionary Changes to Human Stress Biology," in Sherwood L. Washburn (ed.), *Social Life of Early Man*, Chicago: Aldine, 1961, pp. 278–88.

131   Anthony F. C. Wallace, *Culture and Personality*, New York: Random House, 1961, p. 46.

132   Mary Douglas, *Purity and Danger*, New York: Frederick A. Praeger, 1966, p. 84.

132   Vincent J. Fontana, *The Maltreated Child; The Maltreatment Syndrome in Children*, Springfield, Ill.: Charles C. Thomas, 1964.

133   Sam Keen, "Conversation with John Lilly," *Psychology Today*, 4: 75 ff., December 1971.

133   E. Adamson Hoebel, *Man in the Primitive World: an Introduction to Anthropology*, New York: McGraw-Hill, 1949, pp. 150–60.

134   Max Gluckman, *Custom and Conflict in Africa*, Glencoe, Ill.: Free Press, 1955, p. 62.

134   Fred Eggan in Lee and DeVore (eds.), op. cit., p. 95.

134   Peter Gardner in Lee and DeVore (eds.), ibid., p. 95.

134   Interview with Anthony F. C. Wallace, by Cannel, at University of Pennsylvania, Philadelphia, 1969.

135   Marshall H. Sahlins in Lee and DeVore (eds.), op. cit., pp. 85–86.

135   E. Davoren, "Role of the Social Worker," in Ray E. Helfer and C. Henry Kempe (eds.), *The Battered Child*, Chicago: The University of Chicago Press, 1968, pp. 153–68.

135   Konrad Lorenz, *On Aggression*, transl. by Marjorie Kerr Wilson, New York: Harcourt, Brace & World, 1966.

136   Interview with John R. Everett, by Cannel, at the New School for Social Research, New York City, 1971.

136   F. C. Bartlett, *Remembering*, Cambridge, England: Cambridge University Press, 1932, pp. 239–67.

Chapter VII—REFERENCES

Pages   *References*

179–80   Jacques Monod, *Chance and Necessity*, transl. by Austryn Wainhouse, New York: Knopf, 1971 (originally published in French as *Le Hasard et la nécessité*, Paris: Editions du Seuil, 1970).

180–81   D. O. Hebb and W. R. Thompson, "The Social Significance of Animal Studies," in Gardner Lindzey and Elliot Aronson (eds.), *The Handbook of Social Psychology*, 2nd ed., vol. 2, London: Addison-Wesley, 1968, pp. 729–74.

181   Robert B. Zajonc, "Cognitive Theories in Social Psychology," in Gardner Lindzey and Elliot Aronson (eds.), *The Handbook of Social Psychology*, 2nd ed., vol. 1, London: Addison-Wesley, 1968, pp. 320–411.

181   Clifford Geertz, "The Growth of Culture and the Evolution of the Mind," in Jordan M. Scher (eds.), *Theories of the Mind*, New York: Free Press of Glencoe, 1962, p. 719.

181   Claude Lévi-Strauss, *The Savage Mind*, Chicago: The University of Chicago Press, 1966.

182   Noam Chomsky, *Problems of Knowledge and Freedom*, New York: Pantheon Books, 1971.

183   Kenneth J. Gergen, "Personal Consistency and the Presentation of Self," in Chad Gordon and Kenneth J. Gergen (eds.), *The Self in Social Interaction*, New York: Wiley, 1968, pp. 299–308.

184   E. R. Leach, "Time and False Noses," in *Explorations Five*, Toronto, Canada: University of Toronto Press, 1955, pp. 30–35.

184   Edward T. Hall, *The Hidden Dimension*, Garden City, N.Y.: Doubleday & Co., 1966.

185   N. Schoenfeld, "An Experimental Study of Some Problems Relating to Stereotypes," *Archives of Psychology*, 38, 1942.

185–86   Solomon Poll, *The Hasidic Community of Williamsburg, New York*, Glencoe, Ill.: Free Press, 1962.

186   Philippe Aries, *Centuries of Childhood: a Social History of Family Life*, transl. from the French by Robert Baldnick, New York: Knopf, 1962.

186   Herbert J. Muller, *The Children of Frankenstein: a Primer on Modern Technology and Human Values*, Bloomington, Ind.: Indiana University Press, 1970, p. 136.

186   Hebb and Thompson, op. cit., p. 767.

187   Henry Glassie quoted by James Deetz (*vide infra*).

187   James Deetz, "Ceramics from Plymouth, 1635–1835: the Archaeological Evidence," a paper presented at the Ceramics in America Conference, Winterthur, Delaware, March 23–25, 1972.

187   Leonard Schatzman and Anselm Strauss, "Social Class and Modes of Communication," *The American Journal of Sociology*, 60: 329–38, 1955.

188   Alan Dundes, "The Number Three in American Culture," in Alan Dundes (ed.), *Every Man His Way*, Englewood Cliffs, N.J.: Prentice-Hall, 1968, pp. 401–24.

188   G. G. Simpson, "Naturalistic Ethics and the Social Sciences," *American Psychologist*, 21: 27–36, 1966.

189   Zajonc, op. cit., p. 359.

189   Gergen, loc. cit.

189   Monod, op. cit., pp. 144–45.

Chapter VIII—REFERENCES

Pages	References
205	Lewis Carroll, pseud. (Charles L. Dodgson), *Alice's Adventures in Wonderland*, New York: Macmillan Modern Library, 1921, pp. 113–14.
205	Clifford Geertz, "The Growth of Culture and the Evolution of the Mind," in Jordon M. Scher (ed.), *Theories of the Mind*, New York: Free Press of Glencoe, 1962, p. 735.
206	Thomas S. Kuhn, *The Structure of Scientific Revolutions*, Chicago: The University of Chicago Press, 1962, pp. 47–48.
206	Alvin W. Gouldner, *The Coming Crisis of Western Sociology*, New York: Basic Books, 1970.
207	Margaret Mead, "A Working Paper for Man and Nature," *Natural History*, Vol. LXXVIII, No. 4, April 1969.
207	Jules Henry, *Pathways to Madness*, New York: Random House, 1971, p. xvi.
208	Ronald Fisher, *The Genetical Theory of Natural Selection*, 2nd ed., New York: Dover, 1958, p. 189.
208	Alexander Marshack, *The Roots of Civilization: the Cognitive Beginnings of Man's First Art, Symbol and Notation*, New York: McGraw-Hill, 1972.
211	Marshack, ibid., p. 122.
211	Margaret Mead, op. cit.
212	Alan Lomax and Herbert Yahraes, "Music as a Measure of Psychological and Cultural Development," in Eli A. Rubenstein and George V. Coelho (eds.), *Behavioral Sciences and Mental Health: an Anthology of Program Reports*, Washington, D.C.: U. S. Government Printing Office, Public Health Service Publication No. 2064, National Institute of Mental Health, 1970, pp. 381–97.
213	Francis L. K. Hsu, "Psychosocial Homeostasis and Jen: Conceptual Tools for Advancing Psychological Anthropology," *American Anthropologist*, 73: 23–44, 1971.
213	Leo Rosten, *The Joys of Yiddish*, McGraw-Hill, 1968, p. 234.

213   Lister Sinclair, "A Word in Your Ear," in Walter R. Goldschmidt (ed.), *Ways of Mankind*, Boston: Beacon Press, 1954, pp. 23–49.

214   Edward Sapir, *Language: An Introduction to the Study of Speech*, New York: Harcourt, Brace, 1921.

214   Noam Chomsky, *Problems of Knowledge and Freedom*, New York: Pantheon Books, 1971, p. 44.

214   Kuhn, op. cit., pp. 46–47.

216   Peter Berger and Hansfried Kellner, "Marriage and the Construction of Reality: an Exercise in the Microsociology of Knowledge," in Hans Peter Dreitzel (ed.), *Recent Sociology No. 2*, New York: Macmillan, 1970, pp. 49–72.

217   A. Conan Doyle, *Famous Tales of Sherlock Holmes*, New York: Dodd, Mead, 1958.

217–18   Gardner Murphy and Robert O. Ballou (eds.), *William James on Psychical Research*, New York, Viking, 1960.

Chapter X—REFERENCES

Pages	References

249   A. Irving Hallowell, "The Self and Its Behavioral Environment," in Hallowell, *Culture and Experience,* Philadelphia: University of Pennsylvania Press, 1955, pp. 75–110.

250   Claude Lévi-Strauss, *The Elementary Structures of Kinship,* transl. by James Harle Bell, John Richard von Sturmer and by Rodney Needham (ed.), 2nd ed., Boston: Beacon Press, 1969, pp. 52, 56 (originally published in France as *Les Structures Elémentaires de la Parenté,* 1967).

250   Lewis Mumford, *The Transformations of Man,* New York: Harper & Brothers, 1956, p. 18.

251   Isidor Chein, *The Science of Behavior and the Image of Man,* New York: Basic Books, 1972, p. 8.

251   Bernard G. Rosenthal, *The Images of Man,* New York: Basic Books, 1971, p. 31.

251   Mumford, op. cit., p. 24.

252   E. A. Burtt, *The Metaphysical Foundations of Modern Science,* Garden City, N.Y.: Doubleday Anchor Books, 1955, pp. 238–39.

252   A. Irving Hallowell, "Psychology and Anthropology," in John Gillin (eds.), *For a Science of Social Man,* New York: Macmillan, 1955, pp. 160–226.

252   Burtt, loc. cit.

252   Robert K. Merton, *Science Technology and Society in Seventeenth-Century England,* New York: Harper Torchbooks, 1970, p. 87.

252   Floyd W. Matson, *The Broken Image,* Garden City, N.Y.: Doubleday Anchor Books, 1966, p. 12.

253   Michael Foucault, *The Order of Things: an Archaeology of the Human Sciences,* New York: Pantheon Books, 1970, pp. 344–45 (originally published in France as *Les Mots et les choses,* Paris: Editions Gallimard, 1966).

253   Baron d'Holbach quoted in Matson, op. cit., p. 13.

253   Oliver Wendell Holmes quoted in Don M. Wolfe, *The Image*

of Man in America, 2nd ed., New York: Thomas Y. Crowell, 1970, p. 119.

253   William James, *The Varieties of Religious Experience: a Study in Human Nature*, London: Collier Books, 1961, pp. 383–84.

254   B. F. Skinner, *Walden Two*, New York: Macmillan, 1948, p. 214.

255   Ulric Neisser, "Cultural and Cognitive Discontinuity," in Thomas Gladwin and William G. Sturtevant (eds.), *Anthropology and Human Behavior*, Washington, D.C.: The Anthropological Society of Washington, 1962, pp. 54–71.

255   Mary Ellen Goodman, "Influences of Childhood and Adolescence," in Edward Norbeck, Douglass Price-Williams, and William M. McCord (eds.), *The Study of Personality: an Interdisciplinary Appraisal*, New York: Holt, Rinehart & Winston, 1968, pp. 175–93.

255   Clifford Geertz, "The Impact of the Concept of Culture on the Concept of Man," in John R. Platt (ed.), *New Views of the Nature of Man*, Chicago: The University of Chicago Press, 1965, pp. 93–118.

255   A. Irving Hallowell, "The Self . . . ," op. cit., p. 89.

256   Theodore R. Sarbin, "A Preface to a Psychological Analysis of the Self," in Chad Gordon and Kenneth J. Gergen (eds.), *The Self in Social Interaction*, vol. I, New York: Wiley, 1968, pp. 179–88.

256   Franz Boas quoted in Hallowell, "The Self . . . ," op. cit., p. 89.

256–57   George Herbert Mead, "The Genesis of the Self and Social Control," *International Journal of Ethics*, XXXV: 251–73, 1925.

257   Charles H. Cooley, *Human Nature and the Social Order*, New York: Charles Scribner's Sons, 1902, pp. 136–42.

257   Thomas Rhys Williams, *Introduction to Socialization: Human Culture Transmitted*, St. Louis, Mo.: Mosby, 1972, p. 219.

258   Margaret Mead, *Continuities in Cultural Evolution*, New Haven, Conn.: Yale University Press, 1964, p. 106.

258   Ulric Neisser, op. cit.

258   Edward A. Tiryakian, "The Existential Self and the Person," in Chad Gordon and Kenneth J. Gergen (eds.), *The Self in Social Interaction*, vol. I, New York: Wiley, 1968, pp. 75–86.

259   James Fernandez, "Persuasions and Performances: of the

Beast in Every Body . . . and the Metaphors of Everyman," *Daedalus*, 101: 39–60, Winter 1972.

259   Gordon W. Allport, *Personality: a Psychological Interpretation*, New York: Henry Holt, 1937, pp. 159–65.

259   Rosalie H. Wax, *Doing Fieldwork: Warnings and Advice*,
Chicago: The University of Chicago Press, 1971, p. 18.

260   Don M. Wolfe, *The Image of Man in America*, 2nd ed., New
York: Thomas Y. Crowell, 1970.

261   Wolfe, op. cit., pp. 11, 109.

261   James, op. cit.

261   Bruno Bettelheim, *The Empty Fortress: Infantile Autism and
the Birth of Self*, New York: Free Press, 1967, pp. 234 ff.

262   James, op. cit., p. 401.

263   Paul Ramsey, *The Patient as Person: Explorations in Medical
Ethics*, New Haven, Conn.: Yale University Press, 1970,
p. 236.

263   Sherwood Washburn and Sol Tax cited in *Behavior Today*,
December 7, 1970.

264   G. N. M. Tyrrell, *Science and Psychical Phenomena*, New
Hyde Park, N.Y.: University Books, 1961.

264   James, op. cit.

264   Ray E. Helfer and C. Henry Kempe, *The Battered Child*
Chicago: The University of Chicago Press, 1968, p. ix.

264   William Irwin Thompson, *The Edge of History: Speculatic
on the Transformation of Culture*, New York: Harpe
Row, 1971, p. 123.

265   Erving Goffman, *Relations in Public: Microstudies of the
Public Order*, New York: Basic Books, 1971, p. 279.

265   Mark Twain quoted in Wolfe, op. cit., p. 199.

266   Mead, op. cit.

266   Goffman, op. cit., p. 343.

266–67 Ulric Neisser, *Cognitive Psychology*, New York: Appleton-
Century-Crofts, 1967, p. 30.

267   Thomas S. Szasz, *The Myth of Mental Illness: Foundations
of a Theory of Personal Conduct*, New York: Dell, 1967,
p. 42.

268   *The Wall Street Journal*, February 12, 1969.